PASS THE MISSOURI INSURANCE EXAMS:

A STUDY GUIDE FOR

PROPERTY AND CASUALTY PRODUCERS

Pass the Missouri Insurance Exams:
A Study Guide for Property and Casualty Producers

Printed in the United States of America.

ISBN 978-1-7358543-1-1

■P2■

All inquiries should be addressed to:

Prep Training Group
6203 W. Howard
Niles, IL 60714
(847) 613-1300
www.PrepTrainingGroup.com

TABLE OF CONTENTS

INTRODUCTION

Congratulations on choosing to become a licensed insurance producer! Whether you intend to seek new, full-time employment or are looking to supplement other income, being licensed to sell insurance can create worthwhile opportunities for you for the rest of your professional life and even into retirement. However, before you can begin any work as a producer, you'll need to study carefully for your licensing exam(s).

This study guide contains a combination of general insurance material, property insurance material and casualty insurance material. The chapters that deserve your attention will depend on the type of licensing exam(s) you are attempting to pass.

If you are studying for **a property and casualty insurance exam**, we strongly encourage you to read and review all of the chapters in the guide.

If you are studying **only for a property insurance exam**, we strongly encourage you to read and review the following chapters:

- Chapter 1: Risk Management Principles.
- Chapter 2: Insurance Fundamentals.
- Chapter 3: The Insurance Industry.
- Chapter 4: Property Insurance Concepts.
- Chapter 5: Casualty Insurance Concepts.
- Chapter 6: Parts of a Property and Casualty Insurance Policy.
- Chapter 7: Dwelling and Homeowners Insurance.
- Chapter 8: Commercial Property Insurance.
- Chapter 9: Business Interruption Insurance.
- Chapter 10: Marine Insurance (Other than sections pertaining to protection and indemnity [P&I] insurance).
- Chapter 11: Miscellaneous Property Insurance Products.
- Chapter 18: Cyber Insurance.
- Chapter 20: Insurance Regulation.
- Chapter 21: Insurance State Law and Rules.

If you are studying **only for a casualty insurance exam**, we strongly encourage you to read and review the following chapters:

- Chapter 1: Risk Management Principles.
- Chapter 2: Insurance Fundamentals.
- Chapter 3: The Insurance Industry.
- Chapter 5: Casualty Insurance Concepts.
- Chapter 6: Parts of a Property and Casualty Insurance Policy.
- Chapter 10: Marine Insurance (only sections pertaining to protection and indemnity [P&I] insurance).
- Chapter 12: Personal Auto Insurance.

Introduction

- Chapter 13: Commercial Auto Insurance.

- Chapter 14: Commercial General Liability Insurance.

- Chapter 15: Employment Practices Liability Insurance.

- Chapter 16: Workers Compensation and Employers Liability Insurance.

- Chapter 17: Errors and Omissions Insurance.

- Chapter 18: Cyber Insurance.

- Chapter 19: Miscellaneous Casualty Insurance Products.

- Chapter 20: Insurance Regulation.

- Chapter 21: Insurance State Law and Rules.

Multiple practice tests are included in the latter portions of the guide to help you determine your retention of the most important concepts.

Be aware that the information in this book is intended solely for exam preparation and study purposes and shouldn't be viewed as a source of legal advice or as a comprehensive review of common policy language. Upon starting your career as an insurance professional, you should carefully familiarize yourself with any insurance products you are asked to sell and how they might differ from what's presented here. If you have questions about the legality of certain business practices in insurance, you should contact a qualified legal professional who understands the rules and laws in your state.

Good luck!

CHAPTER 1: RISK MANAGEMENT PRINCIPLES

Insurance wouldn't be necessary without the presence of risk and our desire to manage it. Although we tend to view it in negative terms, **risk** can be defined as merely the uncertainty surrounding either the likelihood or impact of an event. In fact, risk can involve a range of possibilities that includes something good possibly happening, something bad possibly happening or something neutral possibly happening. However, at least one of the possibilities must be less desirable than the rest.

Depending on the range of possibilities, a risk can be considered either a pure risk or a speculative risk.

Pure Risks

A **pure risk** is a risk in which none of the potential outcomes is beneficial. At best, this type of risk will result in either a loss occurring or no loss occurring. Unlike with some other risks, there can't be a chance of gain. Pure risks are generally what most people think of when the subject of risk comes up.

Examples of pure risks include the potential for fire, flood, death, liability and accidents. At worst, these risks will materialize and ultimately result in a loss. At best, these risks will merely remain possibilities and won't ultimately result in a loss.

The concept of pure risks (and, in particular, their lack of potential gain) is important within the context of your study because pure risks are generally the only risks that can be managed by traditional forms of insurance.

Speculative Risks

Speculative risks are the opposite of pure risks because, although they involve uncertainty, they include a chance of success or gain rather than just the chance of a negative or neutral outcome. Some examples of speculative risks are listed next:

- The risk of gambling at a casino.
- The risk of investing in the stock market.
- The risk of introducing a new product.
- The risk of changing jobs.
- The risk of committing to a romantic partner.

Although bad outcomes are possible in the above scenarios, the possibility for good outcomes exists, too. These risks are actually very common in life, but they don't receive much attention from the insurance community because they typically cannot be managed through traditional insurance. Instead, someone who is concerned about speculative risks might engage in other protective strategies, such as risk avoidance or risk reduction. You'll learn more about these and other non-insurance forms of risk management later in this chapter.

Loss

A **loss** may be defined as an expense or a decrease in value. In insurance, a loss must generally be the result of an **accident**. In other words, the loss must be an expense or a decrease in value that occurs at an unpredictable moment or in an unpredictable amount. Accidental expenses or decreases in value are often caused by unexpected property damage, bodily injury, death or theft.

By contrast, nonaccidental decreases in value at predictable times—such as property's natural depreciation—are usually not managed by purchasing insurance.

Direct Loss vs. Indirect Loss

Losses might be direct, such as obvious damage to property that must be repaired or replaced. Alternatively, a loss can be indirect, sometimes known as a "consequential loss." An indirect loss can be defined as a loss caused by another loss, such as the extra cost of childcare that a stay-at-home parent might need to pay upon being forced into the workforce by a spouse's unexpected death. Other examples of an indirect loss are the amount of money that a homeowner might spend on a hotel after a housefire and the amount of business that a company might lose after one if its suppliers is shut down by major flooding.

In property insurance, a **direct loss** involves some kind of property damage (such as loss by fire, flood, theft or accidental breakage). Even if one type of property damage causes another form of property damage (such as an earthquake that causes a fire), both types are considered to be direct losses. In property insurance an **indirect loss** usually involves some kind of extra expense or loss of income due to the property damage. Although insurance is most commonly used to address direct losses, indirect losses are sometimes covered, too.

In insurance, the possibility of a loss is sometimes known as **exposure**. An event that actually results in a loss is known as an **occurrence**. Be aware that an occurrence can be a sudden event (such as a vehicle collision) or a series of circumstances that occur over an extended period of time (such as gradual exposure to harmful chemicals).

Perils

A **peril** is the cause of a loss. Examples of perils include fire, flood and illness. Insurance companies are primarily concerned about the risk of perils. In fact, insurance policies will either list the perils that can result in post-loss compensation for the insured party or at least include a special section that explains any excluded perils. If a peril is excluded from a policy, losses caused by it will generally not result in any insurer-provided compensation for the insurance customer.

Named-Peril vs. Open-Peril

With respect to perils, an insurance policy can be categorized as either a named-peril policy or an open-peril policy.

With a **named-peril policy** in force, a loss will only be covered if it has been caused by a peril that is specifically mentioned as a covered peril in the insurance contract. Most kinds of insurance for personal property are named-peril policies.

By contrast, an **open-peril policy** covers losses caused by any peril unless the insurance contract specifically excludes it. Open-peril policies are often called "all-risk" policies. Note, however, that even an open-peril/all-risk policy will contain a lengthy list of excluded perils.

Residential properties, such as dwellings, are often covered by open-peril insurance. Of course, compared to named-peril coverage, insurance provided on an open-peril basis tends to be priced at a higher amount.

Perils and the Proximate Cause of Loss

The **proximate cause of loss** is the peril that logically results in a loss. This can be an important concept when multiple perils contribute to a loss or when one type of loss leads to another. For example, consider a scenario in which an earthquake causes a lit candle to fall onto a carpet and leads to a fire. It might be argued that the earthquake was the proximate cause of loss because the fire wouldn't have occurred without it.

In general, if the proximate cause of a loss is a covered peril, insurance is expected to compensate the consumer for the loss. However, if the proximate cause of a loss is not a covered peril, the insurer might not provide any compensation to the consumer.

Hazards

A **hazard** isn't the cause of a loss but is something that increases a loss's likelihood or scope. This can be important in insurance because someone who is surrounded by too many hazards can struggle to find affordable insurance even if that person has no history of loss.

The broad category of hazards can be broken down into at least three subcategories:

- Physical hazards.
- Moral hazards.
- Morale hazards.

Physical Hazards

A **physical hazard** is an environmental factor that increases the likelihood or severity of a potential loss. Simple examples of physical hazards include frayed wiring (which increases the likelihood and severity of fire) and wet floors (which increase the likelihood and severity of slip-and-fall accidents). Eliminating as many physical hazards as possible can significantly reduce risk and make insurance more affordable.

Moral Hazards

Moral hazards are conditions that increase the temptation to cause a loss on purpose. These hazards are often carefully monitored by the insurance community and have resulted in several long-standing practices within the industry. Safeguards employed by insurance companies to manage moral hazards include the following:

- Requiring policyholders to have an **insurable interest** in the people or things they intend to insure. (An insurable interest is a desire for a person or thing to remain unharmed. For property and casualty insurance, insurable interest must exist at the time of loss rather than merely at the time of an insurance purchase.)
- Constructing insurance contracts so policyholders are made financially "whole" again after a loss, but not any better than they were prior to a loss. (This is known as the **principle of indemnity**.)
- Specifically listing "intentional acts" as an exclusion in nearly every property and casualty insurance policy.

Morale Hazards

Morale hazards (not to be confused with moral hazards) are cases of indifference that make someone not care about preventing or reducing losses. Morale hazards don't involve deception or evil intent, but they foster an environment in which people act irresponsibly. For example, upon believing that a local community is very safe, a homeowner might keep doors unlocked and increase the likelihood of burglary.

Insurance companies have attempted to manage morale hazards by incorporating deductibles, copayments and coinsurance fees into their products rather than paying for insured losses in full. The assumption is that if the insured party is required to pay out of pocket for at least a small portion of a loss (known as "cost-sharing"), the person will work a bit harder to prevent the loss in the first place.

Risk Management Strategies

Although we might be biased in favor of insurance, buying a policy from an insurance company isn't the only way to manage risk. Strategies for addressing risk can be broken down into several categories:

- Risk avoidance.
- Risk retention.
- Risk reduction.
- Risk transfer.

Let's go through each risk management strategy in more detail.

Risk Avoidance

Risk avoidance is a risk management strategy in which a person entirely eliminates a risk by choosing not to engage in an activity. For example, someone who wants to avoid the risk of dying in a plane crash can refuse to ever fly. Someone who wants to avoid the risk of losing money in the stock market can refuse to invest in it. A company wanting to avoid burdensome regulation in a particular industry can choose not to branch out into that industry at all.

Risk Retention

Risk retention (sometimes called "risk assumption") occurs when someone decides to accept a risk and essentially live with the consequences. For example, a driver might choose to retain the risk of damage to his or her old car by not buying collision insurance for the vehicle. Someone might choose to retain the health risk of eating red meat by enjoying a steak whenever he or she chooses and deciding not to worry about the potentially negative dietary effects.

Risk Reduction

Risk reduction (sometimes known as "risk mitigation") occurs when steps are taken to reduce either the likely frequency or likely severity of a potential loss with the understanding that the risk can't be eliminated altogether. Some common examples of risk reduction are listed next:

- Performing preventive maintenance on a house so it is less susceptible to major damage.
- Locking doors and installing alarms so property is less susceptible to burglary.
- Installing sprinkler systems, smoke alarms and fire extinguishers so small fires are less likely to turn into unmanageable ones.
- Diversifying financial investments so downturns in the stock or bond markets don't entirely wipe out someone's savings.
- Implementing mandatory procedures, adequate training and reasonable safeguards at workplaces to reduce human error.
- Exercising and eating well to fight against illness, disability and premature death.
- Setting an alarm clock to reduce the chances of oversleeping and being late for an important appointment.
- Adding warning labels to products in order to reduce lawsuits from a business's customers.

Risk Transfer

Risk transfer (sometimes called "risk shifting") occurs when the consequences stemming from a risk are taken from one party and moved to another. Although risk transfer doesn't eliminate risk, it absolves the original party from certain responsibilities and can let that party concentrate on other goals.

As an insurance professional, risk transfer is probably the method of risk management with which you will have the most familiarity. In fact, insurance is one of the most common forms of risk transfer. The owner of the insurance, often known as the "policyholder," is allowed to transfer the financial risk of premature death, bad health, property damage, costly legal bills and several other possible problems to an insurance company in exchange for paying money called a "premium." Other common examples of risk transfer include warranties and hold-harmless agreements.

Some forms of risk transfer are incomplete and still involve retaining some portion of the risk. This partial transfer of risk is known as **risk sharing** and can be seen in insurance when consumers are required to pay a deductible before the insurer will provide any benefits.

Risk Management Principles in Insurance

Throughout this chapter, we've attempted to emphasize the links between risk management and insurance. Let's spend some time making more specific connections between those topics and highlight some areas in which insurance companies apply risk management principles for their own protection. For example, we'll explain concepts such as uninsurable risks, the pooling of risks and the law of large numbers.

Uninsurable Risks

Given your desire to become a licensed insurance producer, you probably don't need to be told that insurance can be a great tool for dealing with risk. But as much we might hate to admit it, some risks won't be acceptable to an insurance company and can only be managed in other ways.

Risks might be uninsurable for any of the following reasons:

- The size or likelihood of losses associated with the risk can't be calculated by insurance actuaries. (This is common when relatively new risks emerge and tends to last until insurers have enough time and experience to gather sufficient loss-related data about a risk.)

- The probability of losses associated with the risk is too high. (This explains why insurance applicants with a spotty claims history often struggle to obtain good coverage.)

- The size (as opposed to just the probability) of potential losses is considered too high. (This concern is at least partially responsible for the non-competitive insurance market for property situated in coastal areas or on fault lines, where natural disasters are abnormally possible.)

- The risk cannot be spread or diversified across a broad enough range of policyholders. (This is demonstrated by the way insurance companies often use standard coverage forms rather than rewriting their policy language for each customer. Similarly, it somewhat explains why tailor-made insurance solutions might only be available to an applicant at a significant added cost.)

- The risk could result in a gain rather than just a loss. (This explains why it's nearly impossible to insure against an unwise business decision and is what separates the uncertainties in insurance from the uncertainties in gambling.)

The Law of Large Numbers

Insurance companies try to measure risk and predict the probability of losses by applying the law of large numbers to their business.

The **law of large numbers** essentially states that the probability of an occurrence (such as a loss) becomes clearer as it is tested against an increasingly larger sample of data. The more data we have, the more accurate our predictions will be.

Consider, for example, a coin flip and the likelihood of the coin landing "heads" or "tails." If we flip a coin only twice, it's very possible that it will land on "heads" both times. Based only on those two flips, we might incorrectly assume that the probability of a coin landing on "heads" is 100 percent and that the probability of it landing on "tails" is 0 percent. However, if we flip the coin 100 times, 1,000 times or even more, we're likely to see that the coin will land on each side on a fairly even basis and that the real probability is 50 percent for "heads" and 50 percent for "tails."

Insurers use the law of large numbers by only insuring consumers against a risk if there is adequate data to determine the probability or severity of a loss. When an insurer encounters a new type of risk without sufficient data to understand it, insurance for the risk is likely to be either unavailable or unaffordable.

Pooling of Risks

The law of large numbers is tied closely to the pooling of risks.

The **pooling of risks** is a method by which insurers attempt to spread either the same or similar risks across a larger group. For instance, rather than insuring just one person against the risk of premature death, a life insurance company will insure several similar people against that risk. Pooling of risks rather than insuring just one person allows the insurer to be less reliant on the not-entirely-predictable mortality of that one person. In property insurance, the same concept is applied so damage to a single property doesn't cause catastrophic loss for the insurer.

Often, each group of insurance customers who are pooled together will be put into the same "rate class," with all members of the rate class being charged a similar amount. This explains, in part, why a consumer's insurance premiums aren't always a direct reflection of his or her level of risk. For example, a homeowner won't necessarily be charged more after suffering a loss and won't necessarily be exempt from a price increase if he or she experiences no losses. Instead, price increases or lack thereof might depend on the overall change in risk among all the homeowners in the insurer's larger pool.

Adverse Selection

Adverse selection occurs when insurance is purchased disproportionately by people who are at the highest risk of suffering a loss. Unless an insurer can balance its portfolio by attracting low-risk and moderate-risk customers, it will be unable to offer affordable products to the public and might even be unable to serve certain markets at all.

For an example of adverse selection, consider the buying habits that have typified the market for individual health insurance. The people who tend to be most interested in purchasing health insurance are those who already have health problems, whereas the people who tend to be least interested in health insurance are young people with no major medical issues. If a health insurance company is too good at attracting sick customers and unsuccessful at attracting healthy customers, too much adverse selection will exist, and insurance will become unaffordable or unavailable.

One way to combat adverse selection is to carefully evaluate each insurance customer's level of risk (known as **underwriting**) and then charge high-risk customers more than low-risk customers. In theory, lower prices should attract low-risk applicants, while higher prices will make high-risk applicants less likely to pursue insurance.

Adverse selection can also be reduced by requiring people to purchase insurance regardless of their risk. This method diversifies an insurer's pool of risks by bringing more low-risk and moderate-risk customers into the market. Theoretically, the addition of those customers can make it easier for an insurer to absorb high-risk customers. In a controversial example, this approach to addressing adverse selection was tried in much of the U.S. health insurance market in 2010 via the Affordable Care Act and what became known as the "individual mandate."

Chapter Key Points

- Risk is the uncertainty surrounding either the likelihood or impact of an event.
- A pure risk is a risk in which none of the potential outcomes are beneficial.
- A speculative risk is a type of uncertainty in which there is a chance of success or gain rather than just the chance of a negative or neutral outcome.
- A loss is an expense or a decrease in value.
- In insurance, the possibility of a loss is sometimes known as "exposure."
- An event that actually results in a loss is known as an "occurrence." An occurrence can be a sudden event or a series of circumstances that happen over an extended period of time.

- In property insurance, a direct loss involves some kind of property damage. Even if one type of property damage causes another form of property damage, both types are considered to be direct losses.

- In property insurance an indirect loss usually involves some kind of extra expense or loss of income due to property damage.

- A peril is the cause of a loss.

- A named-peril policy will only cover a loss if the peril that caused the loss is mentioned as a covered peril in the insurance contract.

- An open-peril policy covers losses caused by any peril unless the insurance contract specifically excludes it.

- The proximate cause of loss is the peril that logically resulted in a loss. It can be an important factor when a loss was technically caused by multiple perils.

- A hazard is something that increases a loss's likelihood or scope.

- A physical hazard is an environmental factor that increases the likelihood or severity of a potential loss.

- Moral hazards are conditions that increase the temptation to cause a loss on purpose.

- Morale hazards are cases of indifference that make a consumer not care about preventing or reducing losses.

- Risk avoidance is a risk management strategy in which a person entirely eliminates a risk by choosing not to engage in an activity.

- Risk retention is a risk management strategy in which someone decides to accept a risk and live with the consequences.

- Risk reduction is a risk management strategy in which steps are taken to reduce either the likely frequency or likely severity of a potential loss without eliminating the risk.

- Risk transfer is a risk management strategy in which the consequences stemming from a risk are taken from one party and moved to another.

- Risk sharing involves transferring part of a risk and retaining the rest.

- The law of large numbers states that the probability of an occurrence (such as a loss) becomes clearer as it is tested against an increasingly larger sample of data.

- The pooling of risks is a method by which insurers attempt to spread either the same or similar risks across a larger group.

- Adverse selection occurs when insurance is purchased disproportionately by people who are at the highest risk of suffering a loss.

CHAPTER 2: INSURANCE FUNDAMENTALS

Now that you understand the concepts behind risk management, we can focus more precisely on the basics of insurance.

Insurance is a contractual arrangement whereby one party agrees to absorb a risk in exchange for compensation and in an attempt to pool several risks together. Typically, the party absorbing and pooling the risk is an insurance company, and the compensation given to the company is a set dollar amount known as a **premium**. As a condition of keeping the insurance in force, the consumer might need to pay premiums monthly, annually or on some other schedule.

Types of Insurance

Despite the very large number of insurance products available in today's market, most of them fall into one of a few basic categories:

- **Life insurance** helps manage the financial consequences of premature death. Examples of life insurance are term life insurance, whole life insurance, universal life insurance and variable life insurance. Some financial products that are often intended to help people plan for retirement, such as annuities, also contain elements of life insurance.

- **Accident and health insurance** can assist with the payment of medical bills or replace a portion of someone's income after an illness, injury or disability. Examples of accident and health insurance are major medical insurance, disability insurance and long-term care insurance.

- **Property insurance** compensates businesses and individuals when they suffer losses pertaining to their physical assets, such as their building, their home or their belongings. Basic examples of property insurance are homeowners insurance, renters insurance and flood insurance.

- **Casualty insurance** provides financial protection to an insured person or entity upon that person or entity becoming potentially liable for someone else's losses. Examples of casualty insurance are auto liability insurance, malpractice insurance and workers compensation insurance.

Property and casualty insurance can be subdivided further into personal lines insurance and commercial lines insurance.

Personal lines insurance is insurance intended to insure one person or a family in non-business endeavors. Homeowners insurance, renters insurance and personal auto insurance are all kinds of personal lines property and casualty insurance.

Commercial lines insurance is insurance intended to insure either a business or an individual within the context of his or her profession. For example, workers compensation insurance, medical malpractice insurance, product liability insurance and property insurance for office buildings are all examples of commercial lines insurance.

Insurance As a Contract

Insurance policies are contracts between the company issuing the policy and the consumer who is purchasing it. The company issuing the policy is the known as the **insurer** or the "carrier." The consumer in the insurance transaction is often known as the "policy owner," "policyholder," "named insured" or sometimes simply the **insured**.

In general, besides the insurance company, the policy owner/policyholder/named insured is the only person who can make changes to the insurance (such as changing the dollar limits, increasing the deductible, etc.). The owner/policyholder/named insured is also typically the person or entity required to pay premiums on time to keep the coverage in force.

However, you'll note that many insurance products can often provide protection to people besides the policyholder such as the policyholder's family, employees or customers. For this reason, it's important to read policy language very carefully so coverage is clearly understood.

In many policies, "the insured" can mean anyone covered by the insurance regardless of whether a person actually has control over coverage or a contractual relationship with the carrier. By contrast, "the named insured" tends to indicate a particular person who not only is covered by the insurance but also has rights and control over the contract.

Essential Elements to Contracts

In general, a contract requires the following basic elements in order to be valid:

- Legal purpose.
- Competent parties.
- Offer and acceptance.
- Consideration.

Legal Purpose

Contracts or provisions that do not have a lawful purpose are illegal and void if they are contrary to common law, prohibited by statute or against public policy. If someone signs a contract to do something illegal and then breaks the agreement, the contract cannot be enforced by the courts.

Competent Parties

The parties to a contract must have legal capacity to enter into an agreement. Competent parties must be of legal age and of sound mind. The minimum legal age for most contracts in most states is 18 years old. In general, if someone enters into a contract while being of unsound mind or before reaching the minimum legal age, that person might have the option of voiding the agreement.

Offer and Acceptance

Before a contract goes into effect, one party will give the other an offer and some time to accept it. The chance to accept the terms and conditions of a contract will last until the party offering the contract revokes or withdraws it. A contract can be revoked by the person making the offer until that person is notified of the other party's acceptance.

In insurance, the offer is made by the consumer in the form of an insurance application. The insurance company evaluates the application and decides whether to accept or reject it.

Consideration

Consideration is something of value offered in exchange for something else of value. Consideration can include money or merely a promise to perform (or not perform) some type of action.

In insurance, the consideration given to the insurer is a set dollar amount known as the "premium." The consideration given to the consumer in return is the insurance.

Unilateral vs. Bilateral Contracts

A **unilateral contract** is a contract in which only one of the parties makes a legally enforceable promise.

In an insurance transaction, the insurance company promises to compensate a consumer for a loss, and the consumer promises to pay premiums to the insurer. If a loss occurs and the insurer doesn't deliver on its promise to provide compensation, the consumer can take the insurer to court to obtain a financial settlement. However, if a consumer fails to pay premiums, the insurance company generally can't take the consumer to court and demand payment. Instead, the insurer might respond to nonpayment by canceling the person's insurance. Since the consumer can enforce the contract in a court of law but the insurer can't, insurance policies are usually considered to be unilateral contracts.

The opposite of a unilateral contract is a **bilateral contract**. In a bilateral contractual arrangement, both sides promise to do something, and both sides can use the courts to enforce the contract if a promise isn't kept.

Aleatory Contracts

Since compensation from an insurance company is contingent on a loss actually occurring, there is a chance that one party to the insurance contract will benefit significantly more than the other. For example, there is a chance that no loss will occur, in which case the insurer would benefit much more than the consumer. Conversely, there is also the chance that a loss will occur soon after a policy is issued and that the insurer will need to pay significantly more to the consumer than it collects from that person in the form of premiums.

A contract that incorporates elements of chance and thereby makes the exchange of compensation potentially unequal (as is the case with most insurance contracts) is known as an **aleatory contract**.

Personal and Conditional Contract

A property and casualty insurance policy is a personal and conditional contract.

The contract is considered personal because it depends on the insured's relationship to risk and requires an insurable interest from that person and no one else.

The contract is considered conditional because it stipulates several procedures that must be followed for the policyholder to receive compensation from the insurer. If those conditions aren't met (or if a covered loss never occurs), the consumer won't receive compensation from the insurer.

Contracts of Adhesion

A **contract of adhesion** is a written agreement in which one party chooses the language of the contract and the other party merely has the option of either accepting the contract as written or rejecting it. A contract of adhesion involves little or no back and forth regarding the specific wording of the agreement.

Most insurance contracts are contracts of adhesion. Insurance carriers either write their own policy forms or use standard forms common to their line of business. For example, many property and casualty insurers use policy forms with wording from a company called the "Insurance Services Office" (ISO).

On occasion, a consumer will request that something be added to or deleted from a proposed insurance contract, but even the wording that adds or deletes sections of the contract will usually be written by the insurance company or some other insurance entity.

Other than in rare cases involving insurance for very high-profile businesses, the consumer and his or her representatives won't be involved in the drafting of the contractual language. When a consumer or the consumer's representative plays an active role in the writing of an insurance contract, the contract is sometimes referred to as a **manuscript policy** and might not be considered a contract of adhesion by the courts.

Since contracts of adhesion are written by only one of the parties, disputes regarding ambiguities in their wording will usually be resolved in the other party's favor. Within the context of insurance, this means that if an insurer and a consumer are arguing about the meaning of an unclear word or an ambiguous phrase in an insurance policy, a court is likely to rule for the consumer. The general assumption is that the insurance company has more specialized knowledge than the consumer and, as the writer of the contract, already had an adequate chance to protect itself. Thus, when there is more than one way to reasonably interpret the policy, the consumer should generally get the benefit of the doubt.

Warranties and Representations

When entering into an insurance contract, consumers are expected to act in **utmost good faith**. Fulfilling this obligation requires honesty and a willingness to disclose information about the risk being insured. If information provided by a consumer to an insurance company turns out to be incorrect, the options available to the insurance company will depend on whether the incorrect information relates to either a "warranty" or a "representation."

In regard to insurance contracts, a **warranty** is a statement that must continue to be literally true in order for the insured party to keep the policy in force. Alternatively, you can think of a warranty as a promise (such as a promise that a particular fact will remain 100 percent correct) that the consumer agrees to never break. If information related to a warranty is discovered to be incorrect, the insurer might have the ability to void the contract regardless of the consumer's intent.

For example, as part of a warranty, a property insurance application might make the applicant promise to always protect his or her home via a smoke alarm. If insurance is issued and the home ever lacks a working smoke alarm, the insurer might be able to void the policy regardless of whether the failure to have one was intentional or accidental.

By contrast, in insurance, a **representation** isn't a promise but is a statement of fact based on the person's knowledge of a situation at that particular time. If incorrect information from a consumer is considered part of a representation (and not a warranty), the insurer usually can't void the insurance contract unless the information was misrepresented on purpose and is deemed a material fact. In general, a **material fact** is information that, if known, would influence a decision regarding whether to enter into a contract in the first place.

An insurer's ability to act in response to incorrect information from the consumer is often determined by court precedents and state laws. For example, depending on the state and the type of insurance product, information from a consumer might be considered a warranty for a limited amount of time (such as one or two years after the date of application) and then become a representation. In many jurisdictions, the majority of information provided by consumers in insurance transactions will be treated as representations.

Concealment

Concealment occurs when, instead of directly providing false information, a consumer merely fails to disclose something to the insurance company. For concealment to jeopardize a consumer's insurance coverage, the nondisclosure usually must have been intentional and related to a material fact.

Rescission, Cancellation and Nonrenewal

Particularly when discussing the insurer's right to end coverage, it's important to know the differences among policy rescissions, cancellations and nonrenewals.

In a **rescission**, insurance is treated as if it never existed in the first place. In general, all parties must be put back in the position they were in as if the transaction had never occurred. In a rescission, the insurer isn't required to pay for any losses that arose while coverage was in place. However, the consumer might be entitled to a full return of premiums.

In a **cancellation**, the contract is still treated as if it existed, but the agreement ends prior to the intended expiration date. In this case, the insurer might be able to keep premiums in exchange for coverage that it already provided to the consumer. However, insurance compensation for losses occurring after the cancellation will be denied.

In a **nonrenewal**, coverage remains in force during the entire contractually agreed period but cannot be continued for any additional time, even in exchange for a higher premium.

Principle of Indemnity

Particularly in property and casualty insurance, benefits paid by the insurer to the consumer are commonly based on the **principle of indemnity**. The principle of indemnity calls on the insurance company to compensate policyholders to the degree that they are neither worse off nor better off after an insured loss. Rather, within the confines of the contract, the insurer should attempt to make a policyholder "whole" again.

Many property insurance policies apply the principle of indemnity by only insuring items up to their **actual cash value**. An item's actual cash value is the amount it would cost to replace the item minus depreciation.

Coverage that does not subtract for depreciation (and therefore calculates the value of property as if it were brand new) is known as **replacement-cost coverage**. Although replacement-cost coverage technically violates the principle of indemnity, insurers put safeguards in place to protect themselves. For example, replacement-cost coverage usually requires an additional premium. Also, even if replacement-cost coverage is purchased, the policyholder typically won't receive a full amount from the insurance company until he or she proves the property is being repaired or replaced.

Insurable Interest

In order to insure a person or a piece of property, the party who is purchasing the insurance must have an **insurable interest** in that person or property. In general, an insurable interest involves a desire for the insured person or piece of property to remain unharmed.

Insurance companies require insurable interest in order to prevent moral hazard. Without it, unethical people could purchase insurance on the lives of complete strangers and on a stranger's belongings. Then, an unethical person would likely be tempted to harm the insured person or damage the insured property.

In property insurance, insurable interest must exist at the time of loss. For example, if someone insures his or her home but then sells the home, that former owner won't be able to collect money from the insurance company if the house burns down after the sale. This follows the principle of indemnity, as discussed earlier in this chapter, and ensures that a policyholder is made "whole" after a loss rather than any better or worse.

In property insurance, insurable interest tends to exist for the following parties:

- The property's current owner.
- Lenders who accept property as collateral for a loan.
- Renters who make improvements to property and aren't compensated for them by the owner.
- People or businesses that commonly take possession of other people's property with permission.

Waiver and Estoppel

A **waiver** is the intentional or unintentional relinquishment of a right under the law or under a contract.

Waivers are closely linked to the concept of **estoppel**. Estoppel can prevent a party from exercising a right if it led others to reasonably assume that the right had been waived. For example, although an insurance policy might technically require a consumer to pay premiums by a certain deadline, the insurance company might routinely accept payments after the deadline. In that case, by accepting late payment without penalty, the insurance company might be waiving its right to enforce the deadline.

Similarly, if an insurance company's representative provides more lenient instructions about filing a claim than what's stated in the policy, the representative might be waiving that portion of the policy and preventing the insurer from enforcing the more stringent requirements.

When considered together, waiver and estoppel are important concepts for producers because a producer typically acts as an agent of an insurance company. If an agent provides incorrect information about an insurer's products or procedures to a consumer, the consumer might be able to rely on the incorrect information to the detriment of the insurance company. This can lead to strained relationships between agents and insurers and even subject the agent to legal liability.

Chapter Key Points

- Insurance is a contractual arrangement whereby one party agrees to absorb a risk in exchange for compensation and in an attempt to pool several risks together.

- Property insurance compensates businesses and individuals when they suffer losses pertaining to their physical assets, such as their building, their home or their belongings.

- Casualty insurance provides financial protection when the insured becomes potentially liable for someone else's losses.

- The entity that issues an insurance policy is the "insurer" or the "carrier."

- The consumer in the insurance transaction is often known as the "policy owner," "policyholder," "the named insured" or simply "the insured."

- Since the consumer can enforce the contract in a court of law but the insurer can't, insurance policies are usually considered to be unilateral contracts.

- A contract that incorporates elements of chance and thereby makes the exchange of compensation potentially unequal is known as an "aleatory contract."

- A contract of adhesion is a written agreement in which one party chooses the language of the contract and the other party merely has the option of either accepting the contract as written or rejecting it. Most insurance contracts are contracts of adhesion.

- Since contracts of adhesion are written by only one of the parties, disputes regarding ambiguities in their wording will usually be resolved in the other party's favor.

- In regard to insurance contracts, a warranty is a statement that must continue to be literally true in order for the insured party to keep the policy in force. It is generally viewed as a promise that the consumer must keep throughout the contractual relationship. In property insurance, warranties often involve statements about how property will be maintained or protected.

- In regard to insurance contracts a representation is a statement of fact at the time it is given. Unlike a warranty, it is not necessarily a promise that must be kept.

- If incorrect information from a consumer is considered part of a representation (and not a warranty), the insurer usually can't void the insurance contract unless false information was provided on purpose and relates to a material fact. In general, a material fact is information that, if known, would influence a decision regarding whether to enter into a contract in the first place.

- Concealment occurs when, instead of directly providing false information, a consumer fails to disclose something to the insurance company.

- In a rescission, insurance is treated as if it never existed in the first place. In general, all parties must be put back in the position they were in as if the transaction had never occurred.

- In a cancellation, the contract is still treated as if it existed, but the agreement ends prior to the intended expiration date.

- In a nonrenewal, coverage remains in force during the contractually agreed period but can't be continued for any additional time.

- Based on the principle of indemnity, the insurance company is expected to make the consumer "whole" again (neither better nor worse) after an insured loss.

- In general, an insurable interest involves a desire for the insured person or piece of property to remain unharmed.

- In property insurance, insurable interest must exist at the time of loss.

CHAPTER 3: THE INSURANCE INDUSTRY

Before going into further detail about insurance products, let's explore what happens behind the scenes in the insurance industry. By knowing more about the insurance business as a whole, you'll gain a clearer understanding of how a producer fits into the big picture.

Types of Insurers

Most property and casualty insurance in the United States is issued by large insurance companies. Insurance companies can generally be categorized as either stock companies or mutual companies.

Stock Companies vs. Mutual Companies

A **stock company** is owned by investors who might or might not have purchased insurance from that particular company. A **mutual company**, on the other hand, is owned by the same individuals who have purchased insurance from it. In other words, the company's stockholders and its policyholders are the same people.

Fraternal Benefit Societies

Certain non-profit clubs or societies are permitted to provide limited insurance benefits strictly to their members. Historically, "fraternal benefit societies" have catered to members of the same religious group or ethnicity.

The option of obtaining insurance from fraternal benefit societies is relatively rare in in modern times and is usually associated with life insurance rather than property and casualty insurance.

Risk Retention Groups

A "risk-retention group" is an insurance company formed specifically to insure the risks of its members. Those members are either businesses in the same industry or individuals in the same profession. Risk-retention groups are intended to provide liability insurance in markets where traditional insurance options are unaffordable.

Lloyds of London

Lloyds of London isn't an insurance company. Instead, it's an international marketplace where buyers with unique risks can obtain insurance from an investor known as a "syndicate." It's most commonly associated with ocean marine insurance (which manages the risk of overseas shipping) and insurance products that don't exist in the traditional market.

Government Insurers

Government insurance programs exist at the state and federal levels to insure some risks that insurance companies won't accept. These programs might provide insurance directly from the government to the public or might enlist private insurance companies to act as intermediaries.

In health insurance, government insurance programs include Medicare and Medicaid. In property and casualty insurance, the government helps provide flood insurance, terrorism-risk insurance and high-risk auto insurance. Property and casualty insurance for otherwise uninsurable applicants might be available by government order in what's known as the **residual market**.

FAIR Plans

FAIR plans are arrangements whereby the property insurers in a given state provide property insurance in high-risk areas in exchange for federal help with catastrophic losses. They were originally created to meet the needs of residents and businessowners in inner cities where affordable private insurance wasn't widely available.

Reinsurance Companies

Insurance companies help themselves remain financially stable by purchasing **reinsurance**. Reinsurance is essentially insurance sold to insurance companies in case of unexpected catastrophic losses.

Reinsurance is often bought from another private insurance company but is sometimes provided by the government. For example, property and casualty insurers receive reinsurance against terrorism-related risks from the U.S. Department of Treasury.

Insurance Producers

Licensed **insurance producers** act as intermediaries between consumers and insurance companies. Although there are many different ways in which producers can do business, common tasks performed by nearly all active producers include:

- Selling insurance products to the public.

- Analyzing the insurance-related needs of consumers.

- Collecting and/or facilitating the payment of premiums for insurance.

- Providing important insurance-related documents to applicants, policyholders and carriers.

- Facilitating any updates to coverage or policyholder information (dollar limits, deductibles, added coverages, changes of address, changes of names, etc.).

Be aware that the title "insurance producer" is a relatively broad term that can apply to many different kinds of insurance professionals. For example, the term includes someone who acts as an insurance broker as well as someone who acts as an insurance agent.

Concepts of Agency

Agency is the legal relationship created when one person represents another. When an agent represents someone, the person being represented is known as the **principal**.

Agency law provides that the agent is expected to advise and be an advocate for his or her principal. Also, under the common rules of agency, information made known to the agent is generally considered by law to be known by the principal.

Agent Authority

Agency contracts often specify the types of authority given to an agent. For example, an agreement might allow an agent to accept money on a principal's behalf or let the agent enter into contracts on the principal's behalf. Authority that is given unambiguously to an agent by the principal in writing or orally is known as **express authority**.

In addition to express authority, an agent might have **implied authority** in cases where the power to do something wasn't technically granted in writing or conversation but is presumed to exist in order to carry out the agent's express authority. For example, imagine a scenario in which an agent has express authority to sell insurance on a company's behalf. Although the agent's contract might not mention specifically whether the agent can return phone calls received from prospects about the company's products, the agent would likely have the implied authority to do so in order to complete a sale.

Apparent authority exists when a third party reasonably assumes that an agent has been given certain powers by the principal and is acting on the principal's behalf. For example, suppose an insurance producer hasn't yet received express authority to work on an insurer's behalf but is given signage, letterhead and business cards with the insurer's name to display at the producer's office in advance. Despite the lack of express authority, a member of the public who walks into the office and sees these materials could reasonably assume that the producer represents the insurer. Depending on the circumstances, this case of apparent authority might create obligations and liability for the producer and the carrier regardless of their intent.

Insurance Brokers

In an insurance transaction, producers must be mindful of their relationship to their principal and be cognizant of which party (insurer or consumer) they are actually representing at any given moment.

An **insurance broker** (unlike an insurance agent) legally represents the interests of consumers in insurance transactions. Brokers help their clients shop in some of the more complex parts of the insurance market and attempt to secure the best coverage at the best price. Unlike insurance agents, brokers aren't contractually obligated to place business with a specific insurance carrier, and they don't have the authority to accept a risk on behalf of an insurance company. (The ability to accept a risk on an insurer's behalf is known as "binding.")

Insurance brokers don't often specialize in personal insurance for individuals and families and are, therefore, unlikely to be utilized by most consumers. However, brokers commonly play a major part in selling the following types of insurance:

- Property and casualty insurance for businesses.

- Group health and other employee-benefit plans.

- Coverage for special items that isn't sold by typical personal lines insurance carriers (such as insurance for classic cars, art collections or antiques).

Insurance Agents

An **insurance agent** (unlike an insurance broker) legally represents the interests of insurance companies in insurance transactions. Although agents might have ethical obligations to analyze a consumer's needs and help the buyer secure the best coverage at the best price, the agent usually has a contractual duty to only place business with specific insurance companies rather than with any carrier that is willing to accept a risk.

Agents are typically required to engage in good **field underwriting** by knowing an insurer's tolerance for certain risks and applying that knowledge when prospecting for business . They also owe a heightened level of disclosure to the companies they represent.

Under the common rules of agency, information made known to an insurance agent is generally considered by law to be known by the insurance company. In addition, some agents have the authority to issue coverage (known as "binding") on the insurance company's behalf.

Captive Agents

An insurance agent might represent a single insurance company or have contractual relationships with multiple carriers.

A **captive agent** tends to work as an independent contractor for a single insurance company. Assuming a captive agent works for a carrier that is willing to accept a risk, the agent must recommend that company's products and can't help the consumer get a potentially better deal elsewhere. If a captive agent's customers decide to switch their insurance to a different carrier, the captive agent won't be able to collect any more commissions on that business.

In some parts of the insurance industry, an insurance producer works as an employee (rather than an independent contractor) of a single insurance company and sells insurance directly to the public. A carrier selling insurance solely through its employees rather than through independent contractors is sometimes called a **direct writer**.

<u>Independent Agents</u>

Independent agents are producers who represent multiple insurance companies. As a result, if they have contractual relationships with multiple companies that are willing to accept a risk, they can help the consumer choose the best coverage at the best price among those companies. Similarly, if a consumer becomes unhappy with his or her insurance carrier, an independent agent can shop the risk again among several other companies and still continue to collect commissions if the risk is placed elsewhere.

Field Underwriting

Insurance agents are expected to engage in good "field underwriting." This involves a producer being knowledgeable about the types of risks an insurance company will or won't accept and applying those rules (known as the insurer's "underwriting guidelines") when prospecting for sales.

Failure to engage in good field underwriting can waste the time of carriers and consumers and put the insurance company's solvency at risk. Although field underwriting is important in all lines of insurance, it can be even more critical in the property and casualty industry because inspections aren't always required before a risk is accepted by the carrier and because property and casualty agents often have the authority to issue coverage on the company's behalf.

Issuing Binders

Some agents have the contractual authority to issue a **binder**. Through a binder, an agent accepts a risk on a carrier's behalf and gives temporary coverage to a consumer while an insurance policy is still in the process of being issued. If a loss occurs during the period in which the binder is in force (typically no more than 30 days), the insurer generally must cover the loss. If an agent has issued a binder but the carrier ultimately decides not to issue a policy, the binder will remain in effect until its expiration date or until the insurer cancels it in writing.

Although some binders might be provided orally, even an oral binder should be immediately followed by a written version delivered to the consumer. If there are conflicts between an oral binder and a written binder, the written version typically takes precedence.

Since binders impose contractual obligations onto insurance companies, agents must be very careful when issuing them and understand the limits of their binding authority. If a binder is issued inappropriately and a loss occurs, the insurance carrier might take punitive actions against the agent.

In practice, binding authority tends to be more common among property and casualty agents than among life and health agents. In place of a binder, some agents might only be capable of providing a "conditional receipt," which can help cover losses between the time it is received and the time a policy is issued. However, in order for the conditional receipt to provide any coverage after a loss, the insurer's underwriting department must believe the applicant would've ultimately been approved for a policy. If a loss occurs but the underwriting department discovers a serious problem with the consumer's application (such as an undisclosed medical issue pertaining to a life insurance applicant), the conditional receipt might be meaningless.

Product Suitability

Even while representing an insurance company, a producer is often legally required to adhere to a **suitability standard** when selling to the public. In other words, the insurance products, dollar limits and recommendations given to consumers must be appropriate for the buyers.

Meeting this standard requires asking good questions of applicants, listening carefully to the answers and maintaining knowledge about insurance markets and available products. These tasks should be done not only in early stages of the initial transaction but periodically during the producer's professional relationship with the buyer (such as every year as part of the policy renewal process).

Underwriters

Although an insurance producer will solicit business and often provide basic pricing information to prospects, the decision of whether or not to accept a risk at a given price (or at all) Is made by an **underwriter**.

Although an underwriter isn't expected to shield the insurance company from all losses, the underwriter's judgment is expected to be based on a carrier's desire to achieve certain financial benchmarks. Today, an underwriter might be a combination of one person, multiple people and/or an automated computer system.

Applications

Arguably the most important tool used by an underwriter to evaluate a risk is the **application**. The application contains information about the person requesting the insurance, the item being insured and the level of risk posed by the applicant. It typically requires the disclosure of previous losses and is intended to make the underwriter aware of relevant hazards.

Although an application might technically be filled out by an insurance producer, the information contained in it must come from the applicant. The applicant must sign the application and attest to its accuracy and completeness.

As a matter of contract law, the application is considered an offer from the applicant, and the insurance company has the option to either accept or reject it. False information provided on an application can lead to rescission or cancellation of the contract by the insurer.

Inspections and Third-Party Reports

In addition to relying on information provided by the applicant, an underwriter might order an inspection to be conducted by the insurer or a disinterested third party. Depending on the type of insurance, inspections might include property inspections, reviews of financial records, credit checks, criminal background checks, mandatory health examinations or a review of health records. Inspections must relate legitimately to the risk being insured and cannot be accessed otherwise.

In most cases, notice and permission will be required before an insurer can access inspection data about an applicant from a third party. **The Fair Credit Reporting Act** is a federal law that requires insurance companies to inform insurance consumers when negative action is taken against them based on reports from third parties. In general, the consumer must be alerted to the negative action and be given the contact information of the entity that produced the report. The consumer also has a right to a free copy of the report within 60 days of the negative action from the entity that created it. If something in the report is inaccurate, the consumer can request that the information be verified and corrected.

Actuaries

Actuaries use complex math to determine the likelihood of losses for an insurance company and calculate an appropriate set of rates that carriers use to charge their customers.

Compared to an underwriter, who might be charged with evaluating applicants on a case-by-case basis, an actuary pays more attention to an insurer's overall portfolio of risks, loss history and financial status.

Rates and Premiums

Although formulas for calculating the exact premium to be paid by a policyholder are beyond the scope of this study guide, insurers generally start with a number called a **rate** based on the level of perceived risk. Then, the rate is multiplied by another number based on how much insurance will be purchased (often per thousand dollars of coverage). Discounts or other adjustments may or may not be applied as a final step to arrive at the buyer's premium, which might be paid in an upfront lump sum or in multiple installments during the policy period.

Loss Ratios

Insurance companies calculate several ratios to determine their profitability. **Loss ratios** are generally calculated by dividing the insurer's claims-related losses by the amount of earned premiums. The **expense ratio** is generally calculated by combining all of the insurer's costs unrelated to losses (such as marketing, sales commissions and various administrative costs) and dividing them by the amount of premiums. A number known as the insurer's **combined ratio** adds the loss ratio to the expense ratio. High ratios generally indicate low profitability.

Claims Adjusters

After an insured notifies the insurance company of a loss, the person's case will often be passed along to a specially trained **claims adjuster**. A claims adjuster evaluates whether the loss should be covered at all and, if so, for how much.

Adjusters can be classified by the kind of relationship they have with insurance companies. For instance, some adjusters are employees of a single insurance company. Individuals known as **public adjusters** represent claimants during the claims process and don't work for or on behalf of an insurance company. Public adjusters typically must be licensed in their state of business and will earn a percentage of whatever settlement a claimant receives from the insurer.

Chapter Key Points

- A stock insurance company is owned by investors who might or might not have purchased insurance from it.

- A mutual insurance company is owned by the same individuals who have insurance from it.

- FAIR plans are arrangements whereby property insurers provide property insurance in high-risk areas in exchange for federal help with catastrophic losses.

- Reinsurance is essentially insurance sold to insurance companies in case of unexpected catastrophic losses.

- Licensed insurance producers act as intermediaries between consumers and insurance companies.

- Under the common rules of agency, information made known to the insurance agent is generally considered to be known by the insurer.

- An insurance broker represents the interests of consumers in insurance transactions.

- An insurance agent represents the interests of insurance companies in insurance transactions.

- A captive agent tends to work as an independent contractor for a single insurance company.

- Independent agents can represent multiple insurance companies.

- Insurance agents are expected to engage in good field underwriting by knowing the types of risks an insurance company will or won't accept and applying the insurer's underwriting guidelines when prospecting for sales.

- Through a binder, an agent accepts a risk on a carrier's behalf and gives temporary coverage to a consumer while an insurance policy is still in the process of being issued.

- Even when representing an insurance company, a producer is often legally required to adhere to a suitability standard. The insurance products, dollar limits, and recommendations given to consumers must be appropriate for the buyers.

- The decision to accept a risk at a given price is made by an underwriter.

- The most important tool used by an underwriter to evaluate a risk is the application.

- In most cases, notice and permission will be required before an insurer can access inspection data from a third party.

- The Fair Credit Reporting Act is a federal law that requires insurance companies to inform insurance consumers when negative action is taken against them based on reports from third parties. It also provides some protections for people who believe information in a report is inaccurate.

- A claims adjuster evaluates whether the loss should be covered and to what extent.

- Individuals known as "public adjusters" represent claimants during the claims process and don't work for or on behalf of an insurance company.

CHAPTER 4: PROPERTY INSURANCE CONCEPTS

Property insurance is designed to insure against the direct or indirect losses that are possible when property is lost, damaged or destroyed. The property might be real property (such as a building) or personal property (such as a renter's belongings). Property insurance can be used to insure the property itself (such as insurance to rebuild a damaged building) or against the losses that are the result of property damage (such as insurance to replace a business's lost income after a fire destroys an office).

In this chapter, you'll learn and review important concepts common to various types of property insurance.

Actual Cash Value

By default, most property insurance policies only insure items up to their actual cash value. An item's actual cash value is the amount it would cost to replace the item minus depreciation.

For an example of how actual cash value coverage works, imagine a scenario in which you have property insurance on your 10-year-old computer. If your computer is stolen, the insurance company is unlikely to reimburse you for the cost of a brand-new machine. Instead, you're likely to receive an amount equal to the value of a computer that is already 10 years old.

Coverage that doesn't subtract for depreciation is known as "replacement-cost coverage" and is sometimes available to consumers for an additional premium.

Replacement Cost

Property's replacement cost is the amount it would take to rebuild or replace the property as if it were new without taking depreciation into account. If the property is to be replaced, the replacement property and the old property generally must be of "like kind and quality."

Although most residential dwellings (as opposed to personal belongings and commercial property) are insured with replacement-cost coverage rather than with actual cash value coverage, understanding actual cash value can still be important because it's the amount that most insurers will provide until damage to a dwelling has been fixed. After repairs at the home have been completed, the policyholder will receive the difference between the replacement cost and the actual cash value. This delay is intended to reduce moral hazard and prevent homeowners from deciding to damage their own property on purpose.

Note that even an item insured for its replacement cost is still usually subject to a policy's overall dollar limit. If it costs $1 million to replace a dwelling but the policy's limit is only $500,000, the insurer will still only pay up to $500,000 to replace the property.

Functional Replacement Cost

An item's **functional replacement cost** is the amount it would take to replace the property with a new but potentially cheaper alternative that serves the same essential function. In rare cases, homes might only be covered up to this amount if they were constructed from materials that are no longer in widespread use.

Fair Market Value

In all but a few rare cases involving special types of property, insurance doesn't cover an item's "fair market value."

An item's fair market value is the amount owners would receive if they were to sell the item in its current condition. Even if the insured has replacement-cost coverage, the amount to replace an item might be considerably less than the amount it would be worth on the open market. This can be particularly an issue when insuring buildings because the cost to replace a building might be lower than what the building would sell for in the current real estate market. Whereas the market value of a building might be based in part on intangible factors like the desirability of the location, the replacement cost will be based almost exclusively on the cost of materials and labor.

Valued Policies

In contrast to coverage based on an item's actual cash value or replacement cost, a **valued policy** compensates a consumer in an amount already agreed to in advance of a loss.

Valued policies are used in cases where either an insured item would be difficult to replace (such as an antique or a historical artifact) or the financial consequences of a loss can't be calculated with certainty (such as the true cost of losing family to premature death).

Valued policies are very common in life insurance but rarer in other parts of the industry. In property insurance, they usually require a detailed appraisal before coverage can be issued. An **appraisal** is a formal, expert opinion pertaining to an item's authenticity, condition and value. It may entail taking pictures of an item, measuring it and conducting historical and market research.

Pair or Set Coverage

Many property insurance policies have clauses pertaining to pairs or sets. Insurance companies realize that some collections of items (such as earrings) are often worth more as a set than the sum of their parts. However, if part of a pair or set is lost or damaged, the insurer won't provide the value of the complete set. Instead, it will provide the difference between the value of the full pair or set and the value of the remaining pieces that weren't lost or damaged.

Perils Insured Against

Unless the consumer purchases what's known as "open-peril" insurance (also known as "all-risk" insurance), a property insurance policy will specifically list the perils that the insurance will help insure against. In these cases, losses caused by perils other than those listed won't be covered.

Many property insurance policies are based on contractual language from the Insurance Services Office (ISO). In such cases, there tend to be three tiers of perils to choose from:

- **"Basic" coverage** tends to insure against a small handful of perils.
- **"Broad" coverage** tends to insure against an intermediate amount of perils.
- **"Special" coverage** tends to provide coverage against the most perils and is often synonymous with "all-risk" or open-peril coverage. The insurance will respond to all perils other than those specifically excluded in the policy.

You'll learn more about these three levels of coverage when we discuss specific types of property insurance.

Concurrent Causation

Concurrent causation occurs when a loss is created by more than one peril. It becomes an important issue in insurance when one of the perils is covered by the policy but another is not. For example, concurrent causation is a common concern after hurricanes because those storms typically produce wind damage and flood damage at the same time. Although wind damage is covered by practically all forms of homeowners insurance, flood damage is not.

Some insurance contracts contain specific instructions as to how the carrier will respond to losses involving concurrent causation. However, absent contractual language to the contrary, many courts have ruled that a loss caused by both a covered peril and a non-covered peril should be covered by the insurance company.

Coinsurance Clauses

A property policy's **coinsurance clause** is commonly invoked after a partial loss to a building and might result in a reduced amount of compensation for the policyholder.

In property insurance, a coinsurance clause typically states that if a building isn't covered for at least a minimum fraction of its replacement cost (often 80 percent), a loss might not be covered in full. Instead, the insured will typically receive an amount based on how close he or she was to meeting the coinsurance requirement.

For example, if a coinsurance clause states that a building must be insured for at least 80 percent of its replacement cost and the policyholder purchases 5 percent less than this required minimum amount, the policyholder might not be compensated for at least 5 percent of <u>any</u> loss, including small losses that are otherwise far below the policy's dollar limit.

Coinsurance clauses are applied in different ways in different parts of the insurance industry. For example, although these clauses typically base the amount of required insurance on a property's replacement cost, some commercial property insurers might base the figure on actual cash value. In some contexts, the coinsurance clause is also referred to as the "insurance-to-value clause."

Coinsurance clauses are intended to entice consumers to adequately insure their property. In a world where most loses are partial losses, they also help insurers manage the financial inefficiencies involved with small claims. We'll explain coinsurance clauses in greater detail in our chapter about homeowners insurance.

Chapter Key Points

- An item's actual cash value is the amount it would cost to replace the item minus depreciation.

- An item's replacement cost is the amount it would take to rebuild or replace the item without taking depreciation into account.

- If part of a pair or set is lost or damaged, the insurer won't provide the value of the complete set. Instead, it will provide the difference between the value of the full pair or set and the value of the remaining pieces that weren't lost or damaged.

- In property insurance based on ISO coverage forms, "basic" coverage tends to insure against a small handful of perils.

- In property insurance based on ISO coverage forms, "broad" coverage tends to insure against an intermediate amount of perils.

- In property insurance based on ISO coverage forms, "special" coverage tends to provide coverage against the most perils and is often synonymous with "all-risk" or open-peril coverage. The insurance will respond to all perils other than those specifically excluded in the policy.

- Concurrent causation occurs when a loss is created by more than one peril. It becomes an important issue in insurance when one of the perils is covered by the policy but another is not.

- In property insurance, a coinsurance clause (sometimes known as an "insurance-to-value clause") typically states that if property isn't covered for at least a minimum amount specified in the policy, even a small loss might not be covered in full. Instead, the insured will typically receive an amount based on how close he or she was to meeting the coinsurance requirement.

CHAPTER 5: CASUALTY INSURANCE CONCEPTS

Casualty insurance is liability insurance and is used when the insured party is responsible for causing someone else's losses, such as by damaging someone else's property or causing an injury, accident or death.

Negligence

Courts are likely to award money to harmed parties when injury or damage results from someone else's **negligence**. Negligence generally occurs when someone doesn't act with as much care as a reasonable person.

For negligence to exist, several items must be true:

- There must have been a duty of care owed to someone.

- There must have been harm suffered by someone. (If no harm has occurred, no negligence has occurred.) Regarding negligence, harm suffered by someone is sometimes known as **damages**.

- The negligent person's acts must have been the "proximate cause of loss" (an action that logically led to the loss).

Invitee. Licensee, Trespasser

With respect to establishing negligence, the level of care owed to someone will depend on the relationship between the allegedly negligent person and the harmed party. For example, here are a few levels of care that might be owed to a visitor at an owner's property:

- A relatively high level of care is owed to an "invitee." In general, an invitee is someone who is invited onto a property owner's premises largely for the benefit of the owner.

- A somewhat lesser level of care exists for a "licensee." In general, a licensee has permission to be on the owner's property but is doing it largely for his or her own benefit.

- The lowest level of care is owed to a "trespasser." A trespasser is someone who is on property without permission.

Despite these general rules about permission, a heightened level of care might be required from a property owner if potentially dangerous conditions at a location (known as "attractive nuisances") are likely to attract children. As a result, families with pools, trampolines or pets are often encouraged to take special precautions and purchase additional liability insurance.

Contributory Negligence

The theory of **contributory negligence** states that a third party isn't liable for a loss if the injured party's own negligence contributes at all to the loss.

Consider a basic example in which a customer is running in a business's building and slips on a wet floor containing no warning signs. Based on contributory negligence, the business might be entirely free of liability because the customer shouldn't have been running in the first place.

Comparative Negligence

In general, states have determined that contributory negligence laws are too harsh toward injured parties. Instead, most states follow a standard known as **comparative negligence**.

Via comparative negligence, when multiple parties (including the harmed party) have contributed to a loss, each negligent party is only liable for a portion of the loss.

For a basic example, consider again a scenario in which a customer is running through a business's building and slips on a wet floor containing no warning signs. Under comparative negligence, the business might be liable for a fraction of the customer's losses after a fall but be shielded from a portion of liability due to the harmed person's own negligence.

Assumption of Risk

In some scenarios and jurisdictions, a person who might otherwise be liable for somebody else's losses can rely on a defense known as "assumption of risk." This defense might apply if the harmed person actively and freely participated in activities that were already known to be dangerous.

Note that contributory negligence, comparative negligence and assumption of risk generally can't be used as an employer's defense in a workers compensation dispute.

Absolute/Strict Liability

Casualty insurance can often be used to provide compensation to harmed people when the insured has been negligent. However, many types of casualty insurance can provide benefits to harmed people even if negligence hasn't been proven. Negligence isn't necessarily a requirement in order for someone to be legally responsible for a loss.

In certain cases, the law imposes **absolute liability** or "strict liability." In these scenarios, a person can be held legally responsible for losses even if he or she was technically not at fault. For example, in all but a few cases, employers have liability with regard to on-the-job injuries suffered by their employees even when reasonable precautions were taken to prevent harm. Similarly, liability might apply to pet owners in practically all cases when losses are caused by their animals.

Many people use the terms "absolute liability" and "strict liability" interchangeably, but others see a distinction between the two. For example, in some contexts, "strict liability" might mean someone is almost always liable for certain kinds of losses regardless of negligence but that there are a few exceptions to this general rule. Conversely, depending on the context, "absolute liability" might involve liability for which there are practically zero exceptions.

Vicarious Liability

Vicarious liability exists when one party is held responsible for another party's actions. It frequently becomes an issue for businesses when an employee or subcontractor does bad work or causes an accident. Similarly, vicarious liability might exist for parents when a child causes a loss.

Regarding acts committed by an independent contractor, vicarious liability is sometimes referred to as "contingent liability."

Premises and Operations Liability

In commercial liability insurance, **premises and operations liability** can be defined generally as liability arising from accidents at the insured's place of business or while the insured is conducting business.

Liability related to the business premises might arise if the building, office or other space occupied by the insured somehow becomes unsafe. For instance, imagine the insured has erected a sign over its place of business. If the sign falls and damages someone else's property, the business might be legally obligated to replace the broken item.

Liability related to operations occurs when the actions of the insured—not the condition of the premises—cause harm. Suppose a server at a restaurant accidentally splatters hot food over a customer. In this case, the restaurant might be liable for any resulting medical expenses or dry-cleaning bills.

Completed Operations Liability

Completed operations liability arises when work or a service has <u>already been finished</u> by a business and the business's poor performance causes harm.

For example, pretend an electrician has been hired to wire several new circuits at an apartment building. If the wiring causes a fire while the work is still in progress, the electrician would face the kind of operations liability mentioned in the previous section. However, if the wiring causes a fire after the work has concluded, completed operations liability would exist.

Product Liability

Product liability is a concern for businesses that manufacture or sell goods. The potential for product liability exists whenever a product leaves the business premises and causes harm to people or property. If a toy manufacturer sells products that turn out to be dangerous for children, the manufacturer might be liable for injuries, illnesses or deaths. Similarly, if an automotive product actually causes cars to break down, the manufacturer might be liable for the damage.

Contractual Liability

Contractual liability is liability that is accepted as part of an oral or written agreement. For instance, even though a restaurant that rents itself out for a wedding might ordinarily be liable for any injuries sustained at the premises by guests, the couple might sign an agreement in which they agree to accept liability for any accidents during the festivities. In general, casualty insurers are hesitant to cover instances of contractual liability.

Compensatory Damages

Casualty insurance can be purchased to manage potential liability for **compensatory damages**. When one party is deemed responsible for another party's loss, compensatory damages are paid by the responsible party in order to make the wronged party "whole" again. These damages adhere to the principle of indemnity and are intended to make the wronged party no better and no worse than before a loss occurred.

Compensatory damages can be categorized as either special damages or general damages. **Special damages** are damages that are easily quantifiable, such as those awarded to replace damaged property or reimburse an injured person for medical bills. **General damages**, on the other hand, aren't easily quantifiable and might be awarded when someone else is held liable for a death, a long-term disability, a reduced quality of life or a harmed reputation.

Punitive Damages

In addition to having to pay compensatory damages, a liable party might be ordered to provide **punitive damages** to either the harmed party or the government. Punitive damages are sometimes called "exemplary damages" because they're imposed in order to make an example of the liable party and discourage society from engaging in the kind of activity that caused the loss. Whereas compensatory damages are intended to make the wronged party "whole" again, punitive damages are intended to punish the liable party for instances of fraud, major negligence, abusive practices and other negative behaviors.

In order to ensure that punitive damages serve their intended purpose, they usually can't be covered by liability insurance.

Chapter Key Points

- Negligence generally occurs when someone doesn't act with reasonable care.

- For negligence to exist, there must have been a failure to provide a duty of care, the failure of care must have been the proximate cause of loss, and the person owed the duty of care must have suffered damages.

- Via absolute liability, a person can be held legally responsible for losses even if he or she was technically not at fault.

- Vicarious liability exists when one party is held responsible for another party's actions.

- In commercial liability insurance, premises and operations liability can be defined generally as liability arising either from conditions at the insured's place of business or while the insured is conducting business.

- The potential for product liability exists whenever a product leaves the business premises and causes harm to people or property.

- Completed operations liability arises when work or a service has already been finished by a business and the business's poor performance causes harm.

- Contractual liability is liability accepted as part of an oral or written agreement.

- When one party is deemed responsible for another party's loss, compensatory damages are paid by the responsible party to the wronged party. Compensatory damages can include special damages and/or general damages.

- Special damages are for losses that are easily quantifiable.

- General damages are for losses that are not easily quantifiable.

- Punitive damages are imposed to make an example of the liable party. They usually can't be covered by liability insurance.

CHAPTER 6: PARTS OF PROPERTY AND CASUALTY INSURANCE POLICIES

Now that you have a better understanding of some important property and casualty insurance concepts, let's learn some of the most common parts of a property and casualty insurance policy.

Declarations Page

The **declarations page** is often one of the first—if not the very first—pages of an insurance policy. Although insurance policies are generally considered to be contracts of adhesion (and are written by the insurance company with almost no negotiation with the consumer), the declarations page is likely to list those aspects of coverage that either the consumer had the ability to choose or are unique to that person. For example, the declarations page might contain the following information:

- The name of the insured party who controls the coverage (often called the "named insured").
- The overall dollar limit of the coverage (sometimes more generally known as the insurer's "limit of liability").
- The deductible, if any.
- The duration of the policy (often called the "policy period").
- Whether property is covered up to its actual cash value or its replacement cost.
- The policy number.

Let's review a few of a few of those items in more detail.

Understanding the Named Insured

Many insurance policies make several references to the **named insured**. With a few exceptions, the named insured is the only person (besides the insurer) who can make decisions about the coverage. Even if other parties are also technically covered by the policy, the named insured (and not the other parties) will generally be the sole person with the following rights and responsibilities:

- The responsibility to pay premiums.
- The right to receive refunds of premiums (if prompted by a cancellation).
- The ability to change coverage with the insurer's consent.
- The ability to cancel the insurance in writing.
- The ability to assign rights contained in the policy with the insurer's consent.

Understanding the Limit of Liability

A policy's dollar limit is also known as the insurance company's **limit of liability**.

Depending on the policy, the insurance company might list multiple limits of liability. For example, the same policy might have one limit for damage to a building and another limit for damage to personal property. When there are multiple limits of liability, and one of them has been exhausted, the policyholder generally can't dip into another limit of liability to make up the difference.

The limit of liability might apply to each occurrence of loss or be a cumulative limit that applies to all losses during the policy period.

Understanding the Deductible

The **deductible** is the amount of an otherwise insured loss that the consumer must experience and pay out of pocket before a loss can be covered by the insurance policy. In addition to forcing buyers to share in losses, the deductible benefits the insurer by reducing its obligation to pay for many small losses.

Buyers often have some control over the deductible in order to balance the cost of their insurance. Generally, the higher the deductible, the lower the premium.

For an example of how a deductible might be applied, consider someone who has a $200 deductible and suffers a $1,000 loss that would otherwise be covered by insurance. Rather than pay the full $1,000 to the consumer, the insurer would subtract $200 from $1,000 and provide $800 of compensation. The remaining $200 would be the consumer's responsibility.

In another example, assume the same person has a $200 deductible but only suffers a loss of $100. Because the loss is below the deductible, the insurer might provide no compensation at all.

Depending on the policy, the deductible can be enforced after every event that results in a loss ("occurrence") or will only need to be satisfied once per policy period (such as once per year).

Some products, such as homeowners insurance and personal auto insurance, combine property insurance and liability insurance. In these cases, the deductible might only apply to the property insurance portion of the product and not to the liability insurance portion of the product.

Windstorm Deductibles

Most deductibles are a flat dollar amount, but some property losses tend to have deductibles based on a percentage of the loss or a percentage of the damaged property's insured value. For instance, an insurance company in a coastal area might impose a deductible for wind-related losses equal to 5 percent or 10 percent of a home's insured value.

Understanding the Policy Period

The time from the policy's issue date to its expiration date is known as the **policy period**. The length of the policy period can be found on the declarations page and typically spans one year. Losses usually must occur during the policy period in order to be covered by the insurer. Coverage typically starts at 12:01 a.m. on the issue date and is often no longer in effect at 12:01 a.m. on the expiration date.

Near the end of the policy period, the consumer and the insurance company may choose to renew the coverage by mutual consent. Alternatively, either party can refuse to renew the policy and insist on a new contract with different terms and conditions.

When coverage is renewed, a new policy period begins. Like the original policy period, the period for the renewed insurance is usually 12 months.

Definitions

Near either its beginning or end, the insurance policy will contain a set of important definitions that can limit the scope of coverage. Although the insurance industry has worked to improve the readability of its policies, definitions of seemingly common terms (even words like "you") can be more restrictive than what the consumer expects. The policy must be read carefully while keeping the specific definitions in mind.

Insuring Agreement

An insurance policy's **insuring agreement** is the insurance company's basic promise to the consumer. For example, the insuring agreement might say something like, "We will pay for an occurrence of property damage or bodily injury during the policy period." Though this might seem like a fairly straightforward promise, it's impacted (and usually made more complicated) by other parts of the policy, such as definitions and exclusions. In the example referenced here, for instance, the basic promise of the insuring agreement will be dependent on what is actually meant by the terms "occurrence," "property damage," bodily injury" and "policy period." In order to fully understand the scope and limits of the insuring agreement, the entire policy must be read in context.

Package Policies

Note that some insurance policies will contain multiple insuring agreements, particularly in the case of a **package policy**.

A package policy is designed to cover multiple types of risk via the same policy. For example, a homeowners insurance policy is actually a package policy in which one part pertains to property damage while another pertains to personal liability. Similarly, a personal auto policy can sometimes combine casualty insurance (which pays when the insured is liable for an accident) and property insurance (which pays when the insured's own car is damaged or stolen).

Exclusions

An insurance policy will contain a detailed list of perils that will be excluded from coverage. In some scenarios, those **exclusions** can be offset by purchasing additional and/or separate insurance. Other exclusions will generally be uninsurable regardless of how carefully the person shops.

Some common exclusions in most property insurance policies are:

- Intentional damage committed by the insured.
- Floods (often insurable via flood insurance).
- Earth movement (often insurable via earthquake insurance).
- Pollutants.
- Nuclear reactions and radiation.
- War-related damage.
- Orders of destruction or demolition by authorities.
- Wear and tear.

Similarly, unless the contractual language says otherwise, casualty insurance policies often don't provide coverage when liability stems from the following activities:

- Intentional acts committed by the insured.
- War.
- Pollution.
- Operating a vehicle (other than insurance specifically intended for vehicles).
- Scenarios in which the liable party and the harmed person are covered by the same policy.
- Scenarios intended to be covered by workers compensation systems and/or workers compensation insurance.

Exclusions specific to certain types of property and casualty insurance will be addressed later in this book.

Supplementary Payments/Additional Coverages

Most property and casualty insurance policies contain a section or two about **supplementary payments** and/or additional coverages. These parts of a policy can allow the policyholder to receive benefits in addition to the main type of coverage. The specifics will differ from product to product, but they're often designed to keep a loss from getting worse or having a more detrimental impact on the insured. For example, in auto insurance, they might include:

- The cost of a bail bond if a driver is arrested after an accident.
- The cost of taking time off from work to help an insurer in an accident-related court proceeding.

In property insurance, they might include:

- The expense of storing belongings at an offsite location after a building becomes unsecure.
- The cost of temporary repairs.
- The cost of debris removal after a covered peril.
- The cost to replace damaged trees or plants.
- Expenses charged by local fire departments.
- Expenses from credit card theft.

Conditions

The **Conditions** portion of a property and casualty insurance policy lays out many of the requirements for each party to the contract. Most of the statements describe what the insured must do after a loss to collect benefits and what the insurer must do when calculating the amount of an insured loss. For example, as a condition of the contract, the policyholder generally must take the following actions:

- Alert the insurer of a loss within a reasonable time as set by the policy. This is known as **notice of claim**.
- Provide proof of loss to the insurer within a reasonable time.
- Allow the insurer to conduct reasonable investigations and appraisals regarding the loss.
- Take reasonable measures to keep an existing loss from getting worse (such as not abandoning damaged property or allowing damaged property to be harmed further by vandals or burglars).
- Allow the insurer to take legal action against third parties who may have caused the loss.
- Regardless of what appears elsewhere in the policy, the Conditions portion of the policy might limit the insurer's liability depending on the following factors:
- Any applicable deductible or coinsurance requirements that will be the insured's responsibility.
- Where the loss occurred. (In general, losses must occur within the policy's **coverage territory**. The issue of coverage territory is particularly a concern when losses occur in another country or—particularly in workers compensation insurance---another state.)
- Whether the insured has violated any part of the agreement.
- Whether property is insured for its actual cash value, replacement cost or some other amount.
- Other in-force insurance policies that might pay for the same loss.
- Depending on the product, other issues addressed in the conditions section of a policy might include:
- The named insured's ability to cancel the insurance in writing.
- The inability to assign rights under the policy without the insurer's consent.
- If the policy is for a business, the ability of the insurer to examine the business's records during the policy period and up to three years afterward.
- The responsibility of the named insured to pay premiums.
- The ability of the named insured to make changes to the policy.

- Upon death of the named insured, the ability of that person's legal representative to exercise various rights under the policy.
- The ability of the policyholder and insurer to engage in arbitration or mediation in the event of a dispute.

Proof of Loss

Especially in property insurance, an insured who suffers a loss is usually required to provide **proof of loss** to the insurance company. This is often done on special forms provided by the carrier and can involve itemizing various types of damage.

In order to manage its finances and keep enough money in reserve to handle future claims, insurance companies will require proof of loss within a certain amount of time, such as 60 days after a loss occurs. Deadlines for providing proof of loss might be extended in certain cases, such as following a major catastrophe that prevents owners from accessing their damaged property.

Arbitration and Mediation

If a consumer and an insurance company can't come to an agreement about the size or insured nature of a loss, going to court doesn't need to be the next step. Instead, the parties can agree to try some type of "alternative dispute resolution," such as arbitration or mediation.

In **mediation**, attorneys, retired judges or other third-party participants attempt to get both sides of a dispute talking to each other in order to come to a resolution. However, recommendations or proposals made by those third parties aren't binding on the insurer or the consumer, so they don't guarantee an end to the dispute.

In **arbitration**, an impartial "umpire" is designated to resolve the dispute. Unlike in mediation, the results of arbitration are generally considered to be final and can't be appealed or fought again in court.

"Other Insurance" Clause

The **other insurance clause** explains how a loss will be handled if the same loss is insured under multiple policies and/or by multiple insurance companies.

Insurance that will serve as the main source of coverage after a loss is called the "primary insurance." Insurance that will only provide benefits after the primary insurance has done so is called "excess insurance."

When a loss might be covered under multiple policies, each policy might split the loss equally, pay an amount proportional to its portion of the combined coverage limit, or indicate whether it is intended to be primary or excess insurance.

Pro Rata Liability

When the other insurance clause calls for each insurer's payment to be proportional to the carrier's portion of the overall coverage limit, the calculation is based on what's called **pro rata liability**.

For example, suppose the same property is insured by a $90,000 policy and a $10,000 policy. Via pro rata liability, the first insurer in our example would generally be responsible for covering 90 percent of a loss, and the second insurer would be responsible for the remaining 10 percent.

Recovered Property

Imagine a scenario in which insured property is stolen but later recovered. If the owner has already been compensated for the theft by the insurer, the two parties are expected to contact each other. Then, under the policy's "recovered property clause," the insured can usually choose one of two options. Either the insured can return the insurance money and retain ownership of the recovered property, or the insured can keep the money and pass ownership of the property along to the insurance company.

Salvage and Abandonment

When some types of property are damaged beyond repair, the insurer might reserve the right to take possession of it and sell it to a salvage yard or a similar business. The owner might have the opportunity to keep the item for sentimental reasons, but the insurer might be able to deduct whatever amount it would've gotten from the salvage company from the settlement check. (This amount is known as the **salvage value** and can be defined as the value of an item when it is no longer usable for its intended purpose.) The issue of salvage occurs most often in auto insurance, when a driver's insured vehicle is considered "totaled" without another person being at fault.

Note, however, that the insurance company isn't required to take possession of abandoned property. For example, if a property owner is experiencing a financial problem, the owner can't send property to the insurance company and demand its insured value in return.

No Benefit to Bailee

Suppose a policyholder brings property to a business for its repair. If the property is lost or damaged while in the business's custody, the business can't be compensated through the property owner's insurance. If a business is concerned about its liability for damage or loss of someone else's property in its care, custody or control, it must obtain its own insurance. This general rule often appears in a property insurance clause known as "no benefit to bailee."

Liberalization Clause

Often buried near the end of an insurance contract, the policy's **liberalization clause** could make the insured eligible for free additional coverage at a later date. The clause states that if the carrier decides to modify the policy in a way that gives additional insurance to new customers at no cost (either by choice or by law), its existing policyholders must also receive these free benefits.

Cancellation Procedures

Consumers don't need a reason to cancel their insurance. They merely need to give the insurer notice of the cancellation. This can be done by sending the insurer a written statement indicating the exact date when coverage should end. It can also be accomplished by sending the policy back to the insurance company.

Requirements for cancellation are stricter when the insurer is the one ending the relationship. In most cases, an insurer can't cancel a person's property and casualty insurance unless at least one of the following statements is true:

- The person failed to pay premiums.
- The person misrepresented important facts to the insurance company.
- The person violated the terms of the insurance policy.
- The risk being insured has dramatically increased. (However, an increase in risk will typically be handled via nonrenewal rather than a cancellation.)

If an insurer plans on cancelling someone's insurance, the person must receive notice of the cancellation before coverage actually ends. The number of days involved with this notice will depend on state law and the reason for the cancellation.

Be careful not to confuse cancellation and nonrenewal. In cancellation, coverage ends prematurely before the end of the policy period. By contrast, a nonrenewal involves coverage that lasts until the end of the policy period but can't be extended for an additional period.

Pro-Rata Cancellations and Short-Rate Cancellations

In some cases, cancelling coverage will result in a return of premiums to the consumer. The amount returned will depend on who did the cancelling.

When the insurer does the cancelling, it keeps a portion of premium that is proportional to how long coverage has been in force since the previous premium payment. For instance, if premiums have been paid for a year's worth of coverage and the insurer cancels at the midpoint, it might keep roughly half of the paid premium and refund the rest to the consumer.

If the consumer does the cancelling, a **short-rate cancellation** is often occurring. In this case, the insurer will generally be allowed to keep an extra amount of the paid premium in order to compensate for administrative expenses caused by the unexpected cancellation.

If a consumer is entitled to a full return of premium, a "flat cancellation" has occurred.

Since some of the money collected by insurers might need to be refunded back to the consumer after a cancellation, insurers evaluate their financial health in part by differentiating between **unearned premium** and **earned premium**. Unearned premium is the amount of money collected from policyholders that still might be refundable in the event of cancellation. Earned premium is money collected from policyholders that won't be refundable in the event of cancellation. Since premiums are generally paid in advance, the amount of earned premium typically increases as the policy period continues.

Lapse

Lapse occurs when coverage is canceled by the insurer for nonpayment of premiums.

Unlike when cancellation occurs for other reasons, a policy lapse might be proceeded by some type of grace period, during which the consumer can ultimately make late payments and still keep the coverage in force in the meantime. Grace periods might be set by state law or based on a particular carrier's decision.

Assignment

Assignment occurs when some or all of the rights contained within an insurance contract are given by the consumer to a third party. In property and casualty insurance, assignment generally isn't allowed unless the insurance company provides written permission.

Assignment is sometimes requested by the policyholder in order to facilitate payment for professional services after a loss. For example, following a property loss, a homeowner might want to assign some of the policy rights to a building contractor so services can be billed directly to the insurer. Similarly, in many health insurance arrangements, medical patients assign certain rights to health care providers so that the providers can be paid directly by the carrier.

In general, when property is transferred to a new owner, a new owner who wants insurance must enter into a new agreement with his or her insurer of choice. The previous owner can't merely assign ownership of an existing insurance policy to the new owner.

Subrogation

Many insurance policies contain a **subrogation clause** that takes the consumer's right to sue someone for an insured loss and transfers it to the insurance company. Unlike an assignment, subrogation involves the transfer of rights between parties who are already part of the contract rather than transferring rights to a third party.

To understand subrogation, imagine a scenario in which you are the victim of an auto accident. If your own insurance provides coverage for your losses, your insurance company might compensate you and then attempt to be reimbursed by either the at-fault driver or the at-fault driver's insurance company. However, in accordance with the principle of indemnity, you would not be able to sue the at-fault driver for the amount you already received from your own insurer. Instead, your ability to sue was transferred by you to your insurance company via subrogation.

Subrogation saves harmed consumers from having to take expensive legal action in order to collect money from liable parties. It also helps keep the cost of insurance down by providing a way for insurance companies to collect money from people who are truly at fault for losses. But because it can still require time and effort from an insurance company, a carrier will only exercise its right of subrogation when it's cost-effective to do so.

Endorsements

An **endorsement** is an amendment to an insurance company's standard policy. It can either add benefits for the consumer (often in exchange for a higher premium) or subtract benefits in order to make the insurance more affordable.

Certificates of Insurance

A **certificate of insurance** is proof of insurance provided by the insured to a third party. Certificates of insurance are commonly requested in commercial lines when a business is attempting to secure work on a project as an independent contractor. For example, before a land developer hires a construction firm to build something on a vacant lot, it might request a certificate of insurance from the construction firm in order to verify that the firm has its own liability protection. For issues related to convenience and privacy, it's often simpler for an insured to give a third party a certificate of insurance rather than a copy of the insured's entire insurance policy.

Although intended as evidence of insurance, a certificate will contain much less information than a full policy and won't always provide a clear picture regarding what kinds of losses would be covered.

Unlike a binder, a certificate is not a contract and does not alter any of an insurer's obligations under an insurance policy. If the party who requests or provides a certificate wants coverage to be altered or clarified in some way (such as by adding a customer to a business's liability insurance for the duration of a project), changes must first be made to the policy itself. Changes made only to the certificate (and not to the policy) are generally not enforceable.

Chapter Key Points

- The declarations page is often a first-page summary of an insurance policy.

- With a few exceptions, the "named insured" is the only person (other than the insurer) who controls and makes choices about the insurance policy. Although a policy might technically cover multiple parties, the named insured is the person who is ultimately responsible for paying premiums and has the right to cancel or alter the coverage.

- A policy's dollar limit is also known as the insurance company's "limit of liability."

- The limit of liability might apply to each occurrence of loss or be a cumulative limit that applies to all losses during the policy period.

- The deductible is the amount of an otherwise insured loss that the consumer must pay out of pocket before a loss can be covered by the insurance policy.

- In addition to forcing buyers to share in losses, the deductible benefits the insurer by reducing its obligation to pay for many small claims.

- Although most deductibles are a flat dollar amount, some insurers impose a separate deductible when losses are caused by windstorms. This deductible might be based on a percentage of a dwelling's insured value.

- The time between the policy's issue date and expiration date is known as the "policy period."

- The insurance policy will contain a set of important definitions that can limit the scope of coverage.

- An insurance policy's insuring agreement is the insurance company's basic promise to the consumer.

- A package policy is designed to cover multiple types of risk via the same policy.

- Some common exclusions in most property insurance policies are:

  o Intentional damage.

  o Floods

  o Earth movement

  o Pollutants.

  o Nuclear reactions and radiation.

  o War.

  o Wear and tear.

  o Orders of destruction or demolition by authorities.

- Some common exclusions in casualty insurance are:

  o Intentional acts.

  o War.

  o Pollution.

  o Operating a vehicle (other than insurance specifically intended for vehicles).

  o Scenarios in which the liable party and the harmed person are covered by the same policy.

  o Scenarios intended to be covered by workers compensation systems and/or workers compensation insurance.

- Most property and casualty insurance policies contain a section or two about supplementary payments and/or additional coverages. These parts of a policy can allow the policyholder to receive free benefits in addition to the main type of coverage that has been purchased.

- In auto insurance, supplementary/additional coverages might include:

  o The cost of a bail bond if a driver is arrested after an accident.

  o The cost of taking time off from work to help an insurer in an accident-related court proceeding.

- In property insurance, supplementary/additional coverages might include:

  o The expense of storing belongings at an offsite location after a building becomes unsecure.

  o The cost of temporary repairs.

  o The cost of debris removal after a covered peril.

  o The cost to replace damages trees or plants.

  o Expenses charged by local fire departments.

- The Conditions portion of a property and casualty insurance policy lays out many of the requirements for each party to the contract. Most of the statements describe what the insured must do after a loss in order to collect benefits and what the insurer must do when calculating the amount of an insured loss.

- The coverage territory is the geographic area where a loss must occur in order to be covered by insurance.

- The ability of the policyholder and insurer to engage in arbitration or mediation in the event of a dispute can often be found in the Conditions section of the policy.

- An insured who suffers a loss is usually required to provide proof of loss to the insurance company, often within 60 days after a loss occurs.

- The other insurance clause explains how a loss will be handled if the same loss is insured under multiple policies and/or by multiple insurance companies.

- When the other insurance clause calls for each insurer's payment to be proportional to the carrier's portion of the overall coverage limit, the calculation is based on pro rata liability.

- If lost or stolen property is ever recovered, the insurer and the recipient of insurance benefits are usually obligated to contact each other. Either the insured can return the insurance money and retain ownership of the recovered property, or the insured can keep the money and pass ownership of the property along to the insurance company.

- The insurance company is not required to take possession of abandoned property.

- When the insurer cancels on a consumer, it keeps a portion of premium that is proportional to how long coverage has been in force since the previous premium payment.

- If the consumer cancels on the insurer, a short rate cancellation is often occurring. In this case, the insurer will generally be allowed to keep an extra amount of the paid premium in order to compensate for administrative expenses.

- Lapse occurs when coverage is canceled by the insurer for nonpayment of premiums.

- Assignment occurs when some or all of the rights contained within an insurance contract are given by the consumer to a third party. In property and casualty insurance, assignment generally isn't allowed unless the insurance company provides written permission.

- Many insurance policies contain a subrogation clause that takes the consumer's right to sue someone for an insured loss and transfers it to the insurance company. In accordance with the principle of indemnity, a person who is fully compensated for a loss by an insurer can't sue the at-fault person for the same loss.

- An endorsement is an amendment to an insurance company's standard policy. It can either add benefits or subtract them.

- A certificate of insurance is proof of insurance provided by the insured to a third party. Unlike a binder, a certificate isn't a contract and doesn't alter any of an insurer's obligations under an insurance policy.

CHAPTER 7: DWELLING AND HOMEOWNERS INSURANCE

Standard Fire Policy

Modern forms of property insurance can be traced back to the debut of the **New York Standard Fire Policy** in 1943. In order to create some uniformity in the insurance industry and set a baseline of protections for consumers, the language found in this policy was mandatory for property insurance sold in most states.

Although the New York Standard Fire Policy only protected an insured against fire losses, it evolved over time and became a basic template for insurers to build other products, such as the homeowners insurance policies sold in today's market.

Dwelling Policies

Many decades ago, the vast majority of families insured their homes through **dwelling policies**. Although this kind of insurance gave homeowners some basic financial protection against fire and other physical disasters, it still left them exposed to a few big risks. A dwelling policy generally provided no compensation to victims of theft, and it offered no help to homeowners when they were sued by a third party and held responsible for an accident. If consumers were concerned about personal liability or burglaries, they had to make special arrangements with their insurance company.

Who Needs a Dwelling Policy?

Although much less common today, dwelling policies continue to be sold. But rather than catering to owner-occupied, single-family homes, most dwelling policies are intended to cover small rental properties where the owner doesn't reside. In these cases, be aware that the insurance is intended for the building's owner and NOT for any tenants who may be living there.

Dwelling policies may also be used to insure the following types of property:

- A dwelling that is too old or in too much disrepair to qualify for traditional homeowners insurance.

- A dwelling under construction.

- A dwelling used as a vacation home.

To qualify for a dwelling policy, a building generally must have no more than four units and no more than five roomers living in the entire building. For larger properties, either commercial property insurance is obtained, or the insurer might add a series of special endorsements to a dwelling policy.

Parts of a Dwelling Policy

Note that each insurer might offer dwelling policies with different benefits attached to them. However, most insurers use policy forms from an organization called the "Insurance Services Office" (ISO) as a template for creating their own products. The information provided here is based on the common structure and language found in ISO forms.

Like many of the other products discussed later in this chapter, dwelling policies provide multiple kinds of coverage, each of which is commonly categorized by letter and each of which has its own dollar limit.

- Coverage A in a dwelling policy is insurance for the dwelling and attached structures. The dwelling is generally the home itself. Attached structures are properties attached to the home (such as an attached garage). The dollar limit chosen for Coverage A also tends to determine the amount of other types of coverage within the policy.

- Coverage B is insurance for detached structures, such as a detached garage. The dollar limit for Coverage B tends to be equal to 10% of the Coverage A dollar limit.

- Coverage C is insurance for the owner's personal property. However, it doesn't insure the personal property of tenants. It might have its own dollar limit, independent of Coverage A. However, damage to personal property might only be covered up to 10% of the normal limit if damage occurs at a location other than the dwelling.

- Coverage D is for "fair rental value" in case a peril makes the dwelling uninhabitable and the owner loses rent. It's often equal to 20% of the Coverage A dollar limit.

- Coverage E is for additional living expenses that an owner might incur as a result of a loss, such as the cost of having to rent a motel room while damage from a loss is being repaired. However, like Coverage C, it's only for the owner and doesn't provide benefits to a harmed tenant. It's often equal to 20% of the Coverage A limit.

We'll go into greater detail about these lettered coverages later because they can be found in some of the more popular property insurance products, too.

Other Benefits of Dwelling Policies

Along with the main lettered coverages, a dwelling policy typically includes several miscellaneous benefits for policyholders:

- Within Coverage A (insurance for the dwelling), a dwelling policy will often cover the removal of debris caused by a covered peril.

- A dwelling policy will typically cover the cost of temporary repairs done after a loss to keep losses under control. This might include the cost of storing personal property at a temporary location.

- A dwelling policy might cover the cost of damage to trees or plants, but there might be a per-plant dollar limit (such as $500) and an overall limit for multiple losses of plants (such as 5% of Coverage A).

- A small amount of coverage (such as $500) is often provided if a loss forces the insured to incur local fees for fire department services.

Dwelling Policy Exclusions

Some major perils are excluded from dwelling policies unless the consumer makes arrangements to add them in exchange for an additional premium.

For example, without an added endorsement, a dwelling policy will exclude losses caused by theft. Also, without the proper endorsement, a dwelling policy does not cover the property owner for personal liability. These exclusions make dwelling policies inadequate for most homeowners.

Other exclusions in dwelling policies, while not ideal for the consumer, are somewhat standard in other kinds of property insurance, too. For example, like most other kinds of property insurance, a dwelling policy doesn't cover floods, earthquake damage, war-related damage, losses caused by nuclear reactions or losses caused on purpose by the insured.

Dwelling Policy Forms

There are generally three main types of ISO dwelling policies to choose from. The name of each one includes the abbreviation "DP" followed by a number.

DP-1

The most basic dwelling policy is known as the "DP-1" and is, in fact, also called the "basic form." The DP-1 covers the dwelling and the owner's property up to the lesser of the consumer's chosen dollar limit or the property's actual cash value (not replacement cost).

By default, the DP-1 only covers losses caused by fire, lightning and explosions that occur in the dwelling. Unlike other dwelling policies, the DP-1 doesn't cover additional living expenses (such as the cost of renting a hotel room after a fire).

Two common endorsements can be added to the DP-1 to cover a wider range of losses, perhaps in exchange for an additional cost. One endorsement (known as "extended coverage") adds coverage for losses caused by:

- Wind.
- Civil commotion.
- Smoke.
- Hail.
- Aircraft or other vehicles.
- Volcanic eruption.
- Explosions (including outside the dwelling).
- Riot.

(Using the first letter of each peril, many people use the acronym "WC SHAVER" to remember the items on the above list. Be mindful of this list, as it often applies to other forms of property insurance, too.)

Another endorsement adds coverage for losses caused by vandalism and malicious mischief.

Without adding these endorsements, losses caused by the perils other than fire, lightning and internal explosion won't be covered by the DP-1.

DP-2

If the losses covered by the DP-1 seem too narrow for a consumer, coverage under the DP-2 can be considered. The DP-2 covers a broader range of losses than the DP-1 and is, in fact, also known among dwelling policies as the "broad form."

The DP-2 covers the residence and other structures (such as garages) up to the lesser of the policy's dollar limit or the property's replacement cost (not actual cash value). However, personal property belonging to the owner remains covered at actual cash value (not replacement cost).

The perils covered under the DP-2 include all of those covered by the DP-1 (including those that can be added to the DP-1 by the extended coverage/WC SHAVER and vandalism/malicious mischief endorsements) PLUS losses caused by the following perils:

- Falling objects.
- Weight of snow, ice or sleet.
- Accidental discharge or overflow of water.
- Freezing.
- Sudden and accidental tearing, cracking, burning or bulging of heating and water systems.
- Sudden and accidental artificial current.
- Burglary damage.

Note that although the DP-2 covers losses from burglary damage (such as the cost of replacing a window or door after a forced entry), it still doesn't cover theft and doesn't reimburse the owner for the loss of stolen property. Also, for study purposes, be mindful of the extra perils covered under the "broad" form, as they often appear in whole or in large part in other types of similarly intermediate types of property insurance policies.

<u>DP-3</u>

For an even more comprehensive dwelling policy, consumers can opt for the DP-3, also known among dwelling policies as the "special form."

Like the DP-2, the DP-3 covers the dwelling and other structures up to the policy's dollar limit or the property's replacement cost (whichever is less) and covers the owner's personal property up to the lesser of the policy limit or its actual cash value.

Under the DP-3, the owner's personal property is covered against the same types of losses as the DP-2. However, with respect to the dwelling and other structures (such as garages), the owner gets what's commonly known as "all-risk" or "open-peril" coverage. This means the dwelling and other structures will generally be covered no matter the cause of loss, unless the type of loss is specifically excluded by the policy language.

As a reminder, losses specifically excluded from dwelling policies (even the DP-3) include but aren't limited to flood damage, earthquake damage, intentional damage, war-related losses, nuclear reactions and theft.

Dwelling Endorsements for Theft

Although not covered by standard policies, theft can be added as a cause of loss to a dwelling policy as an endorsement. In general, a "broad theft endorsement" can be purchased for an owner-occupied dwelling and can reimburse the owner if theft occurs either at or away from the dwelling. A "limited theft" endorsement is intended for non-owner-occupied dwellings and only insures the owner when theft occurs onsite.

Homeowners Insurance

Since purchasing separate policies for dwelling coverage, theft and personal liability took up too much time and cost too much money, many carriers shifted their attention away from dwelling policies in the 1950s and began encouraging homeowners to buy a multi-part product that had been designed specifically for their insurance needs. That product, known as **homeowners insurance**, built upon the basic dwelling policy and is used to cover most kinds of owner-occupied dwellings today.

Who's Covered by Homeowners Insurance?

In addition to listing other important details, the declarations page of a homeowners insurance policy will contain the name of the "named insured." In most cases, the named insured is the policyholder who is responsible for paying premiums to the insurance company and is eligible for compensation after an insured loss. Though the typical named insured is both the owner and occupant of the entire dwelling, this person can also be someone who owns or occupies just a portion of a dwelling or who owns a building under construction. Even a tenant can be a named insured if he or she takes some initiative and purchases the appropriate policy.

In homeowners insurance, coverage of liability and personal property is often broad enough to apply to individuals other than the named insured. Such protection extends to any relatives who live with the named insured, as well as to a non-relative who is under 21, lives at the insured premises and is being cared for by the named insured or that person's family. This means everyone from the named insured's spouse to the insured's foster child or parent can be covered by homeowners insurance, assuming they reside with the named insured.

Near the start of the new millennium, most insurers clarified coverage for sons, daughters and other young people who may be attending college away from home. Full-time students remain covered for property losses and liability until they turn 24 if they are related to the named insured and lived with the named insured immediately prior to attending school.

It would be unwise, however, to assume that homeowners insurance is a big tent that covers everyone who is remotely affiliated with the named insured. Contrary to popular belief, tenants who aren't related to the named insured aren't protected by their landlord's policy. And even relatives might lack coverage if they're merely guests in the named insured's home instead of permanent residents.

While a named insured's spouse gets coverage if he or she lives on the same premises, former spouses are likely to need their own insurance immediately after a divorce. Similarly, a domestic partner or roommate who isn't related to the named insured might need his or her own insurance.

If the named insured dies, the policy is assigned, in part, to the deceased's legal representative. This transfer of coverage is applicable only in regard to liability at the deceased's residence and to damage to the deceased's property. It doesn't cover the legal representative's belongings and doesn't cover liability stemming from an offsite accident.

Homeowners Insurance Coverages A to F

Most homeowners insurance policies feature six broad types of coverage. In a manner similar to dwelling policies, each of the six kinds of coverage tends to have its own letter:

- Coverage A covers a person's dwelling and any structures attached to it.

- Coverage B covers structures on the named insured's property that aren't attached to the dwelling, such as a stand-alone garage or shed.

- Coverage C covers personal property.

- Coverage D provides compensation when a loss makes a person's dwelling uninhabitable and results in additional living expenses (such as the cost of a hotel room).

- Coverage E is insurance for cases of personal liability (such as being accused of injuring someone or damaging someone else's property).

- Coverage F is no-fault insurance intended to pay for someone else's medical care after an accident regardless of whether the insured is technically liable for an injury.

Each lettered coverage has its own dollar limit, but these limits are generally dependent upon one another. An insurer's limit of liability for Coverage B, for instance, is often equal to 10 percent of its limit for Coverage A. Although each insurer may require its customers to purchase a minimum amount of coverage, people are generally allowed to increase any of the six limits of liability by paying more in premiums.

To better understand the strengths and weaknesses of the standard homeowners insurance policy, let's go through these six kinds of coverage one at a time.

Coverage A

Coverage A insures a person's dwelling. In simplest terms, the **dwelling** is the structure a person lives in. Most often, the dwelling is a one-family building used by the insured and the insured's relatives. However, a multi-unit building might be considered a covered dwelling if it is designed for two, three or even four families and is occupied in part by the policyholder.

In most homeowners insurance policies, the dwelling and all the land and other structures surrounding it are collectively known as the **residence premises**.

In addition to covering the dwelling, Coverage A is used to insure other structures that are both on the residence premises and attached to the home. An attached garage would be insured through Coverage A, as might a deck. Garages and other structures not attached to the dwelling are covered by a different part of the policy.

Coverage B

Coverage B is property insurance for a homeowner's detached structures. A **detached structure** may be defined as a structure that is separate from a dwelling but still situated on the residence premises. Common examples of detached structures are:

- Detached garages.
- Barns.
- Sheds.
- In-ground pools.
- Mailboxes.
- Driveways.
- Sidewalks.
- Satellite dishes.

A little bit of Coverage B is included in most homeowners insurance policies, even in cases where there are no detached structures at the property. By default, this insurance is usually equal in value to 10 percent of the homeowner's dwelling coverage. So, if a dwelling is insured for $100,000 through Coverage A, detached structures on the same residence premises will be insured for $10,000. Coverage for detached structures that are buildings (such as detached garages) tend to be based on a structure's replacement cost. For detached structures that aren't buildings, coverage tends to be based on actual cash value.

Coverage C

Coverage C is **contents coverage**. In general, contents coverage is for all the belongings the insured owns or uses. Although the insurance for these items is part of a homeowners policy, the insured's contents remain covered outside the home, too. In fact, Coverage C is meant to insure people's personal property all over the world.

Like the dollar limit for Coverage B, the dollar limit for Coverage C is expressed as a percentage of Coverage A. Most policies provide the insured with contents coverage equal to at least 50 percent of the person's dwelling coverage. So, if a dwelling is insured for $100,000, the insured will be entitled to no more than $50,000 to repair or replace all damaged or stolen items.

Since tenants and condo owners receive minimal benefits under Coverage A, these individuals are allowed to insure their belongings for a dollar amount of their own choosing. Special polices for these kinds of consumers are mentioned in greater detail elsewhere in this chapter.

Valuation of Contents

There are a few negative aspects of Coverage C that should be disclosed to the consumer. First and foremost, the insured needs to understand that the standard homeowners insurance policy will only reimburse people for their personal property's actual cash value. An item's actual cash value is its replacement cost minus depreciation.

As an example, suppose someone purchases a new television set for $800, uses it for five years and loses it in a fire when its estimated value has dropped to $300. In this case, the insurance company would only need to reimburse the person for a $300 loss. It wouldn't necessarily need to pay for a new TV.

Insurance that doesn't take depreciation into account is known as "replacement-cost coverage" and can be purchased at an additional price.

Limits on Location

Coverage C insures personal property on a worldwide basis. But despite this flexibility, the policy often allows the insurer to limit coverage depending on where the lost or damaged property was normally stored. If an item was normally kept at a dwelling other than what's listed on the policy's declarations page, reimbursement might amount to no more than 10 percent of the person's Coverage C limit or $1,000, whichever amount is greater.

As an example, pretend a homeowner has insured the contents of a country house for $50,000. Let's further suppose the homeowner also keeps an apartment in the city and doesn't have a renters policy for it. If a fire were to break out in the apartment and destroy $50,000 worth of contents, the homeowner would still be able to make a claim but would be reimbursed for no more than $5,000 (10 percent of the Coverage C limit).

Personal Property and Special Limits of Liability

Insurance companies generally have no problem covering basic belongings that are common to the average household. But in an effort to mitigate risk and keep premiums down, they set coverage limits on some highly valued items. These limits are enforced on a per-claim basis and are sometimes known as **special limits of liability**. In most policies, these limits apply to the following kinds of personal property:

- *Jewelry:* Homeowners insurance will often provide no more than $1,500 to replace jewelry after a theft. While there is no special limit of liability when a jewelry claim involves a covered peril besides theft, most policies only cover personal property against perils that are named specifically in the insurance contract. Mysterious losses—including those that occur when a stone comes off its setting or when a ring falls down a drain—are typically not covered by homeowners insurance.

- *Furs:* If a fur is stolen, the insured will receive no more than $1,500 as compensation for the loss. If an insured files claims for stolen jewelry and furs at the same time, the insurer will pay up to $1,500 combined for both kinds of items. It won't apply $1,500 toward the jewelry and another $1,500 toward the furs.

- *Silverware and similar items:* Coverage of silverware, gold-ware, platinum-ware and pewter-ware is limited to $2,500 in the event of theft. There's no specific limit when these items are affected by other covered perils.

- *Money:* Coverage of lost or damaged cash, bank notes, bullion, debit cards and some metals is limited to $200.

- *Valuable documents:* Insurers put a $1,500 limit on manuscripts, passports, stamps, tickets, letters of credit, deeds, securities and other important kinds of documentation. It makes no difference whether these documents are printed on paper or stored electronically.

- *Guns:* Firearms and ammunition are only covered for up to $2,500. This limit applies only to instances of theft.

- *Boats:* All watercraft and their related parts and accessories are covered for up to $1,500. Liability coverage for boaters is dependent on several factors and is addressed elsewhere in this book.

- *Trailers:* Trailers and semi-trailers are insured for up to $1,500.

- *Electronic items and accessories:* Some electronic devices receive limited coverage when kept on or inside a motor vehicle. For a $1,500 coverage limit to apply, a device must be versatile enough to be used with and without the help of the vehicle's electrical system. Presumably, a cell phone or a portable music player would fall under this category. According to the ISO, accessories impacted by the $1,500 limit include audio tapes, CDs, wires and antennas.

- *Tombstones:* Grave markers and mausoleums are covered for up to $5,000 per occurrence.

Scheduling Valuables

People can specially insure their valuables by **scheduling** them. Scheduling involves itemizing a person's valuables and insuring each item for a specific amount. A person with two paintings, for example, might schedule one of them for $50,000 and the other for $100,000. Scheduling can involve either adding a special endorsement to an existing policy (such as a homeowners insurance policy) or buying a stand-alone policy for the specific items.

Scheduling may minimize disputes after a loss because it often forces the owner to prove ownership of an item before insurance can be issued. It's also a relatively simple solution if a person wants to insure only a few items of special value. Scheduling can be less beneficial for people who want to insure large collections, since each item must be appraised and added to the policy individually.

When insurance applies to only one piece of property (as is the case with scheduling), it is sometimes known as **specific insurance**.

Blanket insurance is the opposite of specific insurance. Rather than having each piece of property itemized and covered up to its own dollar limit, it provides broad, generally worded coverage to multiple pieces of property.

Illegal Items and Substances

It probably goes without saying, but Coverage C can't be used to insure illegal items. This exclusion applies to unlawful substances and stolen property.

Coverage D

Having insurance to help replace or repair a dwelling or personal property can be a blessing. But what are homeowners and their families supposed to do between the time a loss occurs and the time they are allowed to move back into a permanent residence? How are they supposed to handle all the expenses that arise from being displaced?

Those questions are answered by Coverage D, which is commonly known as **loss of use coverage**. Loss of use coverage pays money to the insured when the residence premises is made uninhabitable by a covered peril.

Depending on their situation, homeowners are entitled to one of two kinds of benefits while their residence premises is effectively out of service. The most common kind comes in the form of **additional living expenses**. Additional living expenses are those expenses the homeowner encounters as a direct result of not being able to use his or her home. Among other possibilities, these expenses may include the cost of meals and temporary lodging.

A lesser-known benefit is available to landlords when a rented portion of the residence premises becomes unusable. Similar to part of a dwelling policy, this benefit reimburses the insured for the fair rental value of a dwelling until necessary repairs are completed.

Some insurers limit benefits under Coverage D to a set percentage of Coverage A. When a dollar limit is used, it's often equal to 30 percent of the dwelling's insured value. So, if a house is insured for $100,000, the owner will have $30,000 of coverage for loss of use. Renters and condo owners are typically entitled to loss of use coverage equal to 30 percent or 50 percent of their contents coverage.

Acts of Civil Authority

Pretend you and your family are driving back home after a vacation. You're ready to turn down your street when you notice police officers and barricades blocking your way. After getting out of your car, you're told there was a serious fire in the neighborhood. Although your home wasn't damaged, you're forbidden from accessing the residence until local authorities have completed an investigation.

Situations like this are said to involve **acts of civil authority**. An act of civil authority, just like major damage to a dwelling, can produce additional living expenses, such as the cost of food and lodging.

The standard policy pays additional living expenses for up to two weeks when the insured's dwelling becomes inaccessible because of damage to a nearby structure. The damage must be caused by a peril that is covered by the insurance policy. If the damage makes the rented portion of a dwelling inaccessible, the homeowner may be entitled to the property's fair rental value on a prorated level for up to two weeks.

Coverage E

Coverage E is an important yet often overlooked component of homeowners insurance. It typically provides **personal liability insurance** to the homeowner and other insureds in the amount of $100,000 or more.

This insurance applies when third parties suffer accidental harm to themselves or their property because of something an insured did or failed to do. For example, depending on the circumstances, a homeowner might be liable if he or she allows ice to form on the residence premises and a visitor slips on it. Similarly, the insured might be held responsible if the insured's dog is allowed to roam free and attacks a stranger.

Unlike insurance for an insured person's dwelling and belongings, the personal liability insurance found in Coverage E might not require payment of a deductible.

The personal liability insurance made possible through Coverage E can pertain to an insured's liability anywhere in the world with a few exceptions. The worldwide reach of the coverage tends to be applicable when the alleged damage is tied to the insured's actions. So, if an insured accidentally breaks someone's nose by hitting the person with an errant baseball, he or she might be covered for the accident no matter if it occurs in the insured's backyard or at a park across the country.

Geography sometimes does matter when damage isn't caused directly by the insured but is related to conditions at a particular location. Suppose a person owns a house and a condo and has only insured the house. If the person throws a party at the condo and a guest has a serious fall there and sues, the owner might not be covered by homeowners insurance. In this situation, coverage might only be possible if insurance for the house was purchased before the owner bought the condo.

Damage to Other People's Property
Major claims for benefits under Coverage E often involve cases in which bodily harm has been done to another person. However, a homeowner can also file claims under Coverage E when he or she has damaged another person's property.

In addition to the main dollar limit of Coverage E, the standard homeowners insurance policy provides up to $1,000 (sometimes $500) to cover the replacement cost of another person's damaged property even if there hasn't been any negligence. This provision allows benefits to be paid to the owner of the damaged property regardless of whether the insured is technically at fault. The insurance can even be used to pay damages caused by the intentional acts of an insured who is younger than 13. So, if a homeowner's young son intentionally hurls a ball at a neighbor's garage or window and damages the neighbor's property, the parent's insurance company might pay to repair the damage.

Beyond those $1,000 or so, damage caused by an insured to another person's property might not be covered unless the insured is deemed liable for the loss.

Personal Liability Exclusions

The Coverage E portion of a homeowners insurance policy contains several significant exclusions. To prevent conflicts at claim time, insurance producers might want to discuss these exclusions with buyers before a policy is ever issued.

Homeowners insurance doesn't help people manage professional liability risks or business liability risks. If homeowners injure another person or damage another person's property during the course of conducting business or rendering professional services, they are unlikely to be protected by their homeowners insurance in any way. In order to address those kinds of risks, they'll need to purchase other insurance products.

Coverage E also doesn't help the insured deal with liability unrelated to bodily injury or property damage. Therefore, if a person is fearful of being sued for libel, slander or invasion of privacy, homeowners insurance isn't the solution to the problem.

In some cases, the personal liability insurance will be worthless depending on how the insured caused bodily injury or property damage. A homeowner isn't insured for personal liability when the injury or damage is linked to sexual, physical or mental abuse of another person. Also, as a result of AIDS-related lawsuits in the 1980s and '90s, homeowners insurance no longer pays claims for bodily harm when an insured is liable for the spread of a communicable disease. Claims related to the use, creation, possession, delivery or sale of controlled substances will also be denied, including those linked to cocaine, LSD and other illegal drugs.

Sometimes, even the identity of the wronged party in a liability dispute is important to the insurance company. Although Coverage E can be used to cover losses sustained by a guest at a residence premises, it doesn't cover losses sustained by another insured. For example, it generally won't respond if the policyholder causes bodily injury to a family member who lives in the same house.

Defense Costs

With the price of defending oneself in court so high these days, it's important for an insured to know that defense costs are included in nearly all homeowners insurance policies. The insurer has a duty to defend the inured in court against allegations of bodily injury or property damage, no matter if the suit against the person is legitimate or frivolous. The money to pay for this defense comes out of the insurance company's pocket and generally won't run out until the insurer has paid settlement costs or damages in an amount equal to Coverage E's limit of liability. In homeowners insurance, payment of defense costs (as opposed to settlements and judgments) generally won't erode the dollar limits under Coverage E.

Unlike some other kinds of insurance contracts, homeowners insurance policies allow the insurance company to select the legal team that will handle the insured's defense. They also give the insurer the power to settle a liability dispute at a time of its own choosing and conduct its own investigation of the situation.

When an insured participates in the investigation or in the defense process, the insurance company will reimburse the person for lost income, often up to $250 per day.

Coverage F

Coverage F usually provides up to $1,000 for medical expenses when a third party is injured by the insured or on the insured's property. Unlike Coverage E, Coverage F covers these expenses regardless of whether the insured is at fault.

The $1,000 of coverage made available through Coverage F can be applied to medical expenses that an injured third party incurs within three years after an accident. The $1,000 can be used to pay for any of the following:

- Private nursing.
- Hospitalization.
- Ambulance services.
- X-rays.
- Dental work.
- Physician services.
- Surgery.
- Prosthetic devices.
- Funeral expenses.

For an insurer to authorize benefits under Coverage F, at least one of the following circumstances must apply:

- The person was injured while on the insured's property and wasn't guilty of trespassing.
- The person was injured directly by the insured or the insured's activities.
- The person was injured by the insured's household employee while the employee was fulfilling his or her job duties.
- The person was injured by an insured's pet.
- The person was injured near the insured's property because of the condition of the insured's property (such as a tree with hazardous branches that extend into a neighbor's yard).

Coverage F can't be used as medical insurance for anyone who is considered an insured by the insurance company. So, for example, if a husband is mopping his kitchen floor and his wife slips and injures herself, the wife's medical expenses will not be covered by homeowners insurance. Injuries sustained by an insured's domestic employees might represent exceptions to this exclusion, but the insurer will still refuse to pay any expenses when an alternative form of reimbursement is available through disability laws or workers compensation laws.

Common Coverage Forms

Up until now, we've studied homeowners insurance policies and their corresponding terms and conditions in a very general sense. However, producers and consumers need to realize there are several distinct variations on the typical homeowners insurance policy.

Most property insurance companies in the United States use homeowners insurance policies with language written by the Insurance Services Offices (ISO). The ISO's standard policies have names that feature the letters "HO" followed by a number. In theory, a person could purchase an HO-1, HO-2, HO-3, HO-4, HO-5, HO-6, HO-7 or HO-8 policy. All of these forms tend to treat personal liability in essentially the same way, but they differ in how they cover the insured's property.

Let's summarize the most commonly recognized homeowners insurance forms from the ISO.

HO-1

The HO-1 policy form is sometimes referred to as the "basic form." Rarely sold these days, it insures the homeowner's property against fewer perils than the typical homeowners policy, and it contains very broad exclusions by comparison.

An insurance policy modeled after the ISO's HO-1 form insures the homeowner against property losses caused by the following perils:

- Fire.

- Lightning.

- Wind.

- Civil commotion.

- Smoke.

- Hail.

- Aircraft and other vehicles.

- Volcanic action.

- Explosions.

- Riot.

- Vandalism and malicious mischief.

- Theft.

It might be helpful to note that the HO-1 covers someone against the same perils as a fully endorsed version of the DP-1 (other than the added peril of theft).

As mentioned earlier, the dwelling's insured value represents the dollar limit for Coverage A, and many of the policy's other dollar limits are based on this number. With an HO-1 policy in force, detached structures are covered for 10 percent of Coverage A. Coverage of contents is equal to 50 percent of Coverage A. Loss of use coverage is equal to 10 percent of Coverage A.

HO-2

The HO-2 policy form is sometimes referred to as the "broad form." This policy is fairly popular and insures the homeowner against property losses caused by many common perils. In addition to covering losses brought on by all the perils mentioned in the HO-1 form, the HO-2 form reimburses the insured for losses related to the following:

- Falling objects.

- Weight of ice, snow or sleet.

- Accidental discharge of water or steam.

- Freezing.

- Sudden and accidental tearing, cracking, burning or bulging of heating, air conditioning, water or steam systems.

- Sudden and accidental discharge from artificially generated electrical current.

It might be helpful to note the similarities in covered perils under the HO-2 and the aforementioned DP-2. They help explain why both of those forms are considered "broad" coverage.

With an HO-2 policy in force, detached structures are covered for 10 percent of Coverage A. Coverage of contents is equal to 50 percent of Coverage A. Loss of use coverage is equal to 30 percent of Coverage A.

HO-3

The HO-3 policy form is sometimes referred to as the "special form." It's generally considered the standard version of modern homeowners insurance. When phrases such as "the typical policy" and "the standard policy" are used in this chapter, the reader should infer we are talking about the HO-3 policy form.

Unlike previously mentioned homeowners forms, the HO-3 form covers the insured dwelling and detached structures on an "open-peril" basis. This means a loss will be covered by the policy unless the insurance contract specifically excludes it.

It might be helpful to note the similarities in covered perils under the HO-3 and the aforementioned DP-3. They help explain why both of those forms are considered "special" coverage.

When explaining the positive features within HO-3 policies, insurance producers sometimes forget to mention that the open-peril coverage applies only to the dwelling and other structures. By default, HO-3 policies cover personal property on a "named-peril" basis just like HO-1 policies and HO-2 policies. This means a loss pertaining to personal property will only be covered if it's been caused by a peril specifically mentioned as a covered peril in the insurance contract. With respect to personal property, the covered perils in an HO-3 policy are basically the same as those in an HO-2 policy.

With an HO-3 policy in force, detached structures are covered for 10 percent of Coverage A. Coverage of contents is equal to 50 percent of Coverage A. Loss of use coverage is equal to 30 percent of Coverage A.

HO-4

Contrary to popular belief, a renter's personal property is generally not covered by the landlord's insurance policy. This is true no matter if damage to the property is caused by the property's owner or by another tenant in the same building.

From a liability standpoint, tenants without renters insurance might have to pay out of pocket for legal services and court-awarded damages if they are ever sued by a third party. While a landlord might still be held liable for slip-and-fall injuries on the property's steps, adjoining sidewalks or common areas, a renter can be held liable for similar injuries suffered inside his or her portion of the residence premises. The renter might also be liable for hazards—such as a fire—that start in his or her portion of the premises and spread far enough to damage another tenant's property.

All these potential problems may be managed through the HO-4 policy form, which is used to insure renters and their belongings. The HO-4 policy form insures personal property against the same perils named in the HO-2 form. But the typical renters insurance policy is different from other homeowners policies in several respects.

The most significant difference between HO-4 policies and the other forms we've discussed is that the HO-4 policy's emphasis is on contents coverage rather than on dwelling coverage. This makes sense because the responsibility of maintaining the building and fixing structural problems usually belongs to the landlord. Instead of expressing the dollar limit for contents coverage as a percentage of Coverage A, a renters policy is meant to provide as much contents coverage as the tenant wants. It also often provides personal liability protection.

Despite its emphasis on contents coverage, a renters policy may contain a very limited amount of dwelling insurance. This coverage can be used to reimburse tenants when they've made improvements or additions to their rented dwelling and suffer damage to those improvements or additions. This insurance can only be utilized if the tenant paid for the improvements or additions and hasn't been reimbursed by the landlord.

If a person shares a rented dwelling with a roommate who is a non-relative, his or her renters policy probably doesn't cover the roommate's belongings or the roommate's liability. Policies that jointly cover non-related residents of the same dwelling can be obtained from some insurance companies upon request.

With an HO-4 policy in force, the tenant's improvements or additions to the rented portion of the dwelling are covered for 10 percent of Coverage C. Loss of use coverage is equal to 30 percent of Coverage C.

HO-5

The HO-5 policy form gives the insured open-peril coverage for both the dwelling and personal property.

Depending on a carrier's preference, open-peril coverage for both the dwelling and its contents might not be obtained via an HO-5 policy. Instead, the open-peril coverage for personal property will simply be added onto an HO-3 policy as an endorsement for an additional cost.

HO-6

Condominiums are covered by a "master policy," which is purchased by an elected association on behalf of all residents at the complex. The master policy will cover damage to a building's exterior, as well as common areas such as basements and hallways. The extent to which the master policy insures each individual unit is left up to the association.

Those parts of the unit that aren't covered by the master policy are the individual owner's responsibility. Of course, each individual owner is also responsible for obtaining his or her own insurance for personal property and personal liability.

To address the concerns of condo dwellers and townhouse owners, insurance companies sell policies based on the HO-6 form, also known as the "unit-owners" form. The unit-owners form features named-peril coverage for the insured's personal property and a little bit of named-peril coverage for the unit itself. The named perils in an HO-6 policy are the same as those in an HO-2 policy.

With an HO-6 policy in force, the unit and detached structures are often covered by default for $1,000. Loss of use coverage is equal to 50 percent of Coverage C.

HO-7

HO-7 policies are meant to insure mobile homes, which can also be covered by adding endorsements to other homeowners forms.

HO-8

The HO-8 policy form is sometimes known as the "modified" form. It's not used in all states and is typically used to cover older homes in urban areas when the dwelling's market value is considerably lower than its replacement cost.

In many ways, the coverage available through an HO-8 policy is identical to the coverage in an HO-1 policy. However, in a very important difference, HO-8 policies cover the dwelling only up to its actual cash value.

Unlike all other common kinds of homeowners policy forms, the HO-8 form limits coverage of theft to $1,000 per occurrence, and it generally doesn't cover instances of theft in a place other than the residence premises.

With an HO-8 policy in force, detached structures are covered for 10 percent of Coverage A. Coverage of contents is equal to 50 percent of Coverage A. Loss of use coverage is equal to 10 percent of Coverage A.

Replacing the Dwelling

As a reminder, most homeowners insurance policies cover buildings up to their replacement cost and cover contents up to their "actual cash value." The dwelling's replacement cost is the amount it would take to rebuild a new dwelling "of like kind and quality" in the same general area as the existing dwelling.

Until a few decades ago, homeowners had the ability to insure their dwelling at **guaranteed replacement cost**. This meant the insurer would pay to replace the dwelling even if the cost was higher than the policy's Coverage A limit. If, for instance, the price of construction created a situation in which it cost $120,000 to replace a home that was insured for $100,000, the extra $20,000 would still be picked up by the insurance company.

An assortment of catastrophes in the 1990s made it tougher to obtain guaranteed replacement-cost insurance. Instead, insurers began offering **extended replacement-cost coverage**. This insurance will still provide some extra coverage when the cost of replacing the dwelling is larger than the policy's Coverage A limit. However, extended replacement benefits are capped, often at 120 percent or 125 percent of the Coverage A limit. If a person has insured a home for $100,000 and has extended replacement coverage that caps benefits at 125 percent, the insurer will pay up to $125,000 to replace the dwelling. Any costs beyond $125,000 will be the owner's responsibility.

If a homeowner is concerned about the continued accuracy of the dwelling's replacement cost, helpful endorsements can be added to the policy. To guard against increases in local building costs, the insured can opt for **inflation protection**. This feature will recalculate the dwelling's insured value on a regular basis and may increase the policy's Coverage A limit by a few percentage points. It's also possible to obtain a "demand surge endorsement," which can go into effect when construction prices rise after a catastrophic event.

Coinsurance Clauses in Homeowners Insurance

When consumers decide how much replacement-cost coverage to purchase for their dwelling, they need to think about more than just the possibility of a total loss. Smaller losses won't be covered in full if the amount of replacement-cost insurance is less than the amount listed in the policy's coinsurance clause. A coinsurance clause in a homeowners insurance policy is often called an "insurance to value provision."

The typical homeowners insurance policy has a coinsurance clause requiring the insured to cover a dwelling for at least 80 percent of its replacement cost. In this context, the replacement cost would be the cost of rebuilding a similar structure on the same spot at the time of the claim. This is an important point because a person who insures a home at only 80 percent of its replacement cost at the time of purchase won't satisfy the policy's coinsurance requirement if construction costs increase over time.

If a homeowner doesn't insure the dwelling for at least 80 percent of its replacement cost and suffers a partial loss, the insurer won't reimburse the insured for the entire loss. Instead, the insured will be entitled to the actual cash value of the damaged portion of the property or a prorated amount based on how close the person was to meeting the coinsurance requirement. The larger of these two figures will be paid by the insurance company. The rest of the loss won't be covered.

Some Coinsurance Examples

Even for insurance veterans, coinsurance clauses can be confusing. Let's look at a few examples of how this kind of clause might affect a homeowner.

Sally purchased replacement-cost coverage for her home in the amount of $80,000. After a fire, it was determined that the cost to replace the entire home would have been $100,000. Since Sally's amount of replacement-cost coverage ($80,000) was equal to 80 percent of the home's replacement cost ($100,000 × 80% = $80,000), she met her coinsurance requirement and had her claim paid in full, up to her Coverage A limit.

Jim purchased replacement-cost coverage for his home in the amount of $175,000. After a windstorm damaged the dwelling's roof, it was determined that the cost to replace the entire home would have been $200,000. Since Jim's amount of replacement-cost coverage ($175,000) was greater than 80 percent of the home's replacement cost ($200,000 × 80% = $160,000), he met his coinsurance requirement and had his claim paid in full, up to his Coverage A limit.

Mark purchased replacement-cost coverage for his home in the amount of $300,000. After a hailstorm, it was determined that the cost to replace the entire home would have been $500,000. Since Mark's amount of replacement-cost coverage ($300,000) was less than 80 percent of the home's replacement cost ($500,000 × 80% = $400,000), he didn't meet his coinsurance requirement and was only covered for a portion of his losses.

Coinsurance and Prorated Settlements

When a settlement is prorated because of a failure to satisfy coinsurance requirements, an insurance professional can look at the coinsurance clause, plug in the appropriate numbers and determine the amount, in dollars, the insurance company will pay to the policyholder.

To determine the covered portion of a loss, we must first determine the size, in dollars, of the coinsurance requirement. This is accomplished by multiplying the 80 percent coinsurance requirement by the home's replacement cost at claim time. So, for our friend Mark from the preceding example, we would multiply 80 percent by $500,000 and get a result of $400,000.

In the next step, we need to divide the amount of purchased replacement cost coverage by the size of the coinsurance requirement in dollars. For Mark, we would divide $300,000 by $400,000 and get a result of 0.75. This means Mark would be covered for no more than 75 percent of any losses to the dwelling except after a total loss.

Now all we have to do is multiply our answer from the previous step by the actual loss. Suppose the hailstorm caused $40,000 of damage to Mark's home. His insurance company would multiply $40,000 by 75 percent and get a result of $30,000.

Unless the actual cash value of the damaged portion of the property is greater than $30,000, this is the amount Mark will receive from his insurance company. The remaining $10,000 would be considered an uninsured loss.

The preceding steps can be summarized via either of the following equations:

- Prorated settlement = [Coverage A limit ÷ (80 percent × replacement cost at claim time)] × actual loss – deductible.

- Prorated settlement = (Insurance carried ÷ Insurance required) × actual loss – deductible.

As important as the coinsurance clause sometimes is, it's often only a factor in homeowners insurance when there's partial damage to a building. It's often not applicable when a building is completely destroyed, and it doesn't impact coverage of contents, additional living expenses or personal liability claims.

Homeowners insurance and Mortgage Lenders

Even if a prospective homeowner remains unsold on the benefits of having insurance, the person's mortgage lender will require coverage. If the person refuses to abide by the lender's terms, the loan will be canceled.

Since the lender has an insurable interest in the property, it can add itself as an insured to a borrower's homeowners insurance policy. In this case, following a loss to the dwelling or other structures, the insurer will divide the insurance money between the borrower and the lender in proportion to his or her ownership interest in the property. Then, the lender will typically relinquish its portion to the homeowner on the condition that the funds be used to repair any damage.

When named as an insured, the lender maintains certain rights regardless of a homeowner's failure to comply with various parts of the policy. For example, if a borrower suffers a loss to the dwelling but fails to provide proof to the insurer within a reasonable time, the lender can provide it and not lose its share of the insurance money. Similarly, upon learning that a borrower hasn't paid premiums, the lender has the right to provide the owed amount to the insurer and keep the coverage in force.

The rights of lenders can sometimes be found in a policy's "loss payable clause" or "mortgagee clause."

Peril-Specific Information

Now that we've reviewed the basics of the most common homeowners forms, let's get a little more specific and look at how these forms address specific perils.

Water Damage

Coverage of water damage is probably the least understood aspect of homeowners insurance. Even after all the legal back and forth between homeowners and insurers following various hurricanes and other major storms, roughly one-third of households still believe incorrectly that they're covered for flood losses by way of their homeowners insurance.

The kinds of water-related losses that are generally excluded from the standard policy are:

- Flood.
- Surface water.
- Water backup from sewers, drains or sump pumps.
- Foundation seepage.
- Hydrostatic pressure.
- Ignored wear and tear.

Though small leaks that go unaddressed and cause property damage are considered a form of wear and tear and aren't covered by homeowners insurance, policyholders are insured against damage from sudden leaks and overflows. Homeowners can be reimbursed for their losses when there is sudden accidental discharge or overflow of water from a plumbing system, air conditioning system, heating system, sprinkler system or an appliance. Damage stemming from a burst pipe or overflowing toilet, for example, should be covered under many circumstances if the owner has insurance that is at least as extensive as the HO-2.

Sudden kinds of water damage are excluded from coverage if the homeowner hasn't taken reasonable steps to prevent a major loss. Depending on the policy and the nature of the damage, these reasonable steps can pertain to the temperature in the dwelling at the time of the loss. For instance, damage caused by frozen pipes is generally not covered if the homeowner hasn't taken reasonable measures to keep the dwelling heated.

Vandalism and Malicious Mischief

Vandalism and malicious mischief are said to have occurred when someone has done intentional damage to another person's building or belongings. The standard homeowners policy insures the policyholder against vandalism to the dwelling and to contents.

Via a **vacancy clause**, the insurer can refuse to cover losses pertaining to broken glass or vandalism when the dwelling has been vacant for an extended period of time (usually 60 days). However, a home isn't "vacant" just because it's unoccupied. In general, the dwelling is considered vacant only when there's reasonably not enough personal property for a person to live there. The policy also makes it clear that a dwelling isn't vacant if it's still under construction. Note, however, that different definitions of vacancy tend to apply when insuring commercial buildings.

Power Outages and Electrical Surges

Losses brought on by power failures are not covered by homeowners insurance unless an outage is caused by a covered peril that has struck the residence premises.

Although homeowners insurance usually lists artificially generated electrical current as a covered peril, the practical benefits of this coverage can be very narrow. The standard policy doesn't cover electrical damage to tubes, transistors or circuits within computers or appliances.

Earth Movement and Volcanic Eruptions

Earth movement is a broad term used to describe earthquakes, mudslides, landslides and the formation of sinkholes. Damage caused directly by earth movement and nothing else is excluded from coverage in all the standard ISO homeowners policy forms. Still, homeowners receive some compensation when earth movement is followed by any of the following occurrences:

- Fire.
- Theft.
- Explosion.
- Breakage of glass.

Though damage is covered when it's caused by a volcanic eruption, covered property usually must be exposed to a harmful amount of ash or lava. Losses from any tremors or quakes that precede, accompany or follow a volcanic eruption aren't covered. For the purpose of determining a deductible, the insurance company will often consider all eruptions within 72 hours of one another to be a single occurrence.

War

Homeowners insurance policies won't provide compensation for damage caused by war. This exclusion pertains to declared war, as well as to undeclared war, civil war, insurrections and any discharge of a nuclear weapon. Losses caused by riots and civil commotion are addressed elsewhere in these policies and aren't excluded from coverage.

Though insurers didn't invoke war exclusions after the 9/11 terrorist attacks, many carriers began implementing terrorism exclusions in the months that followed. **The Terrorism Risk Insurance Act of 2002** (commonly known as "TRIA") requires that property and casualty insurance companies offer terrorism coverage to businesses, but the law doesn't apply to homeowners insurance.

Nuclear Reactions

Homeowners insurance provides practically no property or liability coverage when losses are caused by a nuclear hazard. A rare exception might be possible if a dwelling sustains fire damage due to a nuclear event. Damage caused by nuclear attacks, whether the attacks are intentional or unintentional, is considered war damage and isn't covered.

Special Coverage Issues in Homeowners Insurance

The next several sections of this chapter address how homeowners insurance caters to people who may have relatively specific coverage concerns. These people include those who have children, those who operate a home-based business and those who have pets.

Information about these and other topics tends to be scattered throughout most policy forms. For the sake of optimum comprehension and convenience, we've gathered up those assorted pieces and attempted to categorize them in an appropriate manner.

Children of the Insured

A person's child is considered an insured under a standard homeowners policy. In essence, the child's property is treated as if it were the parents' property, and any losses the child causes are treated as if they were caused by the child's mother, father or guardian.

Property insurers' treatment of a child's property and personal liability probably seems simple enough while the child is young, living entirely at home and not earning any money. But the child's insurance status might seem less clear when he or she heads off to college or works part time. Let's review how insurers deal with children who are working toward a degree and/or earning their own money.

Children and Personal Property

The standard policy will continue to cover a college-aged child who is away at school if the child is a full-time student and is 23 or younger, a relative of the homeowner and a resident of the residence premises prior to the move. A full-time student who isn't related to the named insured will be covered at school if the student is 20 or younger and was under the care of an insured at the residence premises prior to the move. The meaning of "full-time student" is based on the school's definition of that term.

If the college student's belongings are covered at all away from home, the coverage might still be equal to only a portion of Coverage C's dollar limit. If a covered student's personal property is lost or damaged, the carrier might provide compensation that is no more than $1,000 or 10 percent of the Coverage C limit, whichever is greater.

The student's belongings are covered against the same perils as the parent's belongings, but there may be special conditions that apply in cases of theft. For theft at the school-year residence to be covered at all, the student needs to have lived there within a specific timeframe prior to the loss, such as 45 to 60 days.

Children and Liability

Children who are covered for property losses under their parents' policy are also covered for personal liability. But liability issues can surface much earlier than during the child's college years. This is especially possible if the child does chores for neighbors in exchange for money.

Pretend a homeowner's 14-year-old daughter spends part of her summer mowing lawns and babysitting other people's children. How would an insurer respond if she were to do major damage to a neighbor's yard or accidentally injure a young child?

Though homeowners insurance doesn't cover an individual who causes property damage or physical harm while conducting business, the standard policy makes an important exception for many minors. Specifically, an individual who is under 21 remains covered for personal liability in a business situation if the individual is self-employed, has no employees and only conducts business on a part-time or occasional basis.

Pets of the Insured

The standard homeowners policy doesn't reimburse people for the loss of their birds, animals or fish. If the family dog becomes injured, dies or runs away, the insurance company will provide no financial assistance to the owner.

Homeowners insurance doesn't cover damage to the dwelling when it's caused by the insured's pet or an animal otherwise in the insured's care. Still, the HO-3 policy (as opposed to the other common coverage forms) does cover damage to the dwelling when it's caused by stray creatures. In the case of the HO-3, damage to the dwelling caused by a stray creature still isn't covered when the creature is a bird, insect, rodent or vermin.

An insured is covered anywhere in the world for personal liability when his or her pet harms another person or damages another person's property. If a homeowner is walking his dog and the dog bites a stranger, it's likely the insurance company will pay to defend the insured in court and pick up the cost of a settlement or legal judgment. This coverage is broad enough to also cover a third party who agrees to look after the pet on a temporary basis without charging a fee.

Third parties aren't covered for liability when they care for a person's pet as part of their business or when they care for the pet without the owner's permission. A boarding kennel, for example, would need its own liability insurance. There is also no liability protection when the property damage or bodily injury is suffered by another person who is covered by the same policy.

Home Offices and Business Property

Whether they're paid by an employer or work for themselves, an increasing number of Americans are working from home these days. Working from the comforts of one's own dwelling certainly has its advantages. But doing business beyond the confines of a traditional workplace has its risks, particularly in regard to property losses and personal liability.

Before we look specifically at property and liability risks for at-home workers, we need to know what the word "business" means to most property insurers. It's certainly not surprising that activities related to one's occupation or trade are usually considered business activities. But what about money-making activities that are more casual and sporadic in nature, such as babysitting, tutoring or holding a yard sale?

According to common policy language, a "business" can be operated on a full-time, part-time or occasional basis. An insured is conducting business whenever he or she receives compensation (monetary or otherwise) for performing tasks or providing services. However, an insured isn't engaged in business in any of the following situations:

- The insured is working as a volunteer and is only compensated for the expenses he or she incurs while performing volunteer duties.

- The insured is providing home day-care services to a relative.

- The insured is providing home day-care services to a non-relative but is only receiving home day-care services in return.

- The insured is performing an activity for compensation but didn't receive more than $2,000 in compensation for this activity during the 12 months prior to the policy's inception.

Business Property Losses

When a homeowner suffers a loss related to business property, reimbursement might depend on where the damaged or lost property was stored. The Coverage A section of the standard policy doesn't contain a business exclusion. So, if a person conducts business in a home office that's part of the dwelling and a covered peril causes structural damage to the office, the insurer is likely to pay for repairs. However, there are business exclusions that apply specifically to Coverage B and detached structures. In general, the insurer won't pay to repair or replace a detached structure if any part of it is used to conduct business.

Coverage C insures business property but only up to a certain point. When the business property is lost or damaged while on the residence premises, reimbursement will typically not exceed $2,500. When business property is lost or damaged while off the residence premises, reimbursement will often not exceed $250 or $500.

Businesses and Liability

In general, homeowners insurance doesn't cover individuals who harm other people or other people's property while conducting business. This exclusion represents a major coverage gap, particularly for those home-based businesspeople who deal with customers and clients face-to-face. Possible liability scenarios that might not be covered by homeowners insurance include the following:

- A customer trips over a rug at someone's home office and breaks a toe.
- While conducting business outside the office, the homeowner accidentally damages another person's property.
- While renovating a home office, a contractor slips on the homeowner's wet floor and breaks an ankle.

As the reader might recall, homeowners insurance provides some liability protection for minors who engage in business activities. For coverage to apply, all of the following must be true:

- The insured is under 21.
- The insured is self-employed.
- The insured's business activities aren't part of a full-time job.
- The insured has no employees.

Removing Trees and Debris

Even if a covered peril doesn't make direct contact with a dwelling, the home can still be damaged by debris and trees that get flung about by strong winds or other forces of nature. The cost of removing debris and fallen trees can sometimes amount to thousands of dollars. Fortunately for the homeowner, this expense may be covered by insurance.

The standard homeowners insurance policy covers removal of debris. When the cost of removing the debris and repairing or replacing damaged property is greater than the policy's dollar limit, the homeowner may receive an additional 5 percent of coverage that can be applied specifically to debris removal.

When a tree falls on the residence premises, a homeowner may be reimbursed for its removal. This free additional insurance has a cumulative limit of $1,000 per occurrence, and no more than $500 may be applied to the removal of a single tree. For removal to be covered, the tree needs to have either done damage to the homeowner's property or blocked access to a driveway or a ramp for disabled persons.

Following a windstorm, policyholders often wonder who is responsible for removing a neighbor's tree from their property. Regardless of where a fallen tree once stood, the party who suffers the property damage should file a claim with his or her insurance company. The neighbor would typically be liable for the loss only if the tree was obviously dying or wasn't being maintained properly by its owner.

Motorized Vehicles and Watercraft

The next few sections contain many details about how motor vehicles and boats are addressed in the typical homeowners policy. Yet because the provisions and exclusions mentioned here can be so complex, students shouldn't discuss these coverage issues with the public before reviewing the appropriate policy forms.

Damage of Vehicles and Watercraft
Just in case the exclusion isn't obvious, we'll begin by reminding ourselves that damage to automobiles isn't covered by homeowners insurance. Auto losses are meant to be covered by auto insurance policies.

Despite that general exclusion, Coverage C can be used to repair or replace motor vehicles that don't need to be registered under local law, assuming one of the following statements is true:

- The vehicle is only used to maintain the residence premises.
- The vehicle was made for the benefit of a disabled person.

With those conditions in mind, we can suppose that a pickup truck wouldn't be covered by homeowners insurance but that a riding lawnmower and a wheelchair might be.

As for auto parts and accessories, these items aren't covered if they're already installed. Electronic devices that are only meant to function with the help of the auto's power supply are also excluded from coverage. Conversely, electronic equipment that's in a car but can still be operated via another power source is covered for up to $1,500. Another $1,500 limit applies to all trailers and semi-trailers.

Some boats are covered by homeowners insurance but probably not for their true value. Insurance for a watercraft and all its parts and accessories is often capped at no more than $1,500. A craft or a trailer might not be covered at all if it's stolen from a location beyond the residence premises.

Damage From Vehicles
Damage done to the dwelling or personal property by a vehicle is a covered peril in most homeowners insurance policies. There's also additional insurance that may be utilized when someone else's vehicle damages trees, shrubs or plants on the residence premises. This additional coverage can equal as much as 5 percent of the homeowner's Coverage A limit, but the insurance company will not pay any more than $500 to replace a single tree, shrub or plant.

Vehicle and Watercraft Liability
The liability section of most homeowners insurance policies doesn't provide much coverage for the homeowner when an insured's vehicle is linked to bodily injury or property damage. Based on common ISO language, personal liability protection is only possible if one of the following is true:

- The property damage or bodily injury occurs while the vehicle is in storage at the insured location.
- The vehicle is only being used to help maintain the residence premises.
- The vehicle was made to assist a disabled person and is being used for that purpose.
- The vehicle doesn't belong to the insured and isn't meant to be driven onto public roadways.
- The vehicle belongs to the insured, isn't meant to be driven onto public roadways and causes property damage or bodily injury on the residence premises.
- The vehicle is a golf cart that holds less than four people, goes less than 25 mph and is being operated appropriately at or near a golf course.
- The vehicle is a golf cart that holds less than four people, goes less than 25 mph and is being operated in a private community where the insured lives and where golf carts are permitted.

As if those conditions weren't enough, the typical policy with ISO language won't provide liability protection to the insured if any one of the following statements is true:

- The vehicle is required to be registered with a local authority.
- The vehicle is being used in a contest of some kind, such as a race.
- Property damage or bodily injury occurs while someone was renting the vehicle from the insured.

- The insured is using the vehicle to transport people or property and is requiring passengers to pay a fee for the transportation.

- The vehicle (other than a golf cart) is being used by the insured during a business activity.

Similar conditions and exclusions pertain to watercraft liability, but they also tend to take technical factors, such as a craft's horsepower, into account. Insurance professionals who want to help consumers cover boats should refer back to their policy forms and consider alternative products.

Credit Cards

A little-known provision in homeowners insurance policies covers people for as much as $500 when their credit cards or bank cards are used without their permission. Those same $500 can be used when an insured is the victim of check forgery or unknowingly accepts counterfeit money. The $500 is considered extra insurance and can be utilized by the policyholder without having to pay a deductible.

The $500 for unauthorized use of credit cards and bank cards isn't accessible to an insured if the unauthorized use was committed by another person who lives on the residence premises. The insured's claim will also be denied if the credit or bank card was given to the user with the insured's consent.

Chapter Key Points

- Modern forms of property insurance can be traced back to the debut of the New York Standard Fire Policy in 1943.

- Many decades ago, the vast majority of families insured their homes through dwelling policies. Today, most dwelling policies are intended to cover small rental properties where the owner doesn't reside.

- Coverage A in a dwelling policy is insurance for the dwelling and attached structures.

- Coverage B in a dwelling policy is insurance for detached structures, such as a detached garage.

- Coverage C in a dwelling policy is insurance for the owner's personal property and for family members' personal property. However, it doesn't insure the personal property of tenants.

- Coverage D in a dwelling policy is for fair rental value in case a peril makes the dwelling uninhabitable for tenants.

- Coverage E in a dwelling policy is for additional living expenses an owner might incur as the result of a loss, such as the cost of having to rent a motel room while damage from a loss is being repaired.

- Without an added endorsement, a dwelling policy will exclude losses caused by theft. Also, without the proper endorsement, a dwelling policy doesn't cover the property owner for personal liability.

- There are generally three main types of ISO dwelling policies to choose from. The name of each one includes the abbreviation "DP" followed by a number.

- The most basic dwelling policy is known as the "DP-1" and is, in fact, also called the "basic form."

- The DP-1 covers the dwelling and the owner's property up to the lesser of the consumer's chosen dollar limit or the property's actual cash value (not replacement cost).

- By default, the DP-1 only covers losses caused by fire, lightning and explosion.

- Unlike other dwelling policies, the DP-1 doesn't cover additional living expenses (such as the cost of renting a hotel room after a fire).

- Two common endorsements can be added to the DP-1 to cover a wider range of losses, perhaps in exchange for an additional cost. One endorsement adds coverage for losses caused by wind, civil commotion, smoke, hail, aircraft and other vehicles, volcanic eruption explosions and riot. Another endorsement adds coverage for losses caused by vandalism and malicious mischief.

- The DP-2 covers a broader range of losses than the DP-1 and is, in fact, also known among dwelling policies as the "broad form."

- The DP-2 covers the residence and other structures (such as garages) up to the lesser of the policy's dollar limit or the property's replacement cost (not actual cash value). However, personal property belonging to the owner remains covered at actual cash value (not replacement cost).

- The perils covered under the DP-2 include all of those covered by the DP-1 (including those that can be added to the DP-1 by endorsement) PLUS losses caused by the following perils:

  o Falling objects.

  o Weight of snow, ice or sleet.

  o Accidental discharge or overflow of water.

  o Freezing.

  o Sudden and accidental tearing, cracking, burning or bulging of heating and water systems.

  o Sudden and accidental artificial current.

  o Burglary damage.

- Like the DP-2, the DP-3 covers the dwelling and other structures up the policy's dollar limit or the property's replacement cost (whichever is less) and covers the owners personal property up to the lesser of the policy limit or its actual cash value.

- Under the DP-3, the owner's personal property is covered against the same types of losses as the DP-2. However, with respect to the dwelling and other structures (such as garages), the owner gets open-peril coverage. This means the dwelling and other structures will generally be covered no matter the cause of loss, unless the type of loss is specifically excluded by the policy language.

- The declarations page of a homeowners insurance policy will contain the name of the named insured. In most cases, the named insured is the policyholder who is responsible for paying premiums to the insurance company and is eligible for compensation after an insured loss.

- Coverage of liability and personal property in homeowners insurance is often broad enough to apply to individuals other than the named insured. Such protection extends to any relatives who live with the insured, as well as to a non-relative who is under 21, lives at the insured premises and is being cared for by the insured or the insured's family.

- Most homeowners insurance policies feature six broad types of coverage. In a manner similar to dwelling policies, each of the six kinds of coverage tends to have its own letter. Coverage A covers a person's dwelling. Coverage B takes care of detached structures, such as garages and sheds. Coverage C reimburses people for the loss of their personal property. Coverage D gives them money when their dwelling becomes uninhabitable and results in additional expenses (such as the cost of a hotel room). Personal liability is covered under Coverage E.

Coverage F pays for other people's medical costs after an accident regardless of who is at fault.

- By default, Coverage B in homeowners insurance is usually equal in value to 10 percent of the homeowner's dwelling coverage. But a detached structure isn't insured against property damage if any part of it is used to conduct business.

- Coverage C in homeowners insurance is more commonly referred to as "contents coverage." In general, contents coverage is for all the belongings the insured owns or uses. Although the insurance for these items is part of a homeowners policy, the insured's contents remain covered outside the home, too. In fact, Coverage C is meant to insure people's personal property all over the world.

- Most homeowners policies provide the insured with contents coverage equal to at least 50 percent of the person's dwelling coverage.

- The standard homeowners form will only reimburse people for their personal property's actual cash value. An item's actual cash value is its replacement cost minus depreciation.

- In an effort to mitigate risk and keep premiums down, insurance companies set coverage limits on some highly valued items, such as jewelry, particularly with respect to losses from theft. These limits are enforced on a per-claim basis and are sometimes known as "special limits of liability."

- Scheduling involves itemizing a person's valuables and insuring each item for a specific amount.

- Blanket coverage provides broad, generally worded coverage to multiple pieces of property without itemizing each piece and without having a unique coverage limit for each item.

- Additional living expenses are those expenses the homeowner encounters as a direct result of not being able to use his or her home. Among other possibilities, these expenses may include the cost of meals and temporary lodging.

- In homeowners insurance, some insurers limit benefits under Coverage D (loss of use) to a set percentage of Coverage A. When a dollar limit is used, it's often equal to 20 percent of the dwelling's insured value.

- Coverage E only gives homeowners personal liability insurance. It doesn't help them manage professional liability risks or business liability risks.

- In homeowners insurance, defense costs are included in Coverage E. The insurer has a duty to defend the inured in court, no matter if the suit against the person is legitimate or frivolous. The money to pay for this defense comes out of the insurance company's pocket and generally won't run out until the insurer has paid settlement costs or damages in an amount equal to Coverage E's limit of liability.

- Coverage F in homeowners insurance usually provides up to $1,000 for medical expenses when a third party is injured by the insured or on the insured's property. It covers these expenses regardless of whether the insured is at fault.

- Unlike insurance for an insured person's dwelling and belongings, the personal liability insurance found in homeowners insurance might not require payment of a deductible.

- The HO-1 policy form is sometimes referred to as the "basic form." Rarely sold these days, it insures the homeowner's property against fewer perils than the typical homeowners policy, and it contains very broad exclusions by comparison.

- The HO-2 policy form is sometimes referred to as the "broad form." This policy is fairly popular and insures the homeowner against property losses caused by many common perils.

- The HO-3 policy form is sometimes referred to as the "special form." Unlike the HO-1 and HO-2, the HO-3 form covers the insured dwelling and detached structures on an open-peril basis. This means a loss will be covered by the policy unless the insurance contract specifically excludes it. The open-peril coverage applies only to the dwelling and detached structures. By default, HO-3 policies cover personal property on a named-peril basis.

- Contrary to popular belief, a renter's personal property is generally not covered by the landlord's insurance policy.

- The HO-4 policy form is used to insure renters and their belongings. The HO-4 policy form insures personal property against the same perils named in the HO-2 form.

- The HO-5 policy form gives the insured open-peril coverage for both the dwelling and personal property.

- To address the concerns of condo dwellers and townhouse owners, insurance companies sell policies based on the HO-6 form, also known as the "unit-owners form." The unit-owners form features named-peril coverage for the insured's personal property and a little bit of named-peril coverage for the unit itself. The named perils in an HO-6 policy are the same as those in an HO-2 policy.

- HO-7 policies are meant to insure mobile homes, which can also be covered by adding endorsements to other homeowners forms.

- The HO-8 policy form is sometimes known as the "modified form." It's typically used to cover older homes in urban areas when the dwelling's market value is considerably lower than its replacement cost. HO-8 policies cover the dwelling only up to its actual cash value.

- Extended replacement insurance will provide extra coverage when the cost of replacing the dwelling is larger than the policy's Coverage A limit. Extended replacement benefits are capped, often at 120 percent or 125 percent of the Coverage A limit.

- The typical homeowners insurance policy has a coinsurance clause requiring the insured to cover a dwelling for at least 80 percent of its replacement cost. In this context, the replacement cost would be the cost of rebuilding a similar structure on the same spot at the time of the claim. If a homeowner doesn't insure the dwelling for at least 80 percent of its replacement cost and suffers a partial loss, the insurer won't reimburse the insured for the entire loss. Instead, the insured will be entitled to the actual cash value of the damaged portion of the property or a prorated amount based on how close the person was to meeting the coinsurance requirement.

- When a homeowner hasn't satisfied a policy's coinsurance requirement, the amount provided by the insurer after a partial loss can be calculated via the following formula:
  - (Insurance carried ÷ Insurance required) × actual loss – deductible

- Mortgage lenders can add themselves to a borrower's insurance policy. This lets them control whether insurance money is used to repair property and allows them to provide premiums or proof of loss to the insurer if the borrower fails to do so.

- Homeowners insurance doesn't cover damage to the dwelling when it's caused by the insured's pet or an animal otherwise in the insured's care but can cover pet owner's for liability.

CHAPTER 8: COMMERCIAL PROPERTY INSURANCE

The most common kind of property insurance for businesses is based on contractual language from a document called the **Building and Personal Property Coverage Form**. The form was created by the Insurance Services Office (ISO), a private company specializing in information about property and casualty insurance. This chapter contains explanations of the ISO form. However, be aware that some companies use broader or more restrictive policy forms.

Kinds of Covered Property

There are three basic kinds of covered property addressed by the Building and Personal Property Coverage Form, with each one having its own dollar limit. These three are listed below and will be addressed one at a time in the next few sections:

- The business's building.

- The business's personal property.

- Personal property of others that's in the business's possession.

The Business's Building

The building is the place of business described on the policy's declarations page. Although we generally view buildings as singular structures, a "building" can mean any of the following things:

- The entire structure at a single address.

- Multiple structures described on the declarations page.

- A single unit in a multi-unit building.

Building coverage is for more than just walls, ceilings, windows and doors. It's broad enough to include additions the insured makes to the building and various fixtures, equipment and machinery that are permanently installed in the building.

Building coverage even insures many personal items that the business owns and uses to maintain the building and the surrounding area. Here are a few items that are commonly insured through the policy's building coverage:

- Carpeting and other flooring materials.

- Fire extinguishers and hoses.

- Outdoor furniture.

- Refrigeration and ventilation equipment.

- Appliances used for cooking, dishwashing or laundering.

The Business's Personal Property

Coverage for a business's personal property generally applies to any item inside the insured building or within 100 feet of the premises. More specifically, the typical policy states that the following items are insured:

- Office furniture and fixtures.

- Machinery and equipment used to conduct business.

- Property the insured owns and uses for business purposes.

- Outdoor signs (valued up to $2,500).

- If the insured is a tenant, any improvements the insured has made to the building that weren't paid for by the owner.

- Leased property that the business agrees to insure.

- Improvements made to other people's property, such as replacement parts installed by the business.

Items in stock could also be part of the above list. In regard to the Building and Personal Property Coverage Form, "stock" can be defined as follows:

- Items currently being sold by the business.

- Items the business plans on selling but is keeping in storage.

- Items the business is in the process of producing.

- Any raw materials the business uses to make its products.

Property of Others

Commercial property insurance can cover other people's property while it's in the business's possession. For this kind of property to be covered under the Building and Personal Property Coverage Form, it must be either inside the insured building or within 100 feet of the building.

The insurance for property of others is explained in an early portion of the Building and Personal Property Coverage Form and typically has its own dollar limit, as chosen by the business. It can be capped at any amount and is designed for businesses that commonly keep customers' property on their premises. If customers' property is stored by the business at an offsite location or held in transit, a more specialized insurance product known as "bailee insurance" might be appropriate.

If a business doesn't normally take possession of other people's property and doesn't want to spend extra money to manage a comparatively small risk, it may be able to apply a small amount of its own personal property coverage to "personal effects and property of others." This option is available at no additional expense and reimburses the policyholder and various employees when their personal items are lost or damaged at the business premises. The coverage also applies to the property of others that is in the business's care. However, items pertaining to this optional, extended insurance are only covered for up to $2,500 at each premises.

Replacement Cost v. Actual Cash Value

By default, most kinds of commercial property will only be covered up to their actual cash value. An item's actual cash value is its replacement cost minus depreciation. Replacement-cost insurance can be included for an additional price.

Newly Constructed or Acquired Property

Automatic coverage for newly constructed or acquired property is available if the business satisfies an 80 percent coinsurance requirement (explained later in this chapter).

If a business constructs a new building during the policy period, damage to that building, while under construction, can be covered if the new building is on the premises described on the declarations page.

A newly acquired building can be covered by the same policy if it's used for the same purpose as the building described on the declarations page. Alternatively, the business may cover a newly acquired building if it's used only as a warehouse.

The business also has the option of extending coverage to include its personal property at these new locations. Personal property of others isn't covered in these buildings if it's being serviced in some way by the business.

This extended insurance for newly constructed or acquired buildings is limited to $250,000 per building. The extended insurance for a business's personal property at these buildings is limited to $100,000 per location. The insurance expires when any of the following events occur:

- The policy period ends.
- Thirty days pass after either the time of acquisition or the beginning of construction.
- The insured reports the new property's value to the insurance company.

Covered Perils

Along with choosing how much insurance to buy, a business needs to decide which perils or "causes of loss" should be covered. There are usually three options to choose from.

The most basic kind of property insurance will typically cover businesses against losses caused by the following perils:

- Fire.
- Lightning.
- Windstorm.
- Civil commotion.
- Smoke.
- Hail.
- Aircraft or vehicles.
- Volcanic action.
- Explosion.
- Riot .
- Vandalism and malicious mischief.
- Sprinkler leakage.
- Sinkhole collapse.

You might notice that, with a few exceptions, these perils are very similar to what's covered in some of the basic dwelling and homeowners insurance forms.

An intermediate ("broad") form of property insurance will also help pay for losses caused by a few additional perils:

- Falling objects.
- Weight of snow, ice or sleet.
- Accidental discharge of water or steam.
- You might notice that, with a few exceptions, these perils are very similar to what's covered in some of the "broad" types of dwelling and homeowners insurance policies.

Particularly when tasked with insuring their building, most businesses go a step further and purchase open-peril property insurance via what's known as the "special" coverage form. This covers them against all perils other than those specifically excluded in their policy.

Excluded Perils

Even insurers offering open-peril commercial property insurance will exclude some losses from their policies. The next several sections address those commonly excluded risks.

Water Damage

The Building and Personal Property Coverage Form isn't designed to cover water damage caused by the following perils:

- Floods.
- Waves.
- Mudslides.
- Seepage.
- Sewer backups.

Fungus, Rot and Bacteria

Basic kinds of commercial property insurance don't cover losses related to fungus, rot or bacteria unless the fungus, rot or bacteria is caused by a covered peril.

There is no special limit of liability when fungus, rot or bacteria is caused by fire or lightning. When fungus, bacteria or rot are caused by other covered perils, the insurer's limit of liability is no more than $15,000. Insurance money can be used to remove fungus, rot or bacteria, tear a building apart in order to remove those things, or conduct tests to ensure that the removal of those things has been successful.

Earth Movement

Significant kinds of earth movement can include earthquakes, landslides, volcanic eruptions and sinking. Separate insurance is necessary if a business is concerned about earth movement. However, a business can choose to insure against sinkhole collapse and volcanic action.

Fire damage remains covered even if the fire is caused by earth movement.

Pollutants

Standard kinds of commercial property insurance don't cover pollution losses, other than the cost of cleanup. Furthermore, the cleanup is only covered when it results from a covered peril (such as a windstorm).

The most the insurer will pay for cleanup of pollutants is $10,000 per year. This is additional insurance and has no impact on the insurer's other limits of liability.

Nuclear Reactions and Radiation

Damage done by any kind of nuclear reaction or nuclear radiation is excluded. This exclusion still allows businesses to be reimbursed for losses when a nuclear reaction causes a fire.

War

Commercial property insurance generally doesn't cover damage caused by war or military action. This exclusion applies during declared war, undeclared war, civil war and rebellion.

The Terrorism Risk Insurance Act of 2002 (commonly known as "TRIA") requires that insurance companies offer terrorism coverage to their commercial policyholders. This coverage is available for an additional cost. By signing the appropriate forms, businesses can decline this insurance. In exchange for offering terrorism coverage to businesses, insurance companies receive reinsurance protection from the federal government in case of a catastrophic terrorist attack.

Power Failures and Surges

Businesses receive no insurance benefits when a power failure can be traced back to problems at a utility company. There's also no coverage when artificial current does damage to personal property.

In general, some coverage remains intact when a power failure or power surge causes damage from a covered peril. In other words, if a business experiences a power surge, computers damaged by that surge won't be covered. But if that surge were to cause a fire, the business would generally still be covered for fire losses.

Theft

Losses from theft can often only be covered through open-peril commercial property insurance or by crime insurance. If a business rejects both of those options and a burglary occurs, the insurer might only pay for repairs to the building. Replacing any stolen items will probably be the business's responsibility. Crime insurance will be summarized in a later chapter.

Excluded Property

Often regardless of what causes a loss, commercial property insurance generally doesn't cover the following items:

- Money.
- Vehicles.
- Animals (other than those that are either boarded by the business in exchange for a fee or sold as stock).
- Electronic data (limited to $2,500 per year and must be lost or damaged by a covered peril).

Debris Removal

If a covered peril produces debris of covered property at the business premises, the insurance company will pay to have the debris removed. This provision in the policy doesn't cover the removal of pollutants, and it doesn't cover debris removal when damage is caused by something other than a covered peril.

The amount of money available for debris removal will depend on the size of the loss and the insurer's limit of liability for the damaged property. In general, until the insurer's limit of liability for the property has been reached, a business may file a claim for debris removal equal to 25 percent of the sum of the policy's deductible plus the covered portion of the loss that created the debris.

- 0.25 (deductible + debris-causing loss) = Commercial property debris removal

Suppose a windstorm has created damage and debris for a business. The business has insurance with a $500 deductible, and the business's covered, non-debris losses amount to $49,500. By adding the deductible to the business's covered non-debris losses ($500 + $49,500) and multiplying the sum by 25 percent, we can see that insurance will pay up to $12,500 to remove the debris in this case.

Additional insurance for debris removal (often up to $10,000) might be provided in catastrophic situations.

Coinsurance

Similar to clauses found in homeowners insurance policies, coinsurance requirements in commercial property policies usually state that if property isn't covered up to a certain percentage of its actual cash value (or, in some cases, its replacement cost), the insurance company won't fully compensate the business for a loss. Instead, the insurer will pay a prorated amount based on how close the business was to meeting its coinsurance requirement.

As if the possibility of a partially denied claim wasn't enough, there are plenty of other reasons why a business would consider accepting a coinsurance requirement of at least 80 percent. If the business doesn't comply with a coinsurance requirement of at least 80 percent of the property's value, there might be no coverage at all for the following items:

- Newly constructed property.

- Newly acquired property.

- Personal effects and property of others.

- Valuable papers and records.

- Off-premises property.

- Outdoor property.

- Trailers.

Agreed Value

Insurance companies will typically waive their coinsurance requirements if a business chooses the **agreed-value option**. When the agreed-value option is selected, the insurance company considers the property owned by the business before issuing a policy and arrives at a seemingly suitable dollar limit for the business. This limit is known as the "agreed value."

The business can then choose the agreed value or any other value as the policy's dollar limit. If the business opts for the agreed value or a higher number, the insurer will pay 100 percent of claims up to the policy's dollar limit minus any deductible. If the business opts for a dollar limit below the agreed value, the covered portion of all claims will be determined by dividing the policy's dollar limit by the agreed value.

The agreed-value option can probably be best understood by looking at a few examples. First, let's imagine an insurance company has evaluated a business's property and arrived at an agreed value of $100,000. If the business decides to insure its property for at least $100,000, it will be covered for 100 percent of losses up to $100,000 after satisfying any deductible.

Now imagine the same business has decided to insure its property for $80,000 instead of the agreed value of $100,000. Since the business is only purchasing insurance equal to 80 percent of the agreed value, it will only be covered for 80 percent of any losses.

The agreed value will only remain in effect until a specific date, which may or may not coincide with the end of the policy period. After that date (unless the insurer is contacted), losses will be subject to the policy's coinsurance requirements.

The main difference between the agreed-value option and the coinsurance clause is that the former determines value when coverage is issued. The latter doesn't determine value until after a loss has occurred. The agreed-value option still requires the consumer to purchase at least a minimum amount of coverage in order to have full coverage. However, it shields the consumer from having to worry about an unexpected increase in property value between the time coverage is issued and a loss occurs. Although it's still possible for the consumer to be underinsured for a loss, the agreed-value option makes it more likely that being under-insured was a conscious choice and won't be a post-loss surprise.

Commercial Vacancy Clauses

The insurance company can sometimes deny an otherwise valid claim if the business's building had been vacant for an extended period at the time of the loss. Although similar clauses can be found in homeowners insurance, the insurance rules regarding vacancies tend to be different for commercial properties.

The commercial vacancy clause doesn't impact building owners and tenants in the same way. In the case of an insured tenant, the vacancy clause can go into effect only when the tenant's portion of a building doesn't contain enough property for a tenant to conduct normal business operations. In the case of an insured building owner, it can go into effect when 70 percent or more of the entire building is neither rented to tenants nor used by the owner to conduct regular business. Buildings are not vacant if they are under construction or being renovated.

The commercial vacancy clause is also applied differently depending on the cause of a loss. When a loss is caused by vandalism, theft, water damage or broken glass, the insurance company can deny coverage entirely if the building was vacant for more than 60 consecutive days. For all other perils, a vacancy period beyond 60 days will decrease the insured portion of a loss by 15 percent.

Chapter Key Points

- The most common kind of property insurance for businesses is based on contractual language from a document called the Building and Personal Property Coverage Form.

- There are three basic kinds of covered property addressed by the Building and Personal Property Coverage Form, with each one having its own dollar limit:
    - The business's building.
    - The business's personal property.
    - Personal property of others that is in the business's possession.

- By default, most kinds of commercial property will only be covered up to their actual cash value, not replacement cost.

- Basic commercial property insurance will typically cover businesses against losses caused by the following perils:
    - Fire.
    - Lightning.
    - Explosion.
    - Windstorm
    - Civil commotion.
    - Smoke.
    - Hail.
    - Aircraft or vehicles.
    - Volcanic action.
    - Explosions.
    - Riot or civil commotion.
    - Vandalism and malicious mischief.
    - Sinkhole collapse.
    - Sprinkler leakage.

- An intermediate ("broad") form of commercial property insurance will also help pay for losses caused by a few additional perils:
  - Falling objects.
  - Weight of snow, ice or sleet.
  - Accidental discharge of water or steam.
- Open-peril commercial property insurance covers businesses against all perils other than those specifically excluded in their policy.
- Losses from theft can often only be covered through open-peril commercial property insurance or by crime insurance.
- When a loss is caused by vandalism, theft, water damage or broken glass, the commercial property insurance company can deny coverage entirely if the building was vacant for more than 60 consecutive days. For all other perils, a vacancy period beyond 60 days will decrease the insured portion of a loss by 15 percent. For tenants, a commercial building is considered vacant if it lacks enough property for the tenant to conduct normal business operations. For landlords, property is considered vacant if at least 70 percent of the building is neither rented to tenants nor used by the landlord for normal business.
- Often regardless of what causes a loss, commercial property insurance generally doesn't cover the following items:
  - Money.
  - Vehicles.
  - Animals (other than those that are either boarded by the business in exchange for a fee or sold as stock).
  - Electronic data (limited to $2,500 per year and must be lost or damaged by a covered peril).
- In general, commercial property insurance will cover debris removal up to an amount equal to 25 percent of the sum of the policy's deductible and the covered portion of the loss that created the debris.
  - 0.25 (deductible + debris-causing loss) = Commercial property debris removal

CHAPTER 9: BUSINESS INTERRUPTION INSURANCE

Business interruption insurance typically reimburses policyholders for lost income and the expenses they incur during a break in normal business operations. If, for example, a fire forces a business to shut down for repairs, the owners can be compensated for the money that would've been made, as if the fire hadn't occurred.

Business interruption insurance is a combination of "business income insurance" and coverage of assorted extra expenses. Let's look at the kinds of benefits that are commonly available.

Business Income Insurance

Business income insurance generally pays business owners the amount of money they would have earned if a covered peril hadn't forced them to suspend normal operations. It can compensate a business for expected profits that are impacted by an interruption and can cover expenses that still need to be paid during a shutdown. (In business income terms, the phrase "net income" is sometimes used to mean the business's expected profit before taxes.)

Continuing Normal Operating Expenses

If a business owner plans on ever reopening after an interruption, there will be several bills and other financial obligations to take care of in the meantime. Luckily for that business owner, business income insurance includes coverage of **continuing normal operating expenses**. Continuing normal operating expenses are those expenses that the insured would face regardless of damage to named property. Examples of these expenses include rent, commercial mortgage payments, commercial insurance premiums, utility bills and some taxes.

A normal continuing operating expense isn't covered if the interruption has eliminated it. The cost of electricity, for example, is usually considered a normal continuing operating expense, but it wouldn't be covered if business is interrupted by a blackout.

Payroll Coverage

Choosing to pay employees during a business interruption does more than create goodwill between labor and management. It helps the business owner by making it less likely that valuable workers will leave the company out of financial necessity.

By keeping their experienced employees on the payroll during a suspension of operations, businesses set themselves up for quicker recovery. Their reopening won't be delayed by a shortage of staff, and their productivity won't be hampered by newly hired personnel with inadequate training.

Insurers understand how employee continuity can reduce business interruption losses, and they make it a point to list payroll as a covered continuing normal operating expense. Along with wages and salaries, business interruption insurance can pay for union dues, workers compensation premiums, some employee benefits and the business's required contributions to Social Security and Medicare under the Federal Insurance Contribution Act (FICA). Insurance benefits will be reduced appropriately if an employee is laid off during an interruption.

Businesses concerned about the size of their premiums can drop some of their payroll coverage via an "ordinary payroll limitation or exclusion endorsement." This contractual addition usually provides only a month or two of payroll coverage for nonessential employees or leaves these people with no coverage at all. It doesn't limit or exclude payroll costs pertaining to officers, executives, department managers or contracted workers.

Extra Expenses

Most but not all forms of business interruption insurance reimburse businesses for the extra expenses they incur during a suspension of normal operations. In order to be covered by an insurer, these costs must, in some way, either reduce the duration or scope of the interruption or help eliminate the interruption altogether. Businesses that offer essential services to the public and can't shut down for even a brief period of time will have a heightened need for extra expense coverage as part of their insurance portfolio.

Although each insurer may have its own idea of what constitutes a legitimate extra expense, the insured could probably make a strong case for coverage of the following items:

- The cost of renting a temporary place of business.

- The cost of equipping a temporary place of business with necessary machinery and supplies.

- The cost of making a temporary place of business physically presentable to the public and serviceable for business operations.

- Expedited shipping costs for necessary machinery and supplies.

- Moving costs.

- Overtime pay for employees who assist in the relocation process.

Unlike business income insurance, which usually requires that businesses be shut down for at least three consecutive days before coverage can begin, coverage of extra expenses starts at the very beginning of an interruption. Benefits can continue throughout the "period of restoration," which will be the subject of the next section.

Despite the difference in waiting periods, insurance for extra expenses and coverage of business income are linked to each other in several ways. They're often both subject to the same limit of liability, which means any claim made for an extra expense is likely to reduce the amount of money available for a business income claim.

There's typically no difference between the perils covered by the business income side of a policy and the perils covered by the extra-expense side of a policy. Both parts of the contract require that all claims relate to physical damage at a named property.

Period of Restoration

Coverage of business income and expenses lasts until insured losses exceed the policy's dollar limit or until the end of the **period of restoration**, whichever occurs sooner. In the case of business income, the period of restoration usually begins three days after the start of an interruption. In the case of extra expenses, it starts at the same time as the interruption. In both cases, the period of restoration ends on the earliest of the following dates:

- The day when the damaged premises should've reasonably been repaired, rebuilt or restored.

- The day when the business has reopened at a different permanent location.

- A specific date already identified in the policy language (such as exactly one year after the start of an interruption).

Covered Perils and Benefit Triggers

For a loss to be covered, operations usually need to have been interrupted at the business premises by a covered peril.

The perils covered by business interruption insurance are usually identical to the perils in the business's commercial property insurance policy. This link between property insurance and business interruption insurance usually ensures that interruptions are covered when they're caused by fire, wind, lightning, burst pipes, vandalism, explosions and more. In most cases, it also typically means that interruptions aren't automatically covered when they're caused by a flood or an earthquake. An insurer might agree to cover those commonly excluded perils for an additional premium.

With a few possible exceptions, an interruption will only be covered if a peril has done physical damage to a business's premises. In practical terms, this means a restaurant wouldn't be covered if it shuts down temporarily because of a food-poisoning scare. It also means a business wouldn't be covered if it voluntarily closed its doors in anticipation of a covered peril (such as a windstorm) without sustaining any actual damage to its property.

Waiting/Elimination Periods

Even if a covered peril has clearly caused an interruption, the insured will still have to endure a waiting period, sometimes known as an **elimination period**, before coverage of business income and continuing normal operating expenses can apply. Typically, this elimination period ends when a business has been interrupted for 48 or 72 hours. Elimination periods tend not to apply to coverage of extra expenses.

Regardless of the length of the interruption, businesses aren't reimbursed for the losses they suffer during the elimination period.

Excluded Perils

Perils commonly excluded from business interruption coverage include (but aren't limited to) earthquakes, floods, radiation and acts of war.

Interruptions that aren't caused by physical damage to the business premises are often not covered.

Acts of Civil Authority

Some business interruption products will compensate the insured following an "act of civil authority," in which the business premises can't be accessed due to an order by local government or law enforcement. However, when present, this coverage usually only applies when the reason for the order is related to a covered peril near the business's location, such as a fire at a neighboring building. If authorities prevent access to a business for reasons other than due to a covered peril, the business will be uninsured for the interruption.

When included, coverage for acts of civil authority tends to last for no more than four weeks.

Coinsurance Clauses in Business Interruption Insurance

The coinsurance clause can make a business responsible for a portion of any business interruption loss, even when the loss is far smaller than the policy's dollar limit. The clause exists to protect the insurance company in cases where a business has underreported or underestimated its expected net income (net profit or loss before taxes) and continuing normal operating expenses. It ensures the insurance company will be paid fairly for absorbing risks and that a short interruption won't come close to exceeding the policy's dollar limit.

The coinsurance clause states that the insurer won't honor a claim in its entirety if the policy's dollar limit is less than the policy's coinsurance percentage, multiplied by the business's expected net income and operating expenses for the 12 months following the policy's inception. When the insurance is renewed, its anniversary date will serve as the beginning of a new 12-month period.

Contingent Business Interruption Insurance

Many businesses would struggle to continue if an important vendor, manufacturer or customer were to shut down. This risk can be managed, in part, by purchasing **contingent business interruption insurance.** Similar to traditional forms of business interruption insurance, contingent business interruption insurance compensates a policyholder for a suspension in operations at a particular location due to physical damage. However, benefits are triggered by an interruption at an offsite "dependent property" rather than at the business's own location.

Chapter Key Points

- Business interruption insurance typically reimburses policyholders for lost income and the expenses they incur during a break in normal business operations.

- Business interruption insurance is a combination of business income insurance and coverage of extra expenses.

- Business income insurance pays business owners the profits (net income before taxes) that they would have earned if a covered peril hadn't forced them to suspend normal operations.

- Business income insurance includes coverage of continuing normal operating expenses. Continuing normal operating expenses are those expenses the insured would face regardless of damage to named property (such as mortgage payments, taxes and payroll).

- Most forms of business interruption insurance reimburse businesses for the extra expenses they incur during a suspension of normal operations. In order to be covered by an insurer, these costs must, in some way, reduce the duration or scope of the interruption. Businesses that offer essential services to the public and cannot shut down for even a brief period of time will have a heightened need for extra expense coverage as part of their insurance portfolio.

- Coverage of business income and expenses lasts until insured losses exceed the policy's dollar limit or until the end of the period of restoration, whichever occurs sooner. In the case of business income, the period of restoration usually begins a few days after the start of an interruption. In the case of extra expenses, it starts at the same time as the interruption.

- The period of restoration ends on the earliest of the following dates:
  - The day when the damaged premises should have reasonably been repaired, rebuilt or restored.
  - The day when the business has reopened at a different permanent location.
  - A specific date, as found in the policy language (such as one year from the start of an interruption).

- The perils covered by business interruption insurance are usually identical to the perils in the business's commercial property insurance policy.

- Perils commonly excluded from business interruption coverage include earthquakes, floods, radiation and acts of war.

- In business interruption insurance, the coinsurance clause states that the insurer won't honor a claim in its entirety if the policy's dollar limit is less than the policy's coinsurance percentage, multiplied by the business's expected net income and operating expenses for the 12 months following the policy's inception.

- Some products will cover interruptions when local authorities prevent a business from accessing its premises. To be covered, such interruptions usually must last no longer than three weeks.

- Contingent business interruption insurance compensates a policyholder for a suspension in operations at an offsite "dependent property" rather than at the business's own location.

CHAPTER 10: MARINE INSURANCE

Goods in transit are typically covered by some form of **marine insurance**. Marine insurance can be broken down into many categories and subcategories. The right category of coverage for a business will depend on what's being insured and where.

Broadly speaking, **ocean marine insurance** is property and casualty insurance for people who have a vested interest in a ship's safe journey. Though the ship is usually a waterborne commercial vessel, the insurance can also be used to cover offshore oil rigs and some private yachts.

Property insurance in the ocean marine market can pertain to either the ship itself (**hull insurance**) or the cargo onboard (**cargo insurance**). Liability insurance in the ocean marine market is sometimes known as **protection and indemnity insurance** (P & I) and covers ship owners when they're held responsible for property damage, personal injury, illness or death.

When products are shipped by land rather than by water, they may be covered by **inland marine insurance**. Besides insuring items sent on trucks and trains, this insurance can be used to cover man-made facilitators of transportation, such as bridges and tunnels. Businesses also use it to protect easily movable property of great value.

Cargo Insurance

A good cargo policy can cover seemingly any property transported on a vessel, with the understandable exception of stolen or illegal items. Though the insurance was created to handle losses at sea, today's cargo policies typically extend coverage to include some losses on land. In many cases, ocean cargo insurance can even cover shipments on planes.

A business or individual can insure cargo without owning it and only needs to demonstrate an insurable interest in the property. Within the context of cargo insurance, an insurable interest is merely a valid reason for wanting goods to arrive undamaged from the shipper to the recipient. Thanks to the broadness of insurable interest and the complexities of business relationships, it's possible for transported products to be insured by a seller, a buyer, a freight forwarder or a ship owner.

Hull Insurance

Hull insurance is property insurance that can cover nearly any kind of floating commercial vessel, including cargo ships, tugboats and barges. Though it doesn't cover the cargo onboard, it usually does insure other property that's attached to or used on the craft. More specifically, a hull insurance policy commonly covers the following types of property:

- Hull.
- Lifeboats and rafts.
- Bunks.
- Boilers, machinery and other equipment.
- Furniture and supplies used by the crew.
- Property installed on the vessel but not owned by the insured.

Protection and Indemnity Insurance

Some liability insurance for ship owners is included in hull insurance policies, but that coverage can be very limited. In most cases, the liability insurance only applies to accidental collisions, and even then, it often only covers the insured for damage to property not on the ship. A hull policy provides no coverage for collision liability in cases of bodily injury, death or illness. It also does nothing to help ship owners when they're held responsible for damage to cargo on their own vessel.

Protection and indemnity insurance (P & I) is purchased by ship owners to remove those coverage gaps. In addition to helping policyholders manage their collision liability exposures, the typical P & I policy makes the insurer responsible for many other liability claims relating to property damage, bodily injury, illness or death. Usually renewed every two years, P & I policies aren't purchased by most businesses, but like hull insurance, they can have an indirect impact on a business's shipping costs.

Inland Marine Insurance

- Inland marine insurance began as insurance for shipments on land and evolved into a much broader market for covering nontraditional forms of personal and commercial property. For reasons that are beyond the scope of this guide, inland marine insurance products involve much less standardization than typical property insurance products and aren't always regulated with the same amount of scrutiny.

- To differentiate it from other types of property insurance, regulators have settled on a national definition of inland marine insurance, which includes coverage for the following items:

- Property that has been imported to the United States but hasn't reached its destination.

- Property being warehoused in the United States with the intent of shipping it at a later date.

- Property in the process of being moved from one U.S. location to another U.S. location.

- Man-made property that makes inland transportation possible (such as tunnels and bridges).

- Property entrusted by its owner to a business.

- Highly valued property that is easily portable.

- Property that, by its very nature, has a value that is constantly fluctuating (such as accounts receivable).

Kinds of Inland Marine Insurance Policies

Despite representing only 2 percent or so of the entire property and casualty market, inland marine is an incredibly versatile line that can be broken down into more than 100 types of personal and commercial policies.

Builders Risk Insurance

Builders risk insurance covers a building while it's being rehabilitated or constructed and insures the building materials that have been purchased for the project. It's generally not intended to insure a builder's tools or insure a builder against faulty work. It also doesn't cover builders for liability in case of accidents during construction.

Coverage for a project can last several months to a year and can usually be extended at least once if construction falls behind schedule. Coverage ends when the project is complete, when the building is occupied or when construction has been abandoned.

Property under a builders risk policy is generally insured at its actual cash value. A single dollar limit can be chosen for the duration of the project, or the insured can opt for a "reporting form," which will allow the dollar limit to be increased at various points as the building gets closer to completion. Note that an insurance settlement might be reduced if the insured doesn't choose a dollar limit that reflects the property's actual cash value at the time of loss.

Installation Floaters

Similar to builders risk insurance, an "installation floater" is used to insure materials that are used to install or construct a specific item or feature in an already-constructed building. If, for example, a specialist is hired to install a new electrical system, he or she might rely on an installation floater to cover loss of materials.

Contractors Equipment Policy

Whereas builders risk and installation policies cover materials that will ultimately become part of a contractor's final product, a "contractors equipment policy" insures the tools used to complete the job. Coverage applies at the contractor's workplace, at the worksite and in transit. It also covers commercial vehicles that are exempt from coverage in commercial auto policies, such as bulldozers and forklifts.

Bailee Policies

Bailee insurance is bought by businesses that specialize in servicing other people's property, such as dry cleaners and repair shops. It may help the business compensate the owner of lost or damaged property regardless of whether the business was at fault. Unlike some of the coverage found in usual commercial property policies, it might insure property of others even while offsite or in transit.

Block Policies

Block policies are designed to cover merchandise for businesses that specialize in selling highly valuable and very portable items. Strong candidates for block policies include jewelers, art dealers and music shops. Items covered by block policies are usually very attractive to thieves. Therefore, an applicant's commitment to a strict and thorough security plan might be important to an underwriter.

A jewelers block policy can cover jewelry being sold by the business at its location and jewelry of others that is in the business's care. The policy will likely exclude jewelry being worn by the business or family members. If the jewelry will be sent to someone, it might need to be tracked via registered mail in order to remain insured.

Chapter Key Points

- Goods in transit are typically covered by some form of marine insurance.

- Ocean marine insurance is property and casualty insurance for people who have a vested interest in a ship's safe journey.

- Property insurance in the ocean marine market can pertain to either the ship itself (hull insurance) or the cargo onboard (cargo insurance). Liability insurance in the ocean marine market is sometimes known as protection and indemnity insurance (P & I) and covers ship owners when they are held responsible for property damage, personal injury, illness or death.

- When products are shipped by land rather than by water, they may be covered by inland marine insurance. Besides insuring items that are sent on trucks and trains, this kind of insurance can be used to cover man-made facilitators of transportation, such as bridges and tunnels. Businesses also use it to protect easily movable property of great value.

- Builders risk insurance covers a building while it is being rehabilitated or constructed and insures the building materials that have been purchased for the project. A single coverage limit can be used for the duration of the construction, or a "reporting form" can be used to increase the coverage as the project progresses.

- Bailee policies are bought by businesses that specialize in servicing other people's property, such as dry cleaners and repair shops. They may help the business compensate the owner of lost or damaged property regardless of whether the business was at fault.

- Block policies are designed to cover merchandise for businesses that specialize in selling highly valuable and very portable items. Strong candidates for block policies include jewelers, art dealers and music shops.

- A jewelers block policy can cover jewelry being sold by the business at its location and jewelry of others that is in the business's care. The policy will likely exclude jewelry being worn by the business or family members. If the jewelry will be sent to someone, it might need to be tracked via registered mail in order to remain insured.

CHAPTER 11: MISCELLANEOUS PROPERTY INSURANCE PRODUCTS

Previous chapters have summarized some of the most common property insurance products sought by the public. Other forms of property insurance might not be of much importance to the typical buyer but still serve important purposes in special situations.

Assorted property insurance policies that will be important to your exam preparation—and possibly your career—are explained here.

Commercial Package Policy

In reality, most forms of commercial property insurance are parts of a bigger "package" policy, similar to the manner in which property and casualty insurance is combined for individuals in the form of homeowners insurance.

For instance, a **commercial package policy** combines property insurance with various types of liability insurance. This product can be customized for a wide variety of small, medium and large businesses.

A so-called commercial package policy might include at least two of the following coverages:

- Commercial property insurance.
- Business interruption insurance.
- Farm insurance.
- Commercial inland marine insurance.
- Commercial general liability insurance.
- Boiler and machinery insurance.
- Crime insurance.
- Commercial auto insurance.

Note that a commercial package policy doesn't include life and health insurance. Despite offering several options for property and casualty insurance, it generally won't include workers compensation insurance and might not include certain types of malpractice insurance.

Regardless of which coverages are selected, a commercial package policy will include a **common policy declarations form** that applies to the entire package. The declarations form will contain information about the business and the product such as:

- The business's name and address.
- The policy period.
- The coverages selected by the business.

The commercial package policy will also include **common policy conditions** that explain duties and responsibilities belonging to the named insured. The conditions often pertain to the following topics:

- The named insured's ability to cancel the insurance in writing.
- The inability to assign rights under the policy without the insurer's consent.
- The ability of the insurer to examine the business's records during the policy period and up to three years afterward.
- The responsibility of the named insured to pay premiums.
- The ability of the named insured to make changes to the policy.

- The procedures for mediation or arbitration if the insurer and insured disagree about a claim.
- Upon death of the named insured, the ability of that person's legal representative to exercise various rights under the policy.

Businessowners Policy (BOP)

A **businessowners policy (BOP)** provides a combination of property and casualty coverage to small businesses within relatively low-risk industries.

The BOP will include commercial property and commercial general liability coverage plus any of the following options:

- Crime insurance.
- Outdoor sign insurance.
- Exterior glass insurance.
- Employee dishonesty insurance.
- Boiler and machinery insurance.

Be aware that some business are ineligible for BOPs. A partial list appears next:

- Financial institutions.
- Bars and restaurants that serve alcohol.
- Auto repair shops, auto dealers and service stations.
- Places of amusement (theaters, theme parks, etc.).
- Manufacturers.

Personal Watercraft

Although some insurance for personal watercraft (intended only for private use) is available within a homeowners insurance policy, the property coverage might be limited to only a few hundred dollars, and the liability coverage might be completely nonexistent for boats with most types of motors. Also, coverage of theft, hail and wind damage, among other types of losses, will be extremely limited.

Due to these gaps, special boat owners policies are available for property and liability protection. Yacht insurance is available for larger vessels.

Mobile Homes

Insurance for mobile homes (intended for year-round residency) is handled in different ways depending on the property and the insurer. In some cases, an endorsement can be added to an HO-2 or HO-3 homeowners policy. In others, a separate policy specific to mobile homes (often using the HO-7 form) is used. Mobile homes can usually be insured in the same manner and against the same type of risks (dwelling, contents and personal liability) as traditional homes if the correct forms are used.

Personal Property Floaters

Special items and collections that aren't adequately insured via traditional homeowners insurance can be handled in a number of ways. One common approach is to purchase a policy called a **floater** that is designed to fill in the coverage gaps specific to the special type of property.

The term "floater" relates to the assumption that certain valuables move from place to place and are thereby susceptible to different degrees/types of losses than standard items. For instance, jewelry might be worn outside the home and become more susceptible to theft. Fine art might be loaned to exhibits and be more susceptible to damage in transit.

Several types of floaters and specialty policies exist. They generally insure special property on an open-peril basis and allow for higher coverage limits than homeowners insurance. They often provide first-dollar coverage rather than requiring payment of a deductible. Due to the portability of the property, coverage is often intended to apply on a worldwide basis rather than at a specific location. In the case of small items, the coverage can even include cases of "mysterious disappearance," in which property can't be found and wasn't necessarily stolen.

In the event that the insured already has a floater and acquires an item similar to property already covered by the insurance (such as a new coin purchased by someone who already covers his or her coins via a floater), the new item will often have a limited amount of temporary coverage as long as the acquisition is reported to the insurer within a certain time. Appraisals of property insured by a floater might be required before the coverage is issued or after a claim.

Note that property floaters can also be purchased by businesses for miscellaneous types of risks that aren't sufficiently addressed by commercial property insurance.

Flood Insurance

To guard against the financial consequences of a flood loss, a homeowner is likely to need a flood insurance policy from the **National Flood Insurance Program (NFIP)**. The NFIP is administered by the Federal Emergency Management Agency (FEMA).

The terms and conditions for flood insurance policies are often determined by the federal government, but the policies themselves are usually sold and serviced by private insurers. These insurers are known as "Write Your Own" companies.

The NFIP sets limits on the amount of flood risks it is willing to accept. For most single-family homes, coverage limits for the dwelling can be no more than $250,000, and contents coverage typically won't be available in amounts greater than $100,000. Standard insurance from the NFIP tends not to cover loss of use (such as the cost of renting temporary housing after a flood) or business interruption losses.

Any person who purchases a home in a **special flood hazard area** with the help of a federally regulated lender is required to cover the home with flood insurance. A special flood hazard area is a place where there is at least a 1 percent chance of flooding each year.

Although most buildings that are compliant with modern building codes are eligible for federal flood insurance, a building and most types of contents can't be covered if they're principally below ground level.

Unlike homeowners insurance, flood insurance is a very limited product and will only cover the residence in the event of flooding. According to FEMA, a flood can be defined in the following ways:

- Overflow of inland or tidal waters.
- Unusual and rapid accumulation or runoff of surface waters.
- Mudflow.

In practical terms, these definitions mean that the following types of water damage are generally NOT covered by flood insurance:

- Water damage from plumbing fixtures (such as burst pipes or overflowing bathtubs).
- Sewer backups.
- Overflow of sump pumps.
- Leaks.
- The weight of water.

- Water damage that only impacts the named insured's home and doesn't impact neighboring homes.

There are separate NFIP flood policies for the following properties:

- Residential dwellings.
- Commercial buildings.
- Condominiums (for condo associations).

Dwellings can be covered at replacement cost if they are for a single family and are the family's primary residence. Otherwise, flood policies are likely to cover buildings at actual cash value.

Floods and Contents Coverage

Contents can be covered at their actual cash value, but the insurance might need to be purchased separately and will likely have its own deductible rather than having a single deductible for both the building and any items stored there.

Several types of property will be excluded from contents coverage. For example, the following items are unlikely to be covered by flood insurance even if contents coverage is purchased:

- Personal property that is kept outdoors.
- Trees.
- Decks.
- Driveways.
- Fences.
- Money.
- Crops.

In the event of flood damage to a basement, contents coverage might only apply to the following items:

- Washers and dryers.
- Freezers.
- Portable or window air conditioners.

If contents must be moved to another location to protect them from flood damage, the named insured will typically have coverage of up to $1,000 for storage-related expenses. Meanwhile, the property will be covered against flood damage at the new location for up to 45 days.

Flood Insurance Producers

In accordance with federal rules, producers who wish to sell flood insurance must complete a one-time, three-hour training course. Several states include additional flood-related education requirements as part of the license renewal process.

Agents selling flood insurance from the NFIP lack binding authority, and underwriting decisions will ultimately be made by the NFIP. In order to guard against adverse selection (such as shoppers attempting to time a purchase based on reports of upcoming bad weather), new purchasers of flood insurance will generally need to wait 30 days for their insurance to be in force. The waiting period can be waived if the purchase is prompted by the making, increasing, extension or renewal of a mortgage loan.

Boiler and Machinery and Equipment Breakdown Insurance

Common forms of commercial property insurance usually don't cover explosions of steam pipes, steam boilers, steam engines or steam turbines. Boiler and machinery insurance contains property and liability coverage with respect to such losses.

In time, this coverage evolved to include property coverage for "equipment breakdown," including the malfunctioning of computers, copiers, refrigeration units and HVAC systems. Although those items might be covered under traditional types of property insurance, such coverage might only apply in cases where damage is done by standard perils like fire, windstorms, etc. By contrast, **equipment breakdown insurance** can respond when machinery breaks down unexpectedly due to damage from a power surge, a problem with a motor or defective parts.

A basic boiler and machinery/equipment breakdown insurance policy will at least cover damage to the indicated property but can also be structured to address the following kinds of losses, among others:

- "Expediting expenses" (such as the cost to do emergency repairs).
- Damage to other property due to a breakdown.
- Spoilage of other property due to a breakdown.
- Business interruptions due to a breakdown.
- Extra expenses due to a breakdown (besides expedited expenses).

Note that equipment breakdown coverage generally covers the equipment but not any data on it (such as data or software stored on a computer system). It also generally doesn't cover losses caused by viruses or other malicious acts committed over the internet. Losses due to regular wear and tear or improper maintenance are excluded.

Farm Insurance

Farm insurance is available as a package policy with several coverage options to choose from. Like homeowners insurance, it can combine property insurance and liability insurance in the same product. But unlike homeowners insurance, the same policy can be used to insure someone against personal risks and business risks. For example, property insurance for farms can insure parts of the farm that are used as family dwellings, while other parts of the policy can be used to insure farm-specific structures (such as barns) and farm-specific property (such as grain and livestock).

Common property coverages for farms may include:

- Coverage A: Dwelling (for the residence where farmers and family members reside).
- Coverage B: Other structures appurtenant to dwelling (for detached garages and other non-dwelling structures for personal use).
- Coverage C: Household personal property (for contents belonging to farmers and family members who live at the farm).
- Coverage D: Loss of use (for additional living expenses or fair rental value if the dwelling becomes uninhabitable).
- Coverage E: Scheduled farm personal property (for an extensive list of farm-related items, each of which will only be covered up to a specially chosen dollar amount).
- Coverage F: Unscheduled farm personal property (for farm-related property, all of which will generally only be covered up to one, cumulative dollar amount).
- Coverage G: Other farm structures (such as barns intended for business use).

Note, however, that a farmer's crops are often intended to be covered specifically by crop insurance rather than by the type of farm policy being referenced here.

Similar to other kinds of property, farm property can often be insured via one of three causes of loss forms:

- Basic (insures the property against a limited number of named perils).

- Broad (insures the property against an intermediate number of named perils).

- Special (insures the property on an open-peril basis against all perils, except those specifically excluded by the policy).

Although liability insurance can be included in a farm policy, coverage will likely not apply to business activities other than farming (such as crop dusting, operating a petting zoo or allowing the public to ride horses for a fee).

Common liability/casualty coverages for farms may include:

- Coverage H: Bodily injury and property damage liability (when liable for harm to another person or someone else's property).

- Coverage I: Personal and advertising injury liability (when liable for violating someone's rights or doing harm as part of an advertisement).

- Coverage J: Medical payments (intended as no-fault medical insurance for a third party who is injured on the farm).

The liability coverages mentioned above are very similar to the benefits found in commercial general liability insurance (intended for most businesses and explained in a later chapter of this guide).

Crop Insurance

Farmers may purchase federal crop insurance from private insurers that have been approved by the government. This insurance is designed to protect farmers from natural events out of their control (such as a drought). However, it will generally only insure a farmer against a portion of losses and must be purchased in advance of a growing season. Private crop insurance is also available for broader protection and can be purchased at any time during the growing season.

Earthquake Insurance

Homeowners insurance generally excludes coverage of earthquake-related damage. Many carriers sell special earthquake coverage that can either be added as an endorsement to a homeowners policy or sold as a stand-alone policy.

Earthquake Deductibles

Instead of being based on a flat dollar amount, earthquake insurance deductibles are typically equal to a set percentage of the dwelling's insured value. For example, a policyholder with a 10 percent deductible and a home that's been insured for $100,000 of coverage would ultimately need to suffer $10,000 in damage before the policy benefits could kick in.

In general, earthquake insurance involves one deductible per occurrence, not one deductible per policy period. All earthquakes within a three-day period are usually thought of as a single occurrence for the purpose of deductibles. Some policies broaden that provision to include all quakes within a seven-day period.

Earthquake insurance may require a separate deductible for damaged contents. If so, the deductible may be applied to the insured value of the contents. So, with $50,000 of contents coverage and a 10 percent deductible, the insured would be looking at a minimum of $5,000 in non-reimbursable losses. Other policies might list a flat dollar amount as the contents deductible. Some policies have no deductible for contents coverage if the dwelling deductible has been met.

Earthquakes and Additional Living Expenses

Like homeowners insurance, most earthquake insurance policies include some coverage of additional living expenses, which might arise if a quake makes a home temporarily or permanently uninhabitable. Covered costs usually include those for temporary housing, clothing, meals and laundry services. Additional living expenses don't include those expenses a person would've incurred regardless of an earthquake.

Earthquake Limits and Exclusions

Most types of earthquake insurance exclude damage caused by earthquake-related fires. This damage should be insurable through a standard homeowners policy. Also, detached structures (including pools, garages, spas and greenhouses) often aren't covered by basic earthquake insurance.

Difference in Conditions Insurance

Difference in conditions insurance can have many purposes but is usually used to fill in some of the coverage gaps in typical commercial property insurance policies. Difference in conditions insurance products lack much standardization, but they often exclude the perils covered by the business's other commercial property insurance and include coverage for perils like floods and earthquakes. Coinsurance requirements might not apply to this insurance, and deductibles are often higher than for other policies.

Chapter Key Points

- A commercial package policy combines property insurance with various types of liability insurance and contains at least two coverage parts. The policy is available to a wide range of small, medium and large businesses.

- No matter which coverages are chosen by a business, the commercial package policy will include a common policy declarations form and common policy conditions. The conditions often pertain to the following topics:

    o The named insured's ability to cancel the insurance in writing.

    o The inability to assign rights under the policy without the insurer's consent.

    o The ability of the insurer to examine the business's records during the policy period and up to three years afterward.

    o The responsibility of the named insured to pay premiums and receive any refunds of premiums.

    o The ability of the named insured to make changes to the policy.

    o Procedures for mediation or arbitration if there's disagreement about a claim.

    o Upon death of the named insured, the ability of that person's legal representative to exercise various rights under the policy.

- A businessowners policy (BOP) provides a combination of property and casualty coverage to small businesses within relatively low-risk industries.

- Some ineligible businesses for BOPs are:

    o Financial institutions.

    o Bars and restaurants.

    o Auto repair shops, auto dealers and service stations.

    o Places of amusement (theaters, theme parks, etc.).

- Manufacturers.

- Although some insurance for personal watercraft is available within a homeowners insurance policy, the property coverage might be limited to only a few hundred dollars, and the liability coverage might be completely nonexistent for boats with most types of motors. Coverage of theft, hail and wind damage, among other types of losses, will be extremely limited.

- Special boat owners policies are available for property and liability protection. Yacht insurance is available for larger vessels.

- A personal articles floater can cover personal property on a worldwide basis against more perils and at higher dollar limits than a homeowners insurance policy. The term "floater" is used because the covered property (such as jewelry) is usually very portable and more likely to be taken beyond the policyholder's residence.

- Coverage for a mobile home might be little to nonexistent if damage occurs while the home is in transit. Otherwise, mobile homes can usually be insured in the same manner and against the same type of risks (dwelling, contents and personal liability) as traditional homes if the correct policy forms are used.

- To guard against the financial consequences of a flood loss, a homeowner is likely to need a flood insurance policy from the National Flood Insurance Program (NFIP).

- The premiums, terms and conditions for flood insurance policies are often determined by the federal government, but the policies themselves are usually sold and serviced by private insurers. These insurers are known as "Write Your Own" companies.

- Any person who purchases a home in a special flood hazard area with the help of a federally regulated lender is required to cover the home with flood insurance. A special flood hazard area is a place where there's at least a 1 percent chance of flooding each year.

- Although most buildings that are compliant with modern building codes are eligible for federal flood insurance, a building and most types of contents can't be covered if they're principally below ground level.

- The NFIP sets limits on the amount of flood risks it is willing to accept. For most single-family homes, coverage limits for the dwelling can be no more than $250,000, and contents coverage typically won't be available in amounts greater than $100,000. Standard insurance from the NFIP tends not to cover loss of use (such as the cost of renting temporary housing after a flood) or business interruption losses.

- Flood insurance agents must complete a special training course and don't have authority to bind coverage for the NFIP.

- Buyers of flood insurance must typically wait 30 days before their coverage will be in force.

- Common forms of commercial property insurance usually don't cover explosions of steam pipes, steam boilers, steam engines or steam turbines. Boiler and machinery insurance contains property and liability coverage with respect to such losses.

- A basic boiler and machinery/equipment breakdown insurance policy will at least cover damage to the indicated property but can also be structured to address the following kinds of losses, among others:

  - "Expediting expenses" (such as the cost to do emergency repairs).

  - Damage to other property due to a breakdown.

  - Spoilage of other property due to a breakdown.

  - Business interruptions due to a breakdown.

- o Extra expenses due to a breakdown (besides expedited expenses).

- Farmers may purchase federal crop insurance from private insurers that have been approved by the government. This insurance is designed to protect farmers from natural events out of their control (such as a drought). However, it will generally only insure a farmer against a portion of losses and must be purchased in advance of a growing season. Private crop insurance is also available for broader protection and can be purchased at any time during the growing season.

- Many carriers sell special earthquake coverage that can either be added as an endorsement to a homeowners policy or be sold as a stand-alone product.

- Earthquake insurance deductibles vary depending on where an insured person lives and the amount of risk associated with the area. The deductible is applied to the dwelling's insured value rather than to the value of an insurance claim. For the purpose of deductibles, all earthquakes within a three-day period are usually thought of as a single event.

- Difference in conditions insurance is usually used to fill in some of the coverage gaps in typical commercial property insurance policies. For example, it might cover a business against floods and earthquakes.

CHAPTER 12: PERSONAL AUTO INSURANCE

The most common auto insurance policy for individuals is the **Personal Auto Policy**, which was crafted by the Insurance Services Office in the 1970s and has been revised on several occasions. The policy was designed for private passenger vehicles (as opposed to business vehicles or large trucks) and generally provides four kinds of coverage:

- Liability coverage.

- Medical payments coverage.

- Uninsured motorist coverage.

- Coverage for the policyholder's own car.

Although each auto insurance policy has the potential to be different from all the others, mastering the contents of the Personal Auto Policy will help you answer common questions from motorists and make it easier for you to determine people's insurance needs.

Liability Coverage

Auto liability insurance covers motorists when they cause another person to suffer bodily injury or property damage. The term "bodily injury" can mean any harm to a person's body, including harm that involves an illness or causes death. "Property damage" usually involves harm to a person's vehicle, but it can also mean harm to other property, such as a house, a tree or items stored in a car.

The liability portion of an auto insurance policy doesn't compensate at-fault drivers for their own losses. Rather, it only provides money to other people who are harmed by a liable person's driving activities. Coverage for an at-fault driver's own losses is provided in other parts of the policy.

Auto liability insurance will also compensate drivers or pedestrians when they're faced with extra costs or losses of income that are thought to be the insured's fault. For example, the liable driver's insurer will pay for an accident victim's rental car while the victim's regular vehicle is being repaired. Or if the victim is unable to work because of an accident, the at-fault driver's liability insurance should cover the victim's lost wages.

The maximum amount of money an insurance company will pay on account of liability is listed on the policy's declarations page. The limit might be listed as a single dollar amount or as multiple dollar amounts. When the limit has different limits for bodily injury liability and property damage liability, it's said to have a **split limit**.

A policy with a split limit gives the insured different amounts of liability coverage, with each amount depending on the kind of loss and the number of people impacted by it. The three different kinds of limits are as follows:

- A limit for all bodily injuries sustained by one person.

- A limit for all bodily injuries sustained in a single accident, regardless of the number of people.

- A limit for all property damage in a single accident, regardless of the number of people.

In written form, split limits are often indicated by listing the liability limits per thousand and separating each one with a slash. (For example, "25/50/20" would indicate a bodily injury limit of $25,000 per person, a bodily injury limit of $50,000 per accident and a property damage liability limit of $20,000 per accident.

Consumers can often opt out of purchasing many major kinds of coverage contained in an auto insurance policy, but liability insurance is generally the exception. In most states, people aren't allowed to own a vehicle unless they have an acceptable amount of liability protection.

Who's Covered and in Which Cars?

One of the most important things to realize about auto liability insurance is that it doesn't just cover the driver who purchases it. With a few exceptions, the liability protection can apply to accidents caused by the policyholder or any family members who live with that person. In most auto policies, the term "family member" refers to people who are related to the policy's owner by blood, marriage or adoption. In practice, the term even encompasses unlicensed family members who are too young to drive. People besides family members are covered, too, if they're driving the person's car with permission.

Drivers should also understand that their auto liability insurance extends to cars other than their own. If they borrow a friend's car, their own liability insurance can help pay for damages they cause while driving it. However, coverage beyond their own car generally doesn't extend to cases in which they're driving a vehicle that's readily available to them on a regular basis, such as a company car.

Liability protection for non-family members (as well as family members who don't live with the policyholder) doesn't apply if they're driving a vehicle that doesn't belong to the policyholder. Insurance also rarely offers any help to family members who live with the policyholder but get into accidents in their own cars.

Determining who can be covered under the liability section of an auto insurance policy can be a challenge. Therefore, it may be helpful to go over a few examples. If you have a personal auto policy, here are some hypothetical cases in which your liability insurance is likely to provide at least some financial assistance:

- You hit another vehicle while driving your car.
- Your spouse hits a pedestrian while driving your car.
- Your sister, who lives with you, borrows your car while hers is being repaired and crashes into your neighbor's fence.
- You run over another person's dog while driving a rental car.
- Your friend borrows your car and injures a bicyclist.

On the other hand, here are some examples in which your auto liability insurance probably wouldn't be of much help:

- You injure someone while driving a company car that's frequently available to you.
- Your son, who doesn't live with you, purchases his own car and causes an accident with it.
- A thief steals your car and hits a pedestrian while making his getaway.
- Your roommate rents a car and crashes into your neighbor's tree.

Please note that although auto insurance policies can cover a driver's family members, policyholders may have to inform the insurance company ahead of time about any household family member who will have regular access to their car. Parents, in particular, will want to check in with their auto insurer before giving their children the keys to the family car. At the very least, the policyholder may be required to update the insurer about the number of licensed drivers in a household before the policy is renewed.

Liability Deductibles

When their auto liability insurer provides benefits to an accident victim, at-fault drivers typically don't pay a deductible. This is inconsistent with other types of auto coverage, such as coverage for an at-fault driver's own vehicle.

Defense Costs

If drivers get into an auto accident and are sued for damages, their insurance company can pay to defend them. Defense costs have no effect on a policy's dollar limit for liability, but there are a few restrictions to be aware of. Most importantly, the insurance company will stop paying for a driver's defense if it has already provided compensation to victims in an amount equal to the policy's benefit limit.

As an example, let's suppose Jackie has liability insurance that will pay up to $30,000 for property damage. Jackie hits someone's $30,000 car, and her insurer pays for the loss. However, the other driver also claims Jackie is responsible for $5,000 in damage to antiques that were stored in the trunk. Jackie disputes this and ends up having to defend herself in court. But since the insurer already compensated the other driver in an amount equal to Jackie's limit for property damage liability ($30,000), it won't pay her defense costs.

In exchange for paying their legal expenses, auto insurance companies expect defendants to help them in matters related to their case. At the very least, potentially liable drivers must send the insurer copies of any legal documents involving a demand for money. They may also be required to attend and make statements at legal proceedings.

If drivers incur expenses as a result of assisting the insurer, the company will reimburse them. Coverage of these expenses, such as the cost of travel or lodging, will have no impact on dollar limits for property damage or bodily injury.

Similarly, drivers can receive up to a few hundred dollars per day if their involvement in the defense process forces them to miss work. Like coverage of extra expenses, this benefit doesn't affect the overall dollar limits for property damage or bodily injury.

Since the insurer is the one paying the defense costs, it has the power to settle a legal dispute without the insured's permission. If a matter reaches a judge who rules against the insured, the insurance company is also responsible for paying any court-awarded interest applied to the victim's losses.

Finally, liability insurance will provide a certain amount of money (often $250) for a bail bond. This provision has no effect on dollar limits for property damage or bodily injury, but it does nothing for a driver if an accident hasn't occurred. For instance, if a driver runs a red light without hurting anyone and is arrested for arguing with a police officer, money for bail will likely need to come from another source.

Medical Payments Coverage

Medical payments coverage is probably one of the least understood parts of a personal auto insurance policy. In fact, many motorists may not even know they have it.

If you have medical payments coverage, this insurance can be utilized when you, a family member or anyone else who's riding in or driving your car is injured in an accident. Regardless of who is at fault, this coverage is not for the other driver in an accident or for that driver's passengers. Medical payments for the other driver and people riding with that person are meant to be covered by either your liability insurance or the other driver's medical payments coverage.

Medical payments coverage provides a few thousand dollars or more on a per-person, per-accident basis. The money can be used to pay for all reasonable medical or funeral expenses that are related to an auto accident and are incurred within three years of the accident. It doesn't compensate anyone for pain and suffering.

This traditional form of medical payments coverage usually doesn't exist in states governed by no-fault auto insurance laws. Instead, policies in those states are likely to provide **personal injury protection (PIP)**. PIP is very similar to medical payments coverage but can usually reimburse people for expenses besides medical ones. With PIP, injured motorists might be covered for non-medical household assistance while recovering from an accident, and they might receive payments for lost wages.

Who's Covered Where?

As is the case with auto liability insurance, eligibility for medical payments coverage under an auto insurance policy will depend on who the injured person is and where the injury occurs.

Coverage is broadest for the policyholder and the family members who live with that person. With a few exceptions, these people can receive medical payments whenever they're hurt by a vehicle. This includes instances in which they're driving a car, riding as a passenger in a car, sitting in a parked car or hit by a car while traveling on foot.

People besides those family members can receive medical payments through the policyholder's insurance policy if they're injured while in that person's vehicle. This includes when they're driving it, riding in it or just sitting in it. They're not covered by the policyholder's insurance while in someone else's car or on foot.

This part of the policy provides some broad protection, but it does contain some notable exclusions. If you have medical payments coverage, here are a few things to keep in mind:

- There's no coverage if you're hit by a vehicle while riding something with less than four wheels on it. In effect, this means you might need separate insurance for bicycle accidents.

- There's no coverage if you're injured in your car while transporting goods or passengers for money. In these cases, you'd probably need a commercial auto policy.

- There's no coverage if you're injured while using your vehicle as a residence.

- There might not be coverage if you're injured while using your vehicle for business.

- There's no coverage if you're hit by a vehicle that isn't meant to be driven on public roads. Injuries caused by a snowmobile or golf cart, for example, are matters for your health insurer to deal with.

- There might be no coverage if you're hit by your own car. In other words, if your spouse runs over your foot accidentally in the driveway, don't count on your auto insurer to pay your bills.

Uninsured Motorist Coverage

Whether we like it or not, there will always be people who believe the law doesn't apply to them and who'll drive without liability insurance.

So, what can people do if an uninsured driver hits them? They could, of course, sue the person. But that would probably involve finding a lawyer and rearranging their lives around court dates and other hassles. And even if they take legal action, victims might discover that the at-fault driver lacks enough personal assets to pay for damages in the first place.

A portion of an auto policy known as **uninsured motorist coverage** can help in situations like this one. It makes up for the liability coverage the other driver failed to purchase and can compensate victims for bodily injuries, pain, suffering, and (in some cases) property damage. It doesn't let the at-fault driver off the hook, but it gives injured people the money they need with a minimal amount of effort and frees their insurer to take action against the negligent motorist.

Auto insurers provide these benefits if any of the following circumstances arise:

- The policyholder is hit by someone who has no insurance.

- The policyholder is hit by someone who has less insurance than the law requires.

- The policyholder is the victim of a hit-and-run accident.

- The policyholder is hit by someone whose insurer becomes insolvent.

Overall, the kinds of people and situations covered under the medical payments portion of an auto policy would also be protected by uninsured motorist coverage. If the policyholder or that person's family members are hurt by an uninsured vehicle while in any car or while on foot, they'll probably receive some insurance money. Non-family members (and family members who don't live with the policyholder) are also eligible for these benefits if they're hit while in the policyholder's car.

Policy exclusions for uninsured motorist coverage are nearly identical to those for medical payments coverage. For instance, drivers won't be helped if they're hit while carrying goods or people for money, and they aren't covered for accidents caused by snowmobiles, golf carts and similar vehicles. The main difference, though, is that uninsured motorist coverage isn't no-fault insurance. In order to receive payments, the insured must convince the insurance company that damages were caused by someone else.

Underinsured Motorist Coverage

A somewhat similar policy feature known as **underinsured motorist coverage** can help when an at-fault driver has the required minimum amount of liability coverage but still lacks enough to fully compensate a victim. When this coverage is purchased, the victim may be entitled to the difference between his or her losses and the other driver's liability limit.

For example, let's assume George has $100,000 of underinsured motorist coverage and gets into an accident that costs him $70,000 in medical services. The at-fault driver has complied with the law by purchasing $30,000 of liability insurance for bodily injuries, but this person obviously doesn't have enough to pay for all of George's medical bills. In this case, the other driver would pay his full $30,000 to George, and George's underinsured motorist coverage would handle the additional $40,000 (the difference between George's loss and the other driver's liability limit).

Be aware, though, that in order for underinsured motorist coverage to respond, an accident victim must have underinsured motorist coverage that is greater than the at-fault driver's liability insurance.

Stacking

If drivers insure multiple vehicles under the same policy, some states will allow them to combine the benefit limits for each vehicle and apply the total to a single accident. This option, known as "stacking," can require an additional premium and is most commonly offered as part of a driver's uninsured and underinsured motorist coverage.

Imagine that Sue owns two vehicles and covers them under the same policy with a $100,000 limit for uninsured motorist coverage. If Sue is hit in either car by an uninsured driver and her losses exceed $100,000, she could multiply $100,000 by two and be covered for as much as $200,000. Most states, though, either forbid or put limits on stacking, and even where it's allowed by law, an insurer might still refuse to offer it as an option. When a policy doesn't allow stacking, the driver is said to have "unstacked" coverage.

Coverage for Your Own Car

Property insurance for a driver's own car comes in two varieties. **Collision coverage** pays for damage from crashes. **Comprehensive (or "other-than-collision") coverage** protects the policyholder financially from many other perils, including theft and fire. These two kinds of protection can be purchased individually or together. When both are in effect, a car is generally insured against most risks other than some tire damage, war-related losses, wear and tear and freezing.

Unlike other portions of the typical auto policy, insurance for a driver's car usually includes a deductible, which must be paid by the policyholder whenever an accident occurs. If the insurance company takes action against the other driver and wins, the deductible will usually be refunded to the policyholder.

Unlike liability insurance, property insurance on a driver's own car is usually optional unless an auto loan is still being paid off.

Collision Coverage

Collision coverage is for damage sustained when a car collides with another object. Of course, the most obvious kind of object in this case would be another vehicle, but other kinds of crashes are covered, too. For instance, this insurance is likely to come into play when a driver hits a tree or crashes into a telephone pole.

Practically the only thing a driver can hit and not have the situation count as a collision is an animal. Collisions with deer and other living things are addressed through comprehensive/other than-collision coverage.

Comprehensive/Other-Than-Collision Coverage

Comprehensive coverage (now often referred to as "other-than-collision coverage") is designed to cover the driver against most major risks other than collisions. Drivers who purchase this insurance have open-peril coverage and are typically insured against the following causes of loss plus more:

- Theft (including property damage caused by thieves).
- Fire.
- Falling objects.
- Missiles.
- Explosions.
- Earthquakes.
- Wind.
- Hail.
- Floods.
- Vandalism or malicious mischief.
- Riots or civil commotions.
- Collisions with animals and birds.
- Broken glass.

Calculating Auto Property Losses

When a car is damaged, the owner's insurance company is expected to pay the **least** of the following amounts:

- The cost to repair the vehicle.
- The cost to replace the vehicle.
- The vehicle's actual cash value (replacement cost minus depreciation).

Due to the rapid rate of depreciation, the cost of repairing a vehicle might be higher than the car's actual cash value. When this happens, the car is considered to be a total loss ("totaled") even if it's technically still in drivable condition. Instead of repairing it, the insurer will pay the owner the actual cash value.

If a vehicle is totaled, the insurer might reserve the right to take possession of it and sell it to a salvage yard or a similar business. The owner might have the opportunity to keep the vehicle for sentimental reasons, but the insurer might be able to deduct whatever amount it would've gotten from the salvage company from the insurance settlement.

Auto Accessories

As a general rule, electronic accessories like stereo systems, televisions and GPS devices might be covered by a personal auto policy only if they're permanently installed in the vehicle. Whereas a radio that was put inside the car at the automotive factory will probably be covered if it's stolen, the same can't be said for a personal MP3 player that's hooked up to the car via an adapter. Even covered items might be limited to a certain amount of coverage, such as $1,000.

Creditors and Gap Insurance

In order to protect their interest in a vehicle, lenders who make auto loans can list themselves on an auto insurance policy along with the driver. When this is done, a lender might technically be entitled to a portion of the insurance money if the vehicle is damaged.

Until their auto loans are repaid in full, borrowers are required to maintain full coverage on their vehicles, including collision coverage and comprehensive coverage. Deductibles for property damage can be chosen by the lender.

Even if a vehicle is totaled and worth less than a borrower's loan balance, the driver will remain responsible for the debt. To guard against this undesirable situation, a driver can purchase **gap insurance**, which covers the difference between the remaining loan balance and the totaled vehicle's actual cash value. If a car is leased, the driver might already be paying for this insurance in the form of a built-in fee.

Kinds of Covered Autos

The standard personal auto insurance policy can be used to cover just about any kind of car a person owns and reserves for personal use.

Though there are many situations in which an insurer will pay for damages associated with a car that doesn't belong to the policyholder, a personal auto policy probably doesn't cover that kind of vehicle as comprehensively as it covers the person's "covered auto." In personal auto insurance policies, all of the following vehicles tend to qualify as a "covered auto":

- The vehicle listed on the policy's declarations page. (This is often the vehicle that prompted the policyholder to purchase a policy in the first place.)

- Any other vehicle the policyholder obtains during the policy period. (This allows someone to buy a second car without having to tell the insurer ahead of time. Details can be found in the next section.)

- A vehicle the policyholder uses on a temporary basis while the person's regular car is not available.

- A trailer meant to be pulled by an automobile. (Trailers are covered automatically in regard to liability, but damage to them is not. To ensure that property damage to trailers is a covered loss, ownership must be declared prior to an accident.)

Vans and trucks can be covered by a personal auto policy as long as they weigh less than 10,000 pounds and aren't used as delivery vehicles. When these larger autos don't meet those criteria, they may be covered by a commercial auto policy.

Unless a driver pays an additional premium for the proper endorsement, vehicles with fewer than four wheels, such as motorcycles, will have to be insured by something other than a personal auto policy.

Replacement Vehicles

When drivers replace a car that was covered by their auto insurance policy, their new vehicle automatically receives the same amount of liability coverage as their old one. Although older policies might allow the replacement vehicle to be covered for liability for the remainder of the policy period without being reported to the insurer, newer ones will limit this to 14 days.

Drivers will be covered for physical damage to their replacement vehicle automatically for a limited time if their old car was also covered for the same kind of damage. In other words, if the old car was insured against collision losses, the new vehicle will be covered for those losses, too. This temporary coverage tends to last for 14 days. In order for physical damage to be covered for a longer period, the owner must contact the insurance company.

If the driver's previous car wasn't covered for physical damage, physical damage to the replacement vehicle will probably be covered for no more than a few days (often four). If owners want coverage to extend beyond that short time, they must make arrangements with the insurance company.

Additional Vehicles

When people buy a new car without replacing another one, their liability limit for the car will automatically be equal to the highest liability limit among their other cars.

For example, if Irene already owns one vehicle covered by $100,000 of liability insurance and another car with $50,000 of liability insurance on it, her third car will temporarily be covered by $100,000 of liability insurance. In order to maintain this liability insurance on the additional vehicle, Irene must contact the insurer within a set number of days (often 14).

Physical damage to an additional car is basically treated in the same way as physical damage to a replacement car. If any of a driver's other cars are covered for physical damage, an additional vehicle will be covered, too, if an accident occurs soon after the purchase. This insurance probably won't continue beyond 14 days unless the owner specifically requests it.

If none of a driver's other cars are covered for physical damage, physical damage to an additional vehicle will probably be covered for no more than a few days (often four). If owners want coverage to extend beyond that short time, they must make arrangements with the insurance company.

Driving Other People's Cars

Drivers remain insured by their own insurance while driving other people's cars with their permission. These vehicles are known as "non-owned autos." If a driver has property damage coverage for any of his or her owned vehicles, the property damage coverage can extend to cover the non-owned auto.

If a driver is involved in an accident while operating someone else's vehicle (a non-owned auto), the owner's insurance will usually pay for damages first. Then, the driver's insurance will pick up whatever losses are above the owner's policy limits.

If drivers are involved in an accident while driving a vehicle that isn't theirs but is regularly available to them (such as a company car), their auto insurer will probably not cover the losses unless the regular availability has been disclosed appropriately to the insurance company.

Rental Cars

Many travelers are unsure about whether they should purchase insurance from rental car companies. The decision to buy or not to buy the coverage is often made at the last minute, with some people choosing to leave themselves unprotected from major risks and others paying large sums of money for something they don't really need.

Whether coverage is purchased or not, drivers should definitely consider the risks involved with rented vehicles. If someone has an accident with one of its cars, the rental company might be able to hold the person liable for all the damages regardless of who was at fault. Along with having to pay for another person's injuries and damage to any vehicles involved, the renter can even be held accountable for loss-of-use costs if the accident leaves the rental company without enough cars to meet customer demand. (Some states have passed laws that limit a person's liability while operating rented vehicles.)

Many of these risks can be managed by purchasing a "collision-damage waiver" (also known as a "loss-damage waiver") from the rental company. But such waivers might not always be helpful. For example, some waivers still leave renters liable for damages if they let a companion take the wheel or drive the rental car through rough road conditions. The waivers are also relatively expensive. If drivers buy all the insurance presented to them by the rental company, they might end up paying more for coverage than for use of the vehicle.

Before purchasing a waiver, drivers might want to see if the risks of renting a car are covered by other insurance. If they have a personal auto policy, they are usually already covered for liability while operating a rental car or other non-owned autos on a temporary basis. Most kinds of damage to these non-owned autos will be covered, too, if renters have collision coverage and comprehensive coverage for their own vehicles. Bodily injuries that drivers suffer in an accident will fall under their auto policy's medical payments coverage, and homeowners or renters insurance should cover any belongings damaged in the car.

Once drivers know how their own insurer treats rental cars, they can contact their credit card company and inquire about any additional protection. Many card companies provide free insurance for rental cars if the driver's own policy is insufficient. Of course, in order to receive insurance benefits from a particular creditor, the driver must pay for the rental with the appropriate credit card.

The options available from a renter's auto insurer and credit card company might make coverage from the rental company seem pointless, but these sources of protection do have some limitations. Some of the potential problems with auto insurance or free coverage from a credit card company are listed below and might be avoided by purchasing a loss-damage waiver:

- A personal auto policy might not cover a rental car if it's being used for business purposes.

- Coverage for a rental car might be limited to a specific number of consecutive days.

- A personal auto policy usually doesn't cover vehicles rented outside the United States and Canada. Credit card companies offer broader protection but still tend to exclude vehicles in certain countries.

Business Vehicles

Personal auto policies are meant to cover people's personal vehicles. Coverage for automobiles used in business is either excluded from these policies outright or only provided on a limited basis.

Still, there are plenty of business-related exclusions that ought to be mentioned here. To manage these risks and avoid confusion, people who use their cars in business may want to purchase a commercial auto policy:

- Vehicles owned by a company or some other business-related entity (other than an automobile from a rental company) are usually not covered by a personal auto policy if they're regularly available to an employee.

- Drivers aren't covered while using their personal auto to carry people or things for a fee. (For example, this exclusion has been known to cause problems for drivers who use their personal vehicle to deliver food.)

- Drivers who are part of a ride-sharing service generally don't have coverage beginning at the point when they turn a ridesharing app on.

- A personal auto policy doesn't cover liability while a car is being operated by someone in the course of auto-related business. (For example, a mechanic probably isn't covered while road-testing a vehicle, and a valet might not be covered while parking a car.)

- Under some circumstances, a personal auto policy won't protect a business when one of its employees causes an accident.

For specifics about business auto coverage, you may want to review the ISO's Business Auto Coverage Form. Additional information about commercial auto insurance also appears in a later chapter of this book.

Carpools

If drivers use their own vehicle as part of a carpool and take money from passengers, their personal auto insurance remains in force. This is an exception to the general rule regarding business vehicles, which forbids people from being covered while transporting people for a fee.

Exclusions

Personal auto policies have several exclusions besides the ones involving business vehicles. The most significant exclusions in the typical auto insurance policy are explained in the next several sections.

Wear and Tear

Unfortunately for owners, trips to the mechanic and all the costs of parts and labor are generally not covered by auto insurance unless they're needed after an auto accident. Coverage of weather-related damage and theft are probably the closest a policy comes to protecting an owner against perils other than accidents, and even those protections are only available to people with comprehensive coverage.

Intentional Acts

As should be expected, auto insurers won't compensate a driver who intentionally causes an accident. If drivers intentionally hit someone with their car, they'll be stuck paying for their own property damage and medical expenses, as well as any other reparations awarded to the victim.

Driving Without Permission

Auto insurance doesn't cover people when they drive another person's car without permission. This exclusion often doesn't apply when the driver and the owner are relatives living in the same home.

Damage to Non-Auto Property

Other than the vehicle itself, property that a driver owns or is in the driver's possession at the time of an accident isn't covered by auto insurance. For example, if a driver leaves a suitcase in a car and it's damaged by fire, the insurance company won't pay to replace it. Likewise, if a friend leaves a computer in a driver's car and it's damaged in a fire, the driver isn't covered by auto liability insurance if the friend decides to sue. Personal belongings ought to be covered by some form of homeowners insurance or other type of personal property insurance.

Wars and Nuclear Accidents

Drivers aren't covered for medical payments or property damage if an accident occurs because of war or a nuclear attack. In a somewhat related matter, the Terrorism Risk Insurance Act of 2002 originally required commercial auto insurers to offer government-backed terrorism coverage to their customers, but this requirement ended when Congress revised the law in 2005. The law isn't applicable to personal autos.

Other Restrictions

Personal auto insurance typically doesn't cover people for liability and/or property damage in the following situations:

- When the government seizes or destroys their car.

- When they're involved in an accident while engaging in an automobile race.

- When they're acting as an employer and are liable for an employee's injuries.

Transportation Expenses

If drivers are in an accident and are unharmed, their most immediate problem might be how to get around while their vehicle is being repaired. If their car sustained significant damage, they might be facing several weeks of taking buses and trains or using a rental car.

These unexpected travel expenses can add up, and you may wonder who is responsible for paying them. If another driver caused the accident, the at-fault driver's insurance should pick up the costs of the alternative transportation. But what if the accident wasn't someone else's fault? Or what if the victim doesn't want to bother with the other driver's insurer and just wants expenses to be covered quickly?

Drivers who are in either of those situations might be covered if they purchased collision coverage or comprehensive coverage for their vehicle. If they have comprehensive coverage and their car is stolen, their insurer will give them a limited amount of money for temporary transportation expenses. To be eligible for this benefit, the damaged vehicle often must be unavailable for at least two full days.

If a car is unavailable because of property damage, the owner's insurer might provide a limited amount of transportation coverage after a 24-hour waiting period. To be eligible for this benefit, the owner must have the proper kind of property insurance.

When a vehicle is used on a short-term basis because the driver's own vehicle has been damaged or stolen, the short-term vehicle is known as a "temporary substitute vehicle." When the cost of a temporary substitute auto is covered by someone's auto insurance, the policy might impose a per-day limit and an overall limit (such as $30 per day up to $900 total).

Towing and Labor Charges

If drivers are willing to pay more money, their insurance company will cover them for emergency roadside assistance even if their vehicle simply won't start. This additional insurance will pay for towing a car to a repair shop. The cost of labor is covered, too, but since this only applies to work done at the site of the emergency, coverage will probably be limited to relatively simple tasks like changing a tire.

Auto Insurance Laws

The kind of insurance drivers need to obtain will depend partially on whether their state has tort insurance laws or no-fault insurance laws. Up to now, the information provided in this chapter has assumed a driver is from a tort state. No-fault states take a different attitude toward liability insurance, so coverage in these parts of the country is different in some significant ways.

Tort States

Most states use a tort system for auto insurance. Under a tort system, drivers receive limited or no compensation after an auto accident unless they can prove another person was at fault. If an accident victim suffers bodily injury or property damage, the at-fault driver's liability insurance will cover the losses. Accident victims can also collect compensation from the at-fault driver for non-economic losses, such as pain and suffering.

<u>No-Fault States</u>

Drivers in roughly one-third of the country are governed by a "no-fault" insurance system. Under no-fault laws, losses that drivers sustain as a result of bodily injury are handled by their own insurance company even if an accident is caused by another person. In exchange for the supposed simplicity of having to deal only with their own insurer, drivers give up a significant portion of their right to sue the at-fault individual.

Drivers in a no-fault state are usually required to purchase "personal injury protection" (PIP). PIP is very similar to the medical payments coverage in other personal auto policies, but in addition to reimbursing the insured for medical expenses, it can also help people recoup lost income, funeral costs and other extra expenses linked to an accident.

In no-fault states, any losses related to an injury will first be covered by the injured person's PIP. If the injured person didn't cause the accident and losses exceed his or her PIP dollar limit, the other driver's liability insurance might make up the difference. Compensation for non-economic damages, such as pain and suffering, is often prohibited. As in tort states, compensation for property damage is usually provided to victims by the at-fault driver's insurer.

Drivers in no-fault states are only allowed to sue another driver for pain and suffering if the consequences of an accident are serious (such as by exceeding a particular dollar amount or causing a high level of disability).

Coverage in Other States and Other Countries

As a vehicle travels into another state, the owner's coverage automatically adjusts, insuring the driver for at least the minimum required amount in that other state. However, a personal auto policy usually only pertains to accidents in the United States, Canada or one of those countries' territories. It often doesn't even protect U.S. drivers who cross the border into Mexico.

The Residual Auto Insurance Market

If a state makes auto insurance mandatory, it must ensure that everyone with a valid driver's license has an opportunity to purchase minimum coverage. Each state has a **residual market**, which provides insurance to high-risk drivers who are denied coverage from an insurance company.

Many states operate some form of "assigned-risk program." In an assigned-risk program, all auto insurers in the state are required to cover a certain portion of high-risk drivers. The number of high-risk drivers who must be covered by a particular insurer will generally be proportionate to that company's market share. A large insurer will usually be responsible for covering more high-risk drivers than a small insurer.

A few states have dealt with high-risk drivers by covering them through "joint underwriting associations." A joint underwriting association consists of several insurance companies. When a driver suffers an insured loss, all of the members are financially responsible for covering a portion of it. The size of an insurer's portion will depend on how much business the company does in the state. (Again, large insurers will contribute more than small insurers.) However, only a few members will be held responsible for actually dealing with consumers and doing all the work involved with issuing policies and handling claims.

Since it's meant for high-risk drivers, insurance from the residual market is very expensive. The market exists to make insurance accessible, not to make it affordable. Drivers who find themselves in it will want to improve their driving record so they can eventually obtain cheaper, more comprehensive coverage in the regular market.

Chapter Key Points

- The most common auto insurance policy is the Personal Auto Policy.

- Auto liability insurance covers motorists when they cause another person to suffer bodily injury or property damage.

- Rather than a single dollar limit, a policy with a split limit gives the insured different limits of liability for bodily injury and property damage.

- In written form, split limits are often indicated by listing the liability limits per thousand and separating each one with a slash. (For example, "25/50/20" would indicate a bodily injury limit of $25,000 per person, a bodily injury limit of $50,000 per accident and a property damage liability limit of $20,000 per accident.

- In most states, people aren't allowed to own a vehicle unless they have an acceptable amount of liability protection.

- One of the most important things to realize about auto liability insurance is that it doesn't just cover the driver who purchases it. With a few exceptions, the liability protection can apply to accidents caused by the policy's owner or any family members who live with that person and are driving that person's vehicle.

- Although auto insurance policies can cover a driver's family members, policyholders may have to inform the insurance company ahead of time about any household family member who will have regular access to their car.

- When their auto liability insurer provides benefits to an accident victim, at-fault drivers typically don't pay a deductible.

- If drivers get into an auto accident and are sued for damages, their insurance company can pay to defend them.

- If you have medical payments coverage as part of your personal auto policy, this insurance can be utilized when you, a family member or anyone else who is riding in or driving your car is injured in an accident. Regardless of who is at fault, this coverage isn't for the other driver in an accident or for that driver's passengers.

- Medical payments coverage provides a few thousand dollars or more on a per-person, per-accident basis. The money can be used to pay for all reasonable medical or funeral expenses that are related to an auto accident and are incurred within three years of the accident. It doesn't compensate anyone for pain and suffering.

- Uninsured motorist coverage makes up for the liability coverage the other driver failed to purchase and can compensate victims for bodily injuries, pain, suffering, and (in some cases) property damage.

- Underinsured motorist coverage can help when an at-fault driver has the required minimum amount of liability coverage but still lacks enough to fully compensate a victim.

- Where allowed, "stacking" permits someone to insure multiple vehicles for uninsured and/or underinsured motorist coverage and combine the dollar limits for all of those vehicles after suffering a loss. If an auto insurance policy doesn't allow this type of stacking, the policyholder is said to have "unstacked" coverage.

- Property insurance for a driver's own car comes in two varieties. Collision coverage pays for damage from crashes. Comprehensive (or other-than-collision) coverage protects the policyholder financially from many other perils, including theft and fire. Unlike other portions of the typical auto policy, insurance for a driver's car usually has a deductible.

- Practically the only thing a driver can hit and not have the situation count as a collision is an animal.

- By default, a vehicle will typically only be covered up to its actual cash value.

- Due to the rapid rate of depreciation, the cost of repairing a vehicle might be higher than the car's actual cash value. When this happens, the car is considered to be a total loss (totaled) even if it is technically still in drivable condition. Instead of repairing it, the insurer will pay the owner the actual cash value.

- A driver who borrows money for a vehicle can purchase gap insurance, which covers the difference between the remaining loan balance and a totaled vehicle's actual cash value.

- Drivers remain insured by their own insurance while driving other people's cars with their permission. These vehicles are known as "non-owned autos." If a driver has property damage coverage for any of his or her owned vehicles, the property damage coverage can extend to cover the non-owned auto.

- When a vehicle is used on a short-term basis because the driver's own vehicle has been damaged or stolen, the short-term vehicle is known as a "temporary substitute vehicle."

- If a driver is involved in an accident while operating someone else's vehicle, the owner's insurance will usually pay for damages first. The driver's insurance will pick up whatever losses are above the owner's policy limits.

- If drivers are involved in an accident while driving a vehicle that isn't theirs but is regularly available to them (such as a company car), their auto insurer will probably not cover the losses. However, might they still remain insured while driving a vehicle that is regularly available and owned by a household family member if the insurer has been properly notified.

- Personal auto policies are meant to cover people's personal vehicles. Coverage for automobiles used in business is either excluded from these policies outright or is only provided on a limited basis.

- Most states use a tort system for auto insurance. Under a tort system, drivers receive limited or no compensation after an auto accident unless they can prove another person was at fault. If an accident victim suffers bodily injury or property damage, the at-fault driver's liability insurance will cover the losses. Accident victims can also collect compensation from the at-fault driver for non-economic losses, such as pain and suffering.

- In a no-fault system, losses that drivers sustain as a result of bodily injury are handled by their own insurance company even if an accident is caused by another person. In exchange for the supposed simplicity of having to deal only with their own insurer, drivers give up a significant portion of their right to sue the at-fault individual.

- Drivers in a no-fault state are usually required to purchase personal injury protection (PIP). PIP is very similar to the medical payments coverage in other personal auto policies.

- Drivers in no-fault states are only allowed to sue another driver for pain and suffering if the consequences of an accident are serious.

- As a vehicle travels into another state, the owner's coverage automatically adjusts, insuring the driver for at least the minimum required amount in that other state. A personal auto policy usually only pertains to accidents that occur in the United States, Canada or one of those countries' territories.

- Each state has a residual market, which provides insurance to high-risk drivers who are denied coverage from an insurance company.

CHAPTER 13: COMMERCIAL AUTO INSURANCE

The most popular variety of auto insurance for businesses is based on a document called the "Business Auto Coverage Form." The document was created in the late 1970s by Insurance Services Office and has been revised several times since then. Policies based on that document are known as "Business Auto Policies," BAPs" or "BACs." For simplicity's sake, we'll use the term "BAP" from this point forward.

Covered Vehicles

The specific vehicles insured under a BAP will be indicated by numbers checked on the policy's declarations page. There are nine different numbers for nine different groups of vehicles. The significance of each number is summarized in the list below. <u>For study purposes, rather than attempting to memorize the meaning of each number, merely understand that the numbering system for different kinds of vehicles exists</u>:

- *Symbol 1:* When this symbol is chosen, coverage applies to any vehicle designed for use on public roads, regardless of who owns it. For example, if it's used with regard to liability coverage, the business will be insured if it's sued in connection with practically any auto accident. The only things that would prevent the business from being covered would be either a specific exclusion written into a policy or a previous claim that exhausted the policy's dollar limits. It represents the broadest form of business auto coverage.

- *Symbol 2:* When this symbol is chosen, coverage only applies to autos owned by the "named insured." (In most cases, the named insured is the business.) Unless special arrangements are made, it won't provide coverage for vehicles owned by someone else, such as an employee. It also won't make coverage applicable to vehicles leased or borrowed by the business.

- *Symbol 3:* When this symbol is chosen, coverage only applies to private passenger vehicles owned by the named insured. It won't provide coverage for other people's private passenger vehicles, and it won't cover large trucks.

- *Symbol 4:* When this symbol is chosen, coverage only applies to vehicles that are owned by the named insured and aren't private passenger vehicles. In other words, it can make insurance applicable to a business's large trucks but not its cars.

- *Symbol 5:* When this symbol is chosen, coverage only applies to vehicles registered or stored in states where no-fault auto insurance is mandatory.

- *Symbol 6:* When this symbol is chosen, coverage only applies to vehicles registered or stored in states where uninsured motorist coverage is mandatory.

- *Symbol 7:* When this symbol is chosen, coverage only applies to the specific, individual vehicles listed on the policy's declarations page. It's ideal for businesses that own or have access to multiple vehicles but only want to insure certain ones.

- *Symbol 8:* When this symbol is chosen, coverage only applies to vehicles leased, borrowed, rented or hired by the named insured. It doesn't provide coverage for vehicles owned by employees or by owners of the business or their families.

- *Symbol 9:* When this symbol is chosen, coverage only applies to vehicles that aren't owned, leased, borrowed, rented or hired by the named insured. For example, it might protect the employer if a worker causes an accident in her own car, but it won't cover the employer if that same worker causes an accident in a company car.

A business can request different symbols for each main kind of coverage. For instance, it may want Symbol 1 in regard to liability coverage but only Symbol 7 for property damage to its own vehicles. It's also possible to use multiple symbols at once. So, if a business knows it'll be using its own vehicles and an employee's vehicle but will never rent, lease, borrow or hire any others, it might want liability protection with symbols 2 and 9 selected.

Not every insurer will let businesses choose from all nine symbols under every circumstance. A carrier that's willing to offer Symbol 1 coverage for liability might not make Symbol 1 an option for covering property damage to a business's own vehicles. It's also important to read coverage forms carefully instead of immediately assuming that the symbols correspond with the descriptions listed here. Particularly when not all nine symbols are available, an insurer might renumber the symbols on its forms.

Who's an Insured?

The named insured is the main party who is protected by the commercial auto insurance policy. Unless the policy contains an exception, no one else will be covered for liability if an auto accident causes property damage or bodily injury. And unless the appropriate symbol is chosen (such as symbols 1, 8 or 9), no one else's vehicles will be covered for repairs.

In the vast majority of cases, the named insured in a BAP is the business. Most BAPs will also cover people besides the named insured, but only when certain conditions have been met.

Coverage under a BAP will usually extend to anyone driving a covered auto with the named insured's permission. In a hypothetical example, let's assume Jane is given access to a car that's owned and insured by Real Good Paper Company. Jane causes an accident while driving Real Good Paper Company's car. Since Jane had permission to drive the car, she'll likely be covered for liability along with Real Good Paper Company if an accident victim ever sues. This would likely be true even if Jane doesn't have personal auto insurance of her own.

But as was mentioned in the previous section, the vehicle needs to have been properly listed on the policy's declaration page, either by name or by symbol. In other words, if Real Good Paper Company chose a symbol that doesn't include rental cars, Jane won't be insured under Real Good Paper Company's policy if she rents a car for business.

Who's Not an Insured?

Even when a business allows someone to use one of its vehicles, a few additional exceptions can stop coverage from extending to that individual. Perhaps most significantly, insurance won't apply to employees or business owners when they drive their personally owned vehicles. Suppose Gary is sent by Real Good Paper Company on business trips and uses his own vehicle. If Gary causes an accident on one of these trips and is held personally liable, the BAP usually won't cover him. He'll probably have to seek protection under his personal auto policy.

Liability Coverage

While BAPs and personal auto policies aren't intended for the same audience or the same vehicles, the liability protection they provide to drivers is very similar. Both kinds of insurance can be used to manage liability for bodily injury or damage to someone else's property. They also help potentially liable parties pay to defend themselves.

Defense Costs

If legal action is taken or threatened against an insured party, the liability portion of the BAP will cover defense costs. The insurer's duty to defend is generally greater than its duty to pay for damages. Even if there's only a small possibility that an accident is covered by the policy, the insurance company might still need to provide a defense.

The cost of defending the insured party won't impact the amount of money available for bodily injury or property damage liability. However, the carrier is allowed to stop defending the insured once the policy's dollar limits have been met through any judgments or settlements. For example, imagine a policy covers a company for $200,000 per accident in the event of bodily injury. One of the company's covered employees caused an accident, and the victim claimed to suffer damage to her back and leg. The company's insurer settled with the victim in regard to her back injury for $200,000, but the parties couldn't agree on an amount for the foot problem. Since the insurer already paid out the full $200,000 limit for bodily injury, it won't be obligated to defend the business anymore if the victim sues.

Liability Exclusions

No matter the people or vehicles involved, some injuries and damages won't be covered by the BAP. Many of the exclusions mirror those found in personal auto policies for individuals. Some of the most important exclusions are listed here, and a few will be given more attention in later sections:

- There's no coverage for punitive damages. (Punitive damages are extra court penalties designed to punish people for especially egregious behavior. Covering these damages is usually prohibited by law.)

- There's no coverage for intentionally injuring someone or damaging their property on purpose.

- There's generally no coverage for property damage or bodily injury caused by pollution.

- There's generally no coverage for damage to property in an insured party's care, custody or control. (If a business transports other people's property in its vehicles, it may want to purchase inland marine insurance.)

- There's no coverage if a vehicle is being used as part of an organized racing event or stunt.

Property Damage

If damage to a covered vehicle can't be blamed on someone else, repairs might be covered under the BAP's property damage section. Unlike liability coverage, property damage coverage is usually not required by law.

By default, property damage coverage for covered autos is based on a vehicle's actual cash value. A vehicle's actual cash value is its replacement cost minus depreciation immediately prior to an accident.

Collision, Comprehensive and Other Coverages

Businesses that want to insure vehicles for property damage will usually choose collision coverage, comprehensive (other-than-collision) coverage or both. These two kinds of coverage are also the main options in the market for personal auto insurance.

Collision coverage pays to repair or replace a driver's vehicle if he or she hits another object. Comprehensive/other-than-collision coverage pays to repair or replace a vehicle when damage is caused by something other than a collision. It can also compensate the owner if a vehicle is stolen.

Property Damage Exclusions

Some kinds of damage typically won't be covered by a BAP. Like the liability exclusions, many of these will be familiar to people who sell personal auto insurance. Some common exclusions are as follows:

- There's no coverage for losses caused by war or terrorist attacks.

- There's no coverage for damage from wear and tear.

- There's no coverage for damage from nuclear accidents.

- There's no coverage for lost or damaged media used in the vehicle for enjoyment (such as cassettes or compact discs).

Personal Use

Even if a vehicle is driven primarily for business, people with access to company vehicles are likely to also drive them for personal use. Assuming the appropriate symbol is marked on the declarations page, a business will remain covered for liability even if one of its owned or rented vehicles is being used for non-business purposes. But liability protection for the person driving the vehicle doesn't always exist.

In order for a driver to drive a company vehicle for personal use and still be covered for liability under the BAP, permission must've been granted by the business. In other words, if a company makes it clear that one of its cars is only to be used for conducting business, drivers won't be covered while driving to and from personal errands. Similarly, even if a business allows vehicles to be driven for personal use by an employee, permission might not extend to the employee's spouse, other family members or friends. If anyone besides the permitted driver uses a business's vehicle, the insurance company might not have to cover anyone for liability except the business.

Drive Other Car Coverage

Some business owners and employees rely on company cars and don't actually own a vehicle. Not owning a vehicle usually means they don't have a personal auto insurance policy either. This lack of insurance can create problems if they're ever involved in an accident with a car that they rent or borrow for personal use.

Although the owners of rented or borrowed vehicles are likely to have some auto coverage that the otherwise uninsured driver can rely on, there are no guarantees. The owner of the rented or borrowed vehicle might only have a minimum amount of liability insurance or perhaps no insurance at all. In either of those cases, the driver using the vehicle could have a major liability exposure.

Businesses already furnishing company cars to people can help alleviate this problem by purchasing "drive other car" coverage. Drive other car coverage is added to the BAP for an additional cost and is designed for drivers who don't normally use any other vehicles and don't have personal auto insurance. It covers workers who are held liable for an accident involving practically any vehicle (other than one they own), regardless of whether they're driving for business reasons or personal ones.

A drive other car endorsement covers the individual specifically named in the policy and also extends to the person's cohabitating spouse. Unless requested, it won't cover non-spouses who live with the named driver, and it won't cover a spouse who lives at another location. The endorsement is usually purchased solely for the purpose of covering the driver for liability, but uninsured motorist, physical damage and other coverages may also be available.

Business Auto Insurance and Employee Injuries

A BAP usually won't help pay for bodily injuries to workers who are hurt while doing their jobs. If an injured worker is considered an employee, benefits should be available through the business's workers compensation insurance.

Chapter Key Points

- The most popular variety of commercial auto insurance is based on a document called the "Business Auto Coverage Form."

- The specific vehicles insured under a BAP will be indicated by numbers checked on the policy's declarations page. There are nine different numbers for nine different groups of vehicles.

- Even if a vehicle is driven primarily for business, people with access to company vehicles are likely to also drive them for personal use. Assuming the appropriate symbol is marked on the declarations page, a business will remain covered for liability even if one of its owned or rented vehicles is being used for non-business purposes. But liability protection for the person driving the vehicle doesn't always exist.

- Drive other car coverage is added to the BAP for an additional cost and is designed for drivers who don't normally use any other vehicles and don't have personal auto insurance. It covers workers who are held liable for an accident involving practically any vehicle (other than one they own), regardless of whether they're driving for business reasons or personal ones. A drive other car endorsement covers the individual specifically named in the policy and also extends to the person's cohabitating spouse.

- A BAP usually won't help pay for bodily injuries to workers who are hurt while doing their jobs. If an injured worker is considered an employee, benefits should be available through the business's workers compensation insurance.

CHAPTER 14: COMMERCIAL GENERAL LIABILITY INSURANCE

Many common liability risks for businesses are managed through the purchase of **commercial general liability insurance**. The insurance is relatively broad in scope and was designed to be adaptable for a wide variety of policyholders. Entities that provide services, build property or manufacture goods are all likely to either have it or need it in some form.

In today's market, commercial general liability insurance makes carriers responsible for covering losses related to property damage, bodily injury, medical payments, personal injury and advertising injury. The coverage, which will be described in greater detail over the next several pages, might be purchased independently of other insurance or as part of a multi-layered insurance package.

Bodily Injury and Property Damage

Commercial general liability insurance is used mainly to cover businesses when they're liable for bodily injury or property damage.

Bodily injury can include accidental cases of physical injury, illness or death. Property damage can include physical damage to property as well as the loss of use of undamaged property.

Exclusions to Bodily Injury and Property Damage

Despite being broad in scope and being geared toward a wide range of businesses, commercial general liability insurance policies tend to contain some very important exclusions. Some of the most consequential exclusions are explained next.

Intangible Property

For property damage to be covered by commercial general liability insurance, it must've been done to something tangible. This means the property subjected to damage needs to be something you can actually touch. Computers, discs and flash drives can be touched, but the data stored on them can't. This might create a huge coverage gap when a business is held responsible for the loss or corruption of valuable electronic information.

Economic Losses

Property damage covered by commercial general liability insurance can't be purely economic. Giving bad financial advice to a client might lead to a lawsuit, but it's usually not the kind of suit in which coverage would be triggered. If a financial loss isn't linked directly to bodily injury or physical damage to tangible property, it might only be covered by other insurance, such as errors and omissions insurance.

The Business's Work and Items Being Worked On

A few of the more complex exclusions are designed to ensure the business retains at least some of the risks involved with doing faulty work or making substandard products. For example, if a business is tasked with repairing or servicing property and damages it while performing work, the business might be uninsured for the damage. Similarly, if work has been finished somewhere other than the business premises (such as at a person's home) and is later found to be substandard, the business's insurance company typically won't compensate angry customers who want the work redone. The insurance company can help with accidents, but it isn't interested in covering people who are simply bad at their jobs.

Pollution

Strict exclusions will usually prevent a business from being covered when bodily injury or property damage is caused by a pollutant. The exclusions can pertain to pollution caused by gasses, fumes, liquids, waste, smoke or chemicals.

Property in the Business's Care, Custody or Control

Commercial general liability insurance won't protect a business when it damages someone else's personal property within its care, custody or control. This is a significant coverage gap for repair shops, cleaning companies and just about any other entity entrusted with its customers' belongings. The exclusion can apply if damage is done to the property before, during or after it's been serviced by the insured.

Many businesses opt to cover property in their care with other insurance. Some coverage might be available as part of the business's own property insurance. Alternatively, companies specializing in accepting other people's property for repairs or services are often good candidates for a "bailee" insurance policy, which is specifically designed to cover a customer's belongings.

Intentional Acts

Liability insurance is meant to cover the insured for accidents, not for intentional damage. Doing otherwise would have negative social consequences because it would give people an excuse to commit bad behavior.

Vehicle Liability

Liability arising from the operation of cars and other vehicles is supposed to be covered by commercial auto insurance. With this in mind, commercial general liability policies usually won't cover businesses after accidents involving automobiles, planes or boats. This exclusion also extends to claims alleging that a business was negligent in hiring or supervising drivers or pilots.

Contractual Liability

Many people assume that contractual liability refers mainly to a business's failure to honor an agreement. But in the world of liability insurance, the term is typically used to describe a situation in which liability of one party is assumed by another. In an apartment lease, for example, the tenant might agree to accept liability for all instances of property damage or bodily injury occurring at the property. This includes accidents for which, in the absence of the lease, the landlord would legally be responsible.

Commercial general liability insurance tends to exclude coverage of contractual liability but allows for several complex exceptions, the details of which are beyond the scope of this guide.

Liquor Liability

Liquor liability can be a headache for restaurants, taverns and any business serving alcohol at a party or corporate event. If someone's intoxication results in property damage or bodily injury, the provider or server of alcoholic beverages might be blamed for the trouble.

Commercial general liability insurance won't be of much help when an entity in the business of serving or manufacturing alcohol is accused of contributing to someone's intoxication. Separate insurance is used for that purpose.

Workers Compensation and Disability Benefits

Commercial general liability insurance won't provide any benefits that employers are legally obligated to pay under workers compensation or disability laws.

Employment Practices

Commercial liability insurance rarely covers businesses for employment practices liability. This form of liability usually involves cases in which workers are sexually harassed, discriminated against or wrongfully terminated. Separate insurance exists for some of those risks.

Professional Liability

Professional services are often defined as services requiring special skills that are intellectual rather than physical in nature. Providers of these services include lawyers, doctors, financial planners and insurance producers.

Liability related to professional services is rarely covered by commercial general liability insurance because it hardly ever involves bodily injury or property damage. When a professional gives bad advice or fails to address a client's situation properly, the result is usually limited to economic losses rather than physical harm. Medical professionals are certainly capable of causing bodily injury, but an insurer will often wipe out coverage for that risk by adding an ISO-created endorsement to the standard policy form. Risks associated with professional services can usually be managed more effectively by purchasing errors and omissions insurance or some specific type of malpractice coverage.

No-Fault Medical Coverage

A special section of a commercial general liability insurance policy deals with no-fault medical coverage. This portion of the policy exists so there's a smaller chance of a lawsuit or costly settlement after an accident that harms a member of the public.

The no-fault portion of the policy usually has its own dollar limit. If the insured is accused of being at-fault for bodily injury and runs out of no-fault medical coverage, the main body of the policy (described in the previous sections of this chapter) will take over.

The no-fault medical portion of the commercial general liability insurance policy can cover anything from first aid and x-rays to doctor visits and funeral expenses. The insurer will cover bills for these treatments and services if they're needed within a year of the accident. To be eligible for payments, the injured person may need to agree to an examination by the insurer's chosen physician.

Personal and Advertising Injury

Despite our emphasis so far on property damage and bodily injury, commercial general liability insurance can cover other risks, too. Most notably, it's used to help businesses when they're accused of causing personal injury or advertising injury. Since these terms usually aren't understood by general audiences, we'll explain each of them in their own individual sections.

Personal Injury

In a very basic sense, **personal injury** occurs when people's rights or reputations are taken away from them. Be careful not to confuse personal injury with bodily injury. As far as commercial general liability insurance is concerned, personal injury can occur even if the injured party suffers no bodily injuries or property damage.

The forms of personal injury covered by the typical commercial general liability policy are as follows:

- False arrest, detention or imprisonment. (*Example:* A business believes someone on its premises has broken a law and refuses to let the person leave.)

- Malicious prosecution. (*Example:* A business repeatedly takes unreasonable legal action against a competitor.)

- Wrongful entry. (*Example:* A business renting property to a tenant enters the property and uses it without the tenant's consent.)

- Wrongful eviction. (*Example:* A business changes the locks on rented property without informing a tenant and in violation of a lease.)

- Libel. (*Example:* A business publishes a damaging, untrue statement about a person or another business.)

- Slander. (*Example:* A business says a damaging, untrue statement about a person or other business.)

- Publication of private information. (*Example:* A business publishes something about a competitor's or customer's personal life.)

Advertising Injury

Advertising injury occurs when a business commits an offense against someone in its promotional materials. Examples of advertising injury likely to be addressed by commercial general liability insurance include the following:

- Committing libel or slander in an advertisement.

- Disclosing private information about someone in an advertisement.

- Using copyrighted material in an advertisement without permission.

- Using another business's trademark or slogan without permission.

- Using another business's advertising idea without permission.

Personal and Advertising Injury Exclusions

The personal and advertising injury portion of a commercial general liability insurance policy has its own set of exclusions. Some of the most common exclusions are listed next:

- Copyright infringement in material other than an advertisement.

- Personal or advertising injury that occurs beyond the policy's coverage territory. (This exclusion is usually waived in the case of advertising injury committed over the internet.)

- Copyright infringement or libel committed in materials published before the policy period.

- Knowingly printing false information.

- Intentional acts.

- Libel, slander or any kind of advertising injury committed by advertising agencies, publishing companies, internet service providers, web designers, broadcasters or search engine providers.

- Offenses committed on internet bulletin boards or in chat rooms.

- The use of someone else's name or product in a Web address, email address or metatag. (A metatag is essentially data used by search engines to organize online content.)

- False advertising of products or services.

Defense Costs

Defense costs under the commercial general liability policy will continue to be covered until the amount paid by the insurer for settlements and court-awarded damages equals the policy's dollar limit. Money paid for defense purposes has no effect on the limit.

Since it's responsible for handling defense costs, the insurer behind the commercial general liability policy can settle disputes without the insured's consent. Similarly, the insured isn't allowed to settle disputes without the insurance company's permission.

Occurrence and Claims-Made Policies

Commercial general liability insurance can be issued through the use of either an occurrence policy or a claims-made policy. With an **occurrence policy**, coverage depends mainly on when an accident occurs. With a **claims-made policy**, coverage depends on when an accident occurs AND when a demand for money from an accident occurs. The distinction between the two forms can be extremely important when damage or injuries don't materialize at the same time as the accident that caused them.

With an occurrence policy, a business remains insured for liability even if it cancels coverage before any demand for money is made.

With a claims-made policy, the opposite is often true. Regardless of when an accident actually happens, claims will be denied if they're not made during the policy period.

To better understand the difference between occurrence coverage and claims-made coverage, it may be helpful to know why claims-made forms were introduced. During the 1980s, many people who had occupied buildings with asbestos were experiencing serious health problems. Arguing that asbestos contributed to their conditions, they sued property owners and builders for millions of dollars. In turn, the owners and builders looked to their insurance companies to protect them. Even in cases where the plaintiffs hadn't occupied the properties in several years, and even in cases where the owners and builders had allowed their coverage to lapse 30 years earlier, the insurance companies were expected to pay. This encouraged insurers to stop issuing so many occurrence policies and to start issuing claims-made policies instead.

Retroactive Dates in Claims-Made Policies

A consumer who's considering claims-made insurance should be made clearly aware of the policy's **retroactive date**. Even if a claim is made on a claims-made policy during the policy period, it will be denied if the accident associated with it occurred before the retroactive date.

Think of a claims-made policy that has a retroactive date of January 1, 2020, and is set to expire on December 31, 2021. If a claim is made on December 30, 2021 for an accident from 2019, the policy won't respond. It'll only cover liability for accidents that happened from January 1, 2020, to December 31, 2021.

The retroactive date for a claims-made policy is usually the date when claims-made coverage from that carrier first went into effect for the policyholder. In other words, if a business purchased claims-made coverage from a carrier on January 1, 2020, and renews it every year thereafter, the retroactive date for the renewed policy should continue to be January 1, 2020. If the retroactive date is moved up to a more recent date, the business could be left with a major insurance gap.

Extended Reporting Periods for Claims-Made Policies

Much to the benefit of business owners, claims-made policies typically include an **extended reporting period** at no extra charge. The extended reporting period provides temporary coverage when commercial general liability insurance is canceled, replaced or not renewed. Sometimes known as "tail coverage," It can be particularly helpful when a company goes out of business or switches from one insurance carrier to another.

The basic extended reporting period gives the business 60 days after the end of the policy period to report accidents and have them covered by a claims-made policy. If those accidents are reported in time, claims stemming from them will be covered for five years, up to the policy's dollar limits. For example, if a shopkeeper is scheduled to have her insurance canceled but knows a customer slipped at her premises just prior to the policy's cancellation date, she can report the incident to her insurer and be covered for it for the next five years. However, if the shopkeeper isn't aware of the incident and therefore doesn't report it within 60 days of the policy's cancellation date, she won't be protected by insurance. Although coverage is often available for businesses that want more than 60 days to report accidents or more than five years of protection from those accidents, it isn't included in the typical policy free of charge.

For an incident to be covered as part of the extended reporting period, it still needs to have occurred during the policy period. So, if the policy covering the shopkeeper in our previous example expires on

January 1, she won't be covered at all for accidents occurring on January 2. It makes no difference whether she reports the accident within 60 days of her policy's cancellation date.

Policy Limits

The coverage provided by a commercial general liability insurance policy isn't unlimited. The insurer behind the policy will only be obligated to pay claims up to a certain dollar amount. There may be an overall limit for the policy period regardless of the kind of claim, individual sub-limits for property damage, personal and advertising injury and medical payments and a per-accident limit regardless of the kind of damage. It's also possible for an insurer to have separate limits for completed projects and works in progress, a limit for fire damage and a limit for each of an insured's separate locations.

Chapter Key Points

- Commercial general liability insurance is used mainly to cover businesses when they're liable for bodily injury or property damage impacting the public.

- For property damage to be covered by commercial general liability insurance, it must've been done to something tangible. This means the property subjected to damage needs to be something you can actually touch. Computers, discs and flash drives can be touched, but the data stored on them can't. This might create a huge coverage gap when a business is held responsible for the loss or corruption of valuable electronic information.

- Commercial general liability insurance won't protect a business when it damages someone else's personal property within its care, custody or control. This is a significant coverage gap for repair shops, cleaning companies and just about any other entity entrusted with its customers' belongings.

- Professional services are often defined as services requiring special skills that are intellectual rather than physical in nature. Providers of these services include lawyers, doctors, financial planners and insurance producers. Liability related to professional services is rarely covered by commercial general liability insurance because it hardly ever involves bodily injury or property damage. Risks associated with professional services can usually be managed more effectively by purchasing errors and omissions insurance.

- Commercial general liability insurance can be used to help businesses when they're accused of causing personal injury or advertising injury.

- Personal injury occurs when people's rights or reputations are taken away from them. Be careful not to confuse personal injury with bodily injury. Personal injury can occur even if the injured party suffers no bodily injuries or property damage.

- The forms of personal injury covered by the typical commercial general liability policy are as follows:

  o False arrest, detention or imprisonment.

  o Malicious prosecution.

  o Wrongful entry.

  o Wrongful eviction.

  o Libel.

  o Slander.

  o Publication of private information.

- Advertising injury occurs when a business commits an offense against someone in its promotional materials. Examples of advertising injury likely to be addressed by commercial general liability insurance include the following:
    - Committing libel or slander in an advertisement.
    - Disclosing private information about someone in an advertisement.
    - Using copyrighted material in an advertisement without permission.
    - Using another business's trademark or slogan without permission.
    - Using another business's advertising idea without permission.
- The personal and advertising injury portion of a commercial general liability insurance policy has its own set of exclusions. Some of the most common exclusions are as follows:
    - Copyright infringement in material other than an advertisement.
    - Personal or advertising injury that occurs beyond the policy's coverage territory.
    - Copyright infringement or libel committed in materials published before the policy period.
    - Knowingly printing false information.
    - Intentional acts.
    - Libel, slander or any kind of advertising injury committed by advertising agencies, publishing companies, internet service providers, web designers, broadcasters or search engine providers.
    - Offenses committed on internet bulletin boards or in chat rooms.
    - The use of someone else's name or product in a Web address, email address or metatag.
    - False advertising of products or services.
- With an occurrence policy, coverage depends mainly on when an accident occurs.
- With a claims-made policy, coverage depends on when an accident occurs AND when a demand for money from an accident is made.
- Even if a claim is made on a claims-made policy during the policy period, it'll be denied if the accident associated with it occurred before the retroactive date.
- Claims-made policies typically include an extended reporting period at no extra charge. The extended reporting period provides temporary coverage when commercial general liability insurance is canceled, replaced or not renewed. In order for this coverage to apply, the business must report any incident that has already occurred but not yet resulted in a demand for money from a harmed person.

CHAPTER 15: EMPLOYMENT PRACTICES LIABILITY INSURANCE

Employment practices liability (EPL) insurance aims to protect businesses when they're accused of violating someone's employment rights. The person whose rights might or might not have been violated could be a current or former employee or anyone who unsuccessfully sought work at the business.

Common EPL claims involve allegations of discrimination, retaliation or sexual harassment. Such allegations are often linked to the hiring, firing, layoff, promotion or demotion processes but can occur at seemingly any time.

What Are Covered Acts?

At first, covered acts that could trigger EPL insurance benefits were largely limited to discrimination or sexual harassment alleged by either regular full-time employees or applicants for regular full-time employment. These days, covered acts typically also include alleged retaliation and even accusations made by part-time employees, contractors and other types of workers.

Federal laws prohibiting sexual harassment in the workplace are enforced by the Equal Employment Opportunity Commission (EEOC). According to the EEOC, sexual harassment is occurring if a worker is expected to engage in sexual activity in exchange for a "tangible employment decision" in the person's favor (known as "quid pro quo harassment").

Harassment is also occurring if a worker is forced to endure a "hostile work environment" A hostile work environment is either a work situation that's highly offensive and intimidating or one in which sexual advances unreasonably interfere with an employee's job performance.

Over the years, EPL insurance has evolved to help businesses manage risks besides alleged sexual harassment. Other scenarios that might be addressed by an EPL policy are listed next:

- Alleged discrimination under the Civil Rights Act, Americans With Disabilities Act, Equal Pay Act, Age Discrimination in Employment Act, or Pregnancy Discrimination Act.

- Alleged retaliation for reporting discrimination or harassment.

- Violations related to the Family and Medical Leave Act.

- Alleged libel or slander committed by a supervisor about a current or former employee.

- Alleged privacy violations committed by employers against employees or job applicants.

- Alleged discrimination under applicable state law.

Defense Costs

Like most types of liability insurance, EPL insurance provides coverage for defense costs, including the cost of hiring a qualified legal team.

Unlike some of the other casualty insurance products detailed in this book, basic EPL insurance will include defense costs within the policy's overall coverage limits. In other words, the more money spent to defend the insured, the less money there'll be to pay for settlements or court-awarded damages. If businesses have concerns about how this might create pressure to settle rather than defend a meritless claim, they can often pay extra to have separate limits for defense costs.

Many EPL policies give the insurance company a fairly broad "duty to defend" the insured. In essence, this means the insurance company must pay for and help organize the competent defense of a claim against the insured, as long as the claim isn't obviously excluded by the policy language. However, if further developments (such as a judge's or jury's verdict) later make it clear that the claim is excluded by the policy language, the insurer can stop defending the claim and refuse to pay for any settlements or damages.

Due to its broad duty to defend the insured, the insurance company typically has the authority to choose the defense team or at least require that the insured choose a team from a carrier-approved list. Some EPL products will give the insured greater power over the choice of a defense team, but this might be done only in exchange for either a higher premium from the business or a narrower duty to defend from the carrier.

Deductibles

Compared to other types of liability insurance, such as commercial general liability insurance, EPL insurance is more likely to require payment of a deductible. The deductible is the amount of otherwise covered losses, in dollars, that the insured must pay out of pocket before the insurer will provide benefits.

Coinsurance Fees

Along with paying a per-claim deductible, an EPL-insured business will likely be responsible for a per-claim **coinsurance fee**. Within the context of EPL insurance, a coinsurance fee is the amount, as a percentage of each covered loss, that the insured must pay out of pocket. Research conducted during development of this text unearthed coinsurance fees as low as 5 percent per claim and as high as 35 percent per claim. As with the deductible, the higher the coinsurance fee, the less the business will usually pay in premiums.

Claims-Made Policies

Most EPL policies are claims-made policies rather than occurrence policies. This means that in order to be covered at all, both the incident that prompts a demand for money from an allegedly harmed person and the demand itself must occur within the policy period.

In addition, the incident that leads to a claim must occur no earlier than on the policy's retroactive date. If a policyholder cancels insurance, potential claims might still be covered if they occurred during the policy period and are brought to the insurer's attention during the policy's extended reporting period.

Important details about claims-made policies, retroactive dates and extended reporting periods can also be found in the previous chapter about commercial general liability insurance.

Settlements and Hammer Clauses

Usually, an insurer can't settle an EPL claim without the insured's written consent. Instead, if the carrier wants to settle and the insured disagrees, the claim can continue to be fought in court or via other legal channels but might then be subject to a policy's **hammer clause**. The hammer clause essentially allows the insurer to document the amount for which it wanted to settle the claim and makes the insured responsible for the portion of any eventual settlements or judgments in excess of that amount.

In a simple example, imagine the insurance company proposes a $500,000 settlement for a discrimination claim, but the insured refuses to settle. Under a basic hammer clause, If the claim later results in a judgment against the insured for $700,000, the insured will need to pay the excess of $200,000.

Wage-and-Hour Violations

Most EPL insurance policies won't cover the insured against alleged "wage-and-hour violations." Essentially, these alleged violations involve failing to pay non-salaried employees for the amount they've actually worked or failing to pay them in accordance with applicable overtime rules.

Other EPL Exclusions

Other common exclusions in EPL insurance policies are listed in this section. However, be aware that each EPL insurance product will likely be a bit different from the next. So careful attention should be paid to the exact policy language when explaining gaps in coverage to prospects:

- Assault and battery against workers.

- Disputes regarding unlawful strikes, walkouts or lockouts.

- Employee benefit liability under the Employee Retirement Income Security Act.

- Blatant disregard for federal or state employment laws.

- Fines imposed by regulators (with coverage perhaps depending on the specific type of violation).

- Certain class action suits.

- Punitive damages (unless allowed to be covered by law).

- Damage to employee property.

- Workplace injuries and workers compensation issues.

- Employment violations related to the OSHA, COBRA, the National Labor Relations Act or the Fair Labor Standards Act.

Chapter Key Points

- Employment practices liability insurance aims to protect businesses when they are accused of violating someone's employment rights. The person whose rights might or might not have been violated could be a current or former employee or anyone who unsuccessfully sought work at the business. Common EPL claims involve allegations of discrimination, retaliation or sexual harassment.

- Most EPL policies are claims-made policies rather than occurrence policies. This means that in order to be covered at all, both the incident that prompts a demand for money from an allegedly harmed person and the demand itself must occur within the policy period.

- If a policyholder cancels EPL insurance, potential claims might still be covered if they occurred during the policy period and are brought to the insurer's attention during the policy's extended reporting period.

- If the carrier wants to settle an EPL dispute and the insured disagrees, the claim can continue to be fought in court or via other legal channels but might then be subject to a policy's hammer clause. The hammer clause essentially allows the insurer to document the amount for which it wanted to settle the claim and makes the insured responsible for the portion of any eventual settlements or judgments in excess of that amount.

- Most EPL insurance policies won't cover the insured against alleged wage-and-hour violations. These alleged violations typically involve failing to pay non-salaried employees for the amount they've actually worked or failing to pay them in accordance with applicable overtime rules.

CHAPTER 16: WORKERS COMPENSATION AND EMPLOYERS LIABILITY INSURANCE

Into the first few decades of the twentieth century, workers who became ill or injured on the job were very unlikely to be compensated for their medical care and lost wages. Many low-paid workers didn't want to jeopardize their employment by taking a boss to court over an accident, and those who dared to do it often failed on the basis of three legal defenses:

- Under the "contributory negligence defense," an employer could avoid liability for an accidental injury if the employee in any way caused or helped cause the accident.

- Under the "fellow servant defense," an employer could avoid liability for an accidental injury if the accident was caused by a coworker or some other person besides the employer.

- Under the "assumption of risk defense," an employer could avoid liability for an accidental injury if the nature of the injury was considered common in that line of work. So, for example, a firefighter who was harmed by fire in the line of duty could've been denied compensation because coming into contact with flames was part of the job.

In time, states gradually began creating greater protections for injured workers and ultimately created a system whereby most employees can receive a government-mandated amount of compensation as long as an injury or illness occurred while performing their job duties.

Understanding No-Fault Insurance

Legislators in every state have made workers compensation a no-fault system. In practical terms, this means an injured employee doesn't need to prove negligence by the employer in order to collect benefits. As long as claimants were engaged in work-related tasks at the time of an accident, they can be harmed by the actions of coworkers, bosses, customers or themselves and still have their losses covered. In most cases, the contributory negligence defense, fellow servant defense and assumption of risk defense can't prevent them from receiving compensation.

In exchange for not having to prove negligence by their employer, people who are covered by workers compensation laws generally forfeit their ability to sue their employer after an accident. Employers must provide compensation in the amount prescribed by state law, but they're usually not liable for pain, suffering or punitive damages. The general inability to sue an employer makes workers compensation the **exclusive remedy** for injured or ill employees.

This method of compensating injured employees also limits liability for coworkers. If a worker causes an accident that harms another worker, the injured party will be compensated by the employer in an amount determined by state law. The injured worker doesn't need (and might not have the right) to sue the other worker for damages.

There are, however, a few situations in which the no-fault component of workers compensation is absent. When an employer or coworker harms an employee intentionally or had reason to believe an injury would occur, the employee can take the employer or coworker to court and sue for pain, suffering and punitive damages. The courts are also an option for workers who aren't covered by their state's workers compensation laws. But because these individuals fall outside of the no-fault workers compensation system, they may lose their cases on the basis of the contributory negligence defense, the fellow servant defense or the assumption of risk defense.

Who's Exempt From Workers Compensation?

Workers compensation laws of the past were sometimes geared specifically toward people with highly hazardous jobs. Employers are in a very different situation today and are generally required to purchase insurance covering all workers regardless of risk.

Exceptions to this rule exist in every part of the country and are listed in state statutes and administrative rules. If a certain kind of worker is specifically not protected under state statute or rule, an employer doesn't need to obtain insurance to cover the worker's injuries. Therefore, if all of an employer's workers fall outside of the state's statute and rules, the employer is allowed to conduct business without insurance. If some but not all of the employer's workers aren't covered by statutes or rules, coverage must still be obtained for the other employees.

The next several sections mention classes of people who are often excluded from workers compensation systems. Exclusions differ among states and might not apply to businesses in all industries. Companies involved in accident-prone fields (such as construction and food services) might be required to insure their employees under every circumstance.

Independent Contractors

Workers compensation is for employees, not independent contractors. The exact meaning of "independent contractor" will depend on state and federal law and is generally based on the relationship between the worker and the business. If several of the following statements are true, the worker might qualify as an independent contractor. If several of them are false, the worker is more likely to qualify as an employee:

- The tasks performed by the worker don't relate to the specific nature of the business.
- The business doesn't have the right to determine the worker's schedule.
- The business doesn't have the right to determine where tasks should be performed.
- The worker openly performs similar tasks for other businesses.
- The duration of the relationship between the business and the worker is predefined, rather than indefinite.
- The worker is responsible for providing his or her own tools and supplies.
- The worker doesn't receive employee benefits, such as health insurance or paid vacation days.
- The business provides no training to the worker and doesn't dictate how tasks are to be performed.
- The worker is compensated via a flat fee rather than a regular wage.

When a business hires an independent contractor, it's not required to cover the person for workers compensation or pay various payroll, Medicare and Social Security taxes. This explains why many companies prefer to hire individuals as independent contractors instead of as regular employees. However, business owners must realize a person isn't an independent contractor simply because the company says so. Even a business contract naming the individual as an independent contractor can be irrelevant if the company actually treats the worker like an employee.

When a business inappropriately classifies a worker as an independent contractor on purpose, it's committing fraud and exposing itself to multiple kinds of liability. Depending on the circumstances, such behavior might also result in cancellation or rescission of the business's insurance.

Industry-Related Exemptions

There are some industries and professions that are independent from state workers compensation laws. This independence may exist because occupational injuries in these fields are especially common and severe. Industries are also often exempt from state statutes when they play a direct role in facilitating interstate commerce. In either case, many of the workers in these exempted industries can obtain compensation by way of federal laws.

State workers compensation laws might not be applicable to the following kinds of people:

- *Marine workers:* Dock and harbor workers, as well as those who work on the navigable waters of the United States, may be eligible for workers compensation in amounts allowed by federal law. The Longshore and Harbor Workers' Compensation Act generally covers workers who perform maintenance on ships or who load and unload goods transported on vessels. The Merchant Marine Act (sometimes known as the "Jones Act") provides a simplified way for injured workers to sue employers for work-related damages suffered while at sea.

- *Coal miners:* Miners with black lung disease are compensated in accordance with the Black Lung Benefits Act. Based on this law, mining businesses must pay special taxes toward a federal compensation fund and are required to insure their workers against the disease.

- *Real estate licensees:* In some states, real estate licensees might not be covered by workers compensation laws if they work entirely on commission.

- *Religious organizations:* Some states let these and other non-profit entities operate outside of the workers compensation system.

Before we move on to the kinds of assistance available through workers compensation systems, we should mention that people who aren't included in workers compensation laws can still be eligible for some insurance benefits. This is because the workers compensation insurance bought by businesses is almost always coupled with "employers liability insurance."

Employers liability insurance pays benefits when an employer is held liable for an occupational injury that's not covered by workers compensation laws. Unlike workers compensation insurance, employers liability insurance is limited to a specific dollar amount and can only be used when an employer is believed to be at fault.

Employers liability insurance can help a company cope financially with many kinds of lawsuits related to occupational injuries, but it doesn't fully protect businesses in every industry. The standard policy doesn't cover an employer's liability under the Longshore and Harbor Workers' Compensation Act, the Federal Employees' Compensation Act or other federal laws. Businesses impacted by these laws can add liability protection by endorsement.

Later in this chapter, you'll read more about how employers liability insurance can protect businesses when workplace injuries fall outside of state workers compensation systems.

Workplace Injuries

A person may be eligible for workers compensation after suffering a workplace injury. In order for the individual to be covered for any resulting medical expenses and receive other benefits, the following three facts must be established:

- The person was an employee of the business at the time of the injury.
- The injury was accidental.
- The person suffered the injury in connection with his or her job duties.

Occupational Diseases

In general, a person who contracts a disease is covered for workers compensation if either of the following statements is true:

- The person's assigned tasks or work environment are responsible for causing the illness.
- The person's assigned tasks or work environment are responsible for worsening a pre-existing medical condition.

Despite having grown in recent decades, the list of commonly covered occupational diseases is hardly unlimited. Some illnesses, like the flu, are so common that they're likely to fall outside of workers compensation statutes even when they're contracted from coworkers or customers.

It's more likely for an occupational disease to be covered if job duties made the person more prone to the illness than the average worker. Examples of successful claimants might include firefighters who develop respiratory problems and emergency medical technicians who are exposed to infectious ailments.

Medical Coverage

When an employee is injured or contracts a disease at work, workers compensation pays for the person's medical expenses. Unlike reimbursement for lost income, this coverage begins immediately after an accident and isn't limited to a particular dollar amount. There's no deductible for the employee to worry about, and there are no copayments for medical services. Even when an employee suffers an injury without missing a single minute of work, this nearly unlimited coverage can be utilized to pay for all reasonable medical care.

The medical coverage component of workers compensation can be used for more than just doctor visits, hospital stays and prescription drugs. Covered workers can also receive compensation for rehabilitation expenses and may even be reimbursed for their travel expenses and meals if they go a long way to visit a physician. If a worker is hurt and requires medical equipment (including dentures, leg braces or prosthetic limbs), the cost of these materials will also be paid by the employer or an insurance company.

Wage Replacement

When an injury causes an employee to miss work for more than a few days, the person can make a "lost-time claim." Lost-time claims aren't as common as medical-only claims, but they tend to be much more expensive because they involve payment of lost wages.

For a lost-time claim to be valid, an employee must first miss a certain number of workdays. If the employee comes back to work without having missed the specified number of days, that person won't be compensated for lost wages. The employer or the insurer will only need to pay for the person's medical expenses.

Though some states have required at least a week-long absence, employees are usually eligible for lost-income benefits if an accident has kept them out of work for three days. If absenteeism lasts for a longer period of time (typically two weeks or more), lost wages from those first three days will be provided to the worker. If absenteeism lasts longer than three days but less than two weeks, wages from the first three days will usually be treated like an uninsured loss for the worker.

The amount received for lost wages will depend on the worker's financial situation, as well as on the provisions in the state statute. For most claimants in the United States, the amount will be based on roughly 66 percent of their regular income over the past year. If the person doesn't do any work while recuperating, the entire 66 percent will probably be available to the employee on a weekly, prorated and tax-free basis. If the person does some work while recuperating, wage replacement might be equal to approximately two-thirds of the difference between the employee's pre-accident salary and the employee's post-accident salary. Alternative or additional amounts of compensation may be available if a person is permanently disabled but not unable to work.

States set minimum and maximum amounts for wage replacement in order to benefit their citizens and discourage wrongdoing. Minimum amounts of compensation (such as 66 percent of one's income) have been formulated so injured workers and their families are less likely to live in poverty. Meanwhile, caps on wage replacement have been put in place so injured people have a good reason to eventually rejoin the workforce.

Levels of Disability

Before injured or ill people become eligible to receive compensation for lost wages, they usually must be evaluated by a physician. The physician will determine the severity of the injury or illness, and the severity might determine the duration of wage replacement benefits. The severity might also entitle the person to a predetermined lump sum instead of a weekly income-based award. Predetermined durations of wage reimbursement are very common in cases of permanent partial disability.

Let's quickly go over the different levels of disability and how they relate to workers compensation.

Permanent Total Disability

Employees have a "permanent total disability" when they can't perform any reasonable kind of work and are unlikely to ever improve enough to have another job.

Permanent total disabilities are very rare, with the National Council on Compensation Insurance estimating that they account for only about 1 percent of all lost-time claims. Still, the duration of wage reimbursement in these situations is long and costs insurers a lot of money. In addition to covering the injured person's disability-related medical care for life, the employer or the employer's insurer usually must reimburse the person for lost income until the employee turns 65, depending on the state. Some states allow wage benefits to last throughout the person's lifetime.

Permanent Partial Disability

Employees have a "permanent partial disability" when they will never fully recover from an injury but are still capable of working. Many permanent partial disabilities, such as the loss of a limb, an eye or one's hearing, entitle the employee to a preset amount or duration of wage replacement benefits. These are known as "scheduled" disabilities. Other debilitating conditions have no predetermined amount or duration of wage replacement benefits and are known as "unscheduled" disabilities.

Unlike the basic "two-thirds of wages" formula used for most instances of total disability in the United States, the mathematical operations used for partial disabilities vary greatly from state to state and injury to injury. Some states base compensation on the medically determined degree of impairment, regardless of how an injury impacts a person's work. Others will be concerned mainly with the difference between pre-injury income and post-injury income. Employees in some parts of the country will have their benefits affected by their expected loss of future earnings.

Temporary Total Disability

Employees have a "temporary total disability" when they're incapable of working but will be able to recover and resume their job duties at a later date. Temporary total disabilities are the most common causes of compensation claims for lost income. They usually involve cash benefits based on two-thirds of the employee's salary. Weekly maximum amounts of compensation are typically based on a certain percentage of the average income in the area, and minimum amounts might be based on the local minimum wage multiplied by 40 hours.

Temporary Partial Disability

Employees have a "temporary partial disability" when they're able to return to work in some capacity but are still in the process of full recovery. If their reduced duties or reduced hours cause a drop in their income, they might be entitled to two-thirds of the difference between their pre-injury income and their post-injury income.

Death Benefits

When workers die as a result of a workplace accident, their family members and dependents are likely to receive a death benefit from the employer's insurance company. In most states, the death benefit will usually be provided on a weekly basis and based on roughly 66 percent of the worker's wages. It generally will be close to the amount the worker would've received for a permanent total disability. Like disability payments, death benefits may be capped at a certain percentage of the state's average weekly income.

Funeral Expenses

Survivors of deceased workers receive a few thousand dollars for funeral, burial and other end-of-life expenses. The employer or insurer provides this money even if the worker had no dependents.

Finding Workers Compensation Insurance

For the most part, employers who had to comply with early workers compensation laws did not have a private insurance market to help them manage their risks. When a statute granted compensation to an injured worker, money for the person's medical care and lost wages often came out of the business's own pocket.

Since many employers lacked the resources to self-insure for workers compensation, insurance companies began marketing policies to businesses and agreed to take on workers compensation risks in exchange for a premium. When some high-risk companies could still not obtain coverage from private insurers, states started stepping in as insurers of last resort.

State Funds and Assigned-Risk Programs

When states started passing workers compensation laws, there were concerns that there would be a negative impact on local economies. If a high-risk business couldn't secure insurance from a private carrier, would it move to another state or close down completely?

In response to these concerns, every state has developed a system that guarantees coverage for all employers. The system might involve a monopolistic state fund, a competitive state fund or a residual market overseen by a non-governmental third party. These funds and markets generally operate without support from the typical taxpayer and are regulated in many of the same ways as private insurance companies. The insurance they offer is often more expensive than coverage in the open market, but they give their policyholders the chance to comply with state law and remain in business.

A few states operate a "monopolistic" workers compensation fund. When a fund is monopolistic, it's the only source of workers compensation insurance for employers. Private insurers aren't allowed to compete against a monopolistic state fund.

In most states, high-risk businesses can obtain workers compensation insurance as a last resort from an "assigned-risk program." When employers are denied insurance from a specific number of private insurers, they can send proof of the denial to the administrator of the assigned-risk program, and the administrator will select an insurer to provide the mandatory coverage.

Because assigned-risk programs are utilized by high-risk employers, the insurance they offer is often very expensive.

Private Insurance

Most employers are covered for workers compensation by private insurance. Private insurance is usually less expensive than insurance from the state or an assigned-risk program, and the coverage might be more comprehensive.

The positive features of private insurance aren't available to everyone who wants them. In order to offer quality coverage and remain in business, insurance companies sometimes must refuse to accept high-risk applicants.

Though one insurer's underwriting guidelines will be different from its competitors', an employer might be denied a workers compensation insurance policy for any of the following reasons:

- The employer's company has a history of serious workplace accidents.
- The employer's industry has a history of serious workplace accidents.
- The applicant is a new business, and the insurer can't determine the likelihood of a workplace accident.

As was mentioned in the previous section, an employer who is unable to purchase private insurance in the voluntary market can often obtain coverage through an assigned-risk program. Employers who apply for assigned-risk coverage must be able to prove that a private carrier is unwilling to insure them.

Workers Compensation Premiums

To better understand how certain factors can impact the cost of workers compensation insurance, let's examine how premiums for this coverage are determined.

Job Classifications Codes

Insurance companies start calculating workers compensation premiums by looking up a company's four-digit "classification code." There are several hundred classification codes, and each code is shared by all businesses in the same line of work. All wineries, for example, will have the same classification code, and all shoe manufacturers will have another classification code.

Each classification code has a numerical rate attached to it. The rate has been calculated by actuaries and is a mathematical representation of the basic risk level for all employers who share that classification code. Because underwriters often verify this rate by looking it up in a manual, the rate is known as the "manual rate." Manual rates in most states are based on the loss histories of similar businesses over the past five years.

The manuals featuring classification codes also contain summaries. The summaries explain the kinds of tasks that fall under each code. If the summary doesn't mention the tasks performed by a particular employee, the employee might have to be classified and rated separately. Depending on the nature of the employee's job duties, this could have a positive or negative effect on the employer's insurance premiums. Intentional misclassification of an employee in order to reduce insurance costs is a form of fraud.

Once the manual rate is known, insurers can focus on calculating the "manual premium." The manual premium is calculated by dividing the employer's payroll by $100 and multiplying the result by the manual rate.

Experience Modification Factors and Premium Discounts

Next, the insurer needs to account for the business's unique experience with safety or losses. This is represented by a number called the "experience modification factor" Although calculating this number is beyond the scope of this course, it's generally designed to reward businesses that are less risky than similar businesses while penalizing those that are more loss-prone than their peers. Also, it may be worth noting that the calculation cares more about frequency of losses than severity of losses. In general, a business with several small workers compensation claims will be deemed riskier than a similar business with one large claim.

Ultimately, the experience modification factor is multiplied by the aforementioned manual premium in order to obtain a basic estimate of the employer's premium. This estimate is sometimes known as the "modified premium." The modified premium might be adjusted by the insurer in order to reflect administrative costs and policy discounts. For example, the modified premium might be reduced if the business agrees to implement safety measures requested by the insurance company.

Regardless of any initial calculation, it's not uncommon for insurance in commercial lines to be issued in exchange for a **deposit premium**, which will be held by the insurer until the business's level of risk becomes clearer. Then, upon obtaining more data and being able to examine the business's records, the insurer may readjust the premium to be more in line with the actual risk. If the risk ends up being lower than the original estimate, the business might receive a credit on its account. If the risk ends up being higher than the original estimate, the business might be required to pay an additional amount.

Standard Workers Compensation Insurance Policies

Workers compensation insurance is almost always paired with employers liability insurance. Workers compensation insurance covers employers for the medical costs and lost wages they must pay to employees in accordance with state statutes. Employers liability insurance covers the employer for damages and defense costs when an employer is believed to be liable for an occupational injury that isn't covered by workers compensation insurance. The coverage provided by most insurers in the

United States is based on the "Workers Compensation and Employers Liability Insurance Policy" as written by an entity called the National Council on Compensation Insurance (NCCI).

A workers compensation insurance policy serves as a contract between the insurance company and the employer. Although the policy makes the insurer responsible for providing money to injured employees, the phrase "the insured" refers, in general, to the business paying for the policy.

The specific people or businesses covered by the policy are identified on the policy's "information page." The information page is like the declarations page in other lines of insurance and can be thought of as a policy summary. In addition to naming the insured, the information page is likely to contain the following pieces of information:

- The policy number.

- The policy period (typically lasting one year).

- The insured's mailing address.

- The states where coverage applies (also known as the "coverage territory").

- The dollar limit for employers liability insurance.

- The estimated premium.

The policy itself is divided between a workers compensation section, an employers liability section and several other sections. We'll spend the next few pages summarizing the important points of those sections.

Workers Compensation Insurance

The workers compensation portion of the policy is relatively short. It covers the employer for nearly every medical expense and wage reimbursement that must be paid to employees in accordance with state statutes. If an employee is entitled to workers compensation, the insurance company must provide it. If an employee or an injury is excluded from state workers compensation laws, this portion of the policy doesn't force the insurer to pay anything.

Workers compensation insurance was designed to be flexible and easily adaptable to laws in different states. If anything in this portion of the policy differs with the kind of compensation that must be paid in accordance with state workers compensation laws, the wording in the policy can be disregarded. As long as a business has purchased insurance, its out-of-pocket expenses for workers compensation will almost always be limited to its insurance premium and deductible.

One of the few coverage restrictions in this part of the policy relates to the date of the worker's injury. Bodily injuries (including occupational deaths) are only covered by the insurance company if they occur during the policy period. So, if an employee is injured on December 23, for example, and the employer's policy doesn't go into effect until December 24, the employer will be solely responsible for the person's medical expenses and lost wages. Claims made to the insurer will be denied. Similarly, occupational diseases are only covered if the worker's last exposure to the cause of the disease occurred during the policy period.

The date of an injury is also important when a worker's medical expenses and lost wages span several years. As long as the injury occurs during the policy period, compensation that must be paid after the policy period will remain the insurer's responsibility. The employer doesn't need to keep renewing the insurance until the injured person recovers.

The workers compensation portion of the policy isn't subject to any dollar limit. This is different from the second portion of the policy, which addresses employers liability insurance.

Employers Liability Insurance

Employers liability insurance covers an employer when a worker is injured but isn't protected by workers compensation laws. It also can be utilized in situations where a worker's injury leads to legal action by a third party, such as the worker's family. (Note that, within the context of this chapter, the term "employers liability insurance" refers to a very specific portion of a workers compensation insurance policy and isn't intended to mean something more general, such as any type of liability insurance that will cover a business in a variety of different legal disputes.)

Like workers compensation insurance, employers liability insurance pays claims related to occupational injury, occupational disease or occupational death. The injury or death must have occurred during the policy period. Claims related to occupational diseases are only covered if the worker's last exposure to the disease or harmful work environment took place during the policy period.

Employers liability insurance doesn't make the insurer responsible for paying benefits that are required by workers compensation laws. Nor does it make the insurer responsible for paying damages when an employee's lawsuit isn't related to a workplace injury, illness or death.

Unlike workers compensation insurance, employers liability insurance has dollar limits. Unless the employer agrees to pay more for additional insurance, coverage is usually provided in the following amounts:

- Up to $100,000 for each event causing an occupational injury (no matter how many people are injured in the event).

- Up to $100,000 for each employee who suffers an occupational disease.

- Up to $500,000 total for all instances of occupational disease arising during the policy period.

Policy Exclusions

Sometimes even insurance isn't enough to keep an employer from having to pay for work-related injuries. Situations in which liability isn't entirely transferable from employer to insurer are summarized in the next few sections.

Intentional Injuries by Employers

When an employer does intentional harm to a worker, the worker can sue for damages. Defense costs, settlements and damages related to intentional harm aren't covered by insurance.

Willful Misconduct

Workers compensation insurance doesn't cover any extra benefits or fines that employers must provide due to willful misconduct. This exclusion might be cited in cases where the employer didn't specifically intend to injure someone but willfully engaged in unsafe behavior.

Multi-State Coverage

When employees suffer an occupational injury, their benefits might be based on the workers compensation laws in any one of the following states:

- The state where the injury occurred.

- The state where the employee resides.

- The state of the employer.

Most of the time, the injury, the employer and the employee's residence will all be in the same state. But when business trips are made, when a company expands, or when telecommuters are hired, the employer might need coverage that can be used in other parts of the country. The appropriate kind of multi-state insurance can exist within a single policy if application forms are filled out properly and if multi-state activities are communicated promptly to the insurer.

In most scenarios, there will be two separate places on the policy's information page where states must be listed.

The first place (often known as "3A") should list those states where the business currently has a legitimate workers compensation exposure (such as all states where the business has an office, all states where it has offsite employees and all states where its workers engage in regular, repeated business travel).

The second place (often known as "3C") should list all states where the business expects to have incidental exposures (such as bordering states where onsite workers reside, all states to where there are likely to be infrequent business trips, and all states where the business is in the process of opening a new office). Typically, insurance professionals will suggest careful language that allows this section to pertain to as many states as possible.

Note, however, that these methods might not be possible for "monopolistic states." In a monopolistic state, coverage must be purchased from the state rather than from a private insurance company.

Similarly, it might not be possible to get coverage for additional states if a business's workers compensation insurance is from an assigned-risk plan for high-risk businesses.

Regardless, it's extremely important that the business contact the insurer whenever its activities in a state change. For example, the insurer must be notified as soon as possible if the company opens an office in another state, allows an employee to work regularly from another state, etc.

Chapter Key Points

- Legislators in every state have made workers compensation a no-fault system. In practical terms, this means an injured employee doesn't need to prove negligence by the employer in order to collect benefits. In exchange for not having to prove negligence by their employer, people who are covered by workers compensation laws generally forfeit their ability to sue their employer after an accident. This makes workers compensation the "exclusive remedy" for injured or ill employees.

- Workers compensation is for employees, not independent contractors. The exact meaning of independent contractor will depend on state and federal law and is generally based on the relationship between the worker and the business.

- When an employee is injured or contracts a disease at work, workers compensation pays for the person's medical expenses. Unlike reimbursement for lost income, this coverage begins immediately after an accident and isn't limited to a particular dollar amount. There's no deductible for the employee to worry about, and there are no copayments for medical services.

- Though some states have required at least a week-long absence, employees are usually eligible for lost-income benefits if an accident has kept them out of work for three days. For most claimants in the United States, compensation will be based on roughly 66 percent of their regular income over the past year.

- Workers compensation insurance is almost always paired with employers liability insurance. Workers compensation insurance covers employers for the medical costs and lost wages they must pay to employees in accordance with state statutes. Employers liability insurance covers the employer for damages and defense costs when an employer is believed to be liable for an occupational injury that isn't covered by workers compensation insurance.

- Unlike workers compensation insurance, employers liability insurance has dollar limits imposed by the insurer.

- When calculating workers compensation premiums, insurers will be focused mainly on the type of business, the work performed by employees, the size of the business's payroll and the business's history of losses. Although some industries will have higher premiums than others, a number known as the "experience modification factor" helps perceivably safer businesses pay less than their riskier competitors in the same field.

- Intentional misclassification of an employee's job duties in order to reduce insurance costs is a form of fraud.

- If a risk can't be fully calculated at the start of a policy term, a business might pay a deposit premium, and the insurer will reserve the right to audit the business's records and adjust the premium at a later date.

- Although workers compensation insurance can apply to accidents in multiple states, businesses must ensure that they disclose any exposures (such as the opening of a new office or the hiring of an out-of-state worker) to their insurer in a timely manner.

CHAPTER 17: PROFESSIONAL LIABILITY/ERRORS AND OMISSIONS INSURANCE

Errors and omissions insurance is a type of liability insurance that covers various professionals when their services don't meet clients' or customers' expectations.

"Malpractice insurance" is another name for errors and omissions insurance specific to doctors, lawyers and a few other professions with a long tradition of needing job-specific liability insurance.

Malpractice insurance, errors and omissions insurance and a few other specialized casualty products are collectively known as **professional liability insurance**.

Who Needs E & O?

Errors and omissions insurance is intended to help professionals when they're accused of negligence or incompetence in their work. This type of accusation might arise whenever a professional either provides services that don't meet a client's or customer's expectations or fails to provide an expected service at all.

In general, for most types of errors and omissions coverage to apply (assuming we are putting medical malpractice insurance in a separate category), the harm to the client or customer must be financial in nature rather than a case of property damage or bodily injury.

Basic examples of scenarios that might ultimately result in an errors and omissions claim include the following:

- Giving bad professional advice.
- Failing to complete an important task before an important deadline.
- Committing a seemingly minor but ultimately costly clerical error.
- Performing an inadequate analysis of a client's needs.

An abbreviated list of professionals who tend to be good candidates for E & O (or, in some cases, malpractice) insurance appears next:

- Medical professionals.
- Legal professionals.
- Accountants.
- Architects.
- Engineers.
- Funeral directors.
- Real estate agents.
- Stockbrokers.
- Insurance agents and brokers.
- Web and software designers.
- Various types of "consultants," who are typically hired for advisory roles because of their alleged expertise.

Who Is the Insured?

The broadest forms of errors and omissions insurance will cover the business or person specifically named on the policy's declarations page, as well as all past, present and future owners, employees and independent contractors when conducting business on the named entity's behalf. However, agreeing to insure so many people under the same policy can raise the amount of risk to the carrier and, consequently, can require the named insured to pay relatively high premiums. As a result, a business's errors and omissions insurance might not cover employees or its independent contractors at all. Alternatively, the insurance from the business might only cover an employee or contractor if the individual is willing to pay for some or all of the premiums. In many cases an individual who serves in a professional capacity will need to find and purchase errors and omissions insurance independently.

Covered Professional Services

In general, errors and omissions insurance is only applicable in cases in which the insured is performing "professional services" or "professional acts." If an error or omission arises from an activity beyond the scope of professional acts or professional services, the insured will need to find another way to deal with any resulting damages.

Note that an E & O policy's definition of "professional services" is likely to be specific to a particular profession. For example, in a policy for insurance agents, the definition might apply to various activities associated with selling insurance but not to the various activities that are instead commonly associated with other professions, such as accounting, selling real estate or providing legal advice. If someone works in multiple professions, separate insurance might be needed for each job.

Defense Costs

Errors and omissions insurance isn't just for cases in which a professional is officially deemed at fault for a loss. It can also be extremely helpful when an ethical, competent and law-abiding person becomes ensnared in a frivolous suit with an overly combative customer. In fact, regardless of whether someone wins a lawsuit, loses a lawsuit or agrees to an out-of-court settlement, errors and omissions insurance will usually help pay for the defense.

Most forms of errors and omissions insurance include a duty to defend the insured. Note that this duty to defend is different (and significantly more beneficial to the insured) than a mere "right" to defend. Unless a scenario is obviously unrelated to professional services or the performance of professional acts, the duty to defend makes the insurer obligated to provide competent legal counsel. In exchange, the insured is obligated to cooperate with the insurance company in regard to his or her defense, which might include providing evidence to attorneys, appearing at legal proceedings and answering attorneys' questions.

The issue of defense costs should be a factor in evaluating and choosing an errors and omissions product's coverage limits. Though E & O insurance is purchased mainly to deflect the cost of judgments and settlements against the insured, significant legal fees might be incurred while a case or complaint is still being disputed. Whereas many other types of liability insurance will cover such interim expenses without impacting a policy's dollar limits, these costs might reduce the amounts available for judgments and settlements under an E & O insurance contract. If a carrier is willing to cover these costs in ways that won't reduce the amounts available for judgments and settlements, it will typically do so in exchange for a higher premium from the insured.

Deductibles

A deductible is the amount, in dollars, that an insured must pay after a loss in order for the insurer to start paying benefits. If an insurance product has no deductible, the insured has what is known as "first-dollar coverage."

Errors and omissions insurance might have a single deductible for the policy period or a per-claim deducible that essentially must be paid in connection with every single loss. Similarly, the deductible might only apply to settlements and judgments against the insured or might also need to be paid before the carrier will cover any defense costs.

Regardless of the specifics, the more the insured is willing to absorb in the form of a deductible, the lower the cost of insurance is likely to be.

Exclusions

Several common exclusions that might apply to E & O insurance are listed next:

- Libel or slander.
- Theft.
- Embezzlement, commingling or misappropriation of funds (including any premiums collected from consumers).
- Property damage and bodily injury. (Insurers generally prefer that liability for property damage or bodily injury be addressed via different types of coverage, such as commercial general liability insurance.)
- Fraud or dishonesty.
- Cyber liability (such as the loss or disclosure of personal data).
- Intentional acts.
- Employment liability.
- Violations of antidiscrimination laws.
- Regulatory fines and punitive damages. (Depending on the state, insurance companies might be prohibited by law from covering these fines or damages.)
- Violations of securities laws.
- Violations of the Employee Retirement Income Security Act (if the producer is helping to administer employee benefit programs for businesses).
- Claims by the insured against another insured (assuming the policy covers more than one person).
- Any allegations that don't relate to professional services or professional acts (as defined elsewhere in the policy).

Claims-Made Policies vs. Occurrence Policies

Until the 1970s or so, E & O and other types of professional liability insurance were commonly issued as occurrence policies. Under an occurrence policy, the insured is generally covered for liability as long as the alleged error or omission occurred while the policy was in force.

As an example, consider a professional who was insured under an occurrence policy and provided bad advice to a client a year ago. Since then, the professional has allowed his or her insurance to lapse. If the client who received the bad advice suddenly decides to sue the professional tomorrow, the lapsed occurrence policy could still be relied upon to help pay for any judgments or settlements stemming from the advice.

Casualty insurers eventually determined that occurrence policies exposed them to too much liability and have stopped making these types of insurance products widely available. Casualty insurance companies in today's professional liability market typically provide claims-made policies.

Under a claims-made policy, the insured is covered for liability if the claim that resulted from an error or omission occurred while the policy was in place. (In general, within the context of E & O insurance, a "claim" is a written demand for money as compensation for the insured's allegedly negligent actions.) In most cases, the alleged error and omission must occur during that timeframe as well.

Consider our previous example of a professional who gave bad advice a year ago, gets sued tomorrow and allowed his or her E & O coverage to lapse in the meantime. If the lapsed coverage involved a claims-made policy and not an occurrence policy, the insurer would generally be under no obligation to help the professional pay for defense costs, judgments or settlements stemming from the allegedly bad advice.

Retroactive Dates and Prior Acts

A claims-made policy's "retroactive date" is the earliest date on which an error or omission can occur in order for the insurer to cover any resulting claim. In most instances, this date will be identical to the date on which the policy was first issued to the insured. If the policy is renewed on time, the retroactive date will remain unchanged and will continue to be identical to the date on which the policy was first issued to the insured.

If someone allows his or her errors and omissions insurance to lapse (or cancels the coverage in the middle of a policy period) and then decides to purchase a policy again at a later date, the retroactive date will be moved up and usually be identical to the date on which the new policy (not the old one) is issued. A potential exception to this rule about having a new retroactive date after a lapse or cancellation might exist if the professional is merely having one carrier's policy replaced with another carrier's policy and isn't going a single day without being covered by one policy or the other.

Tail Coverage and Extended Reporting Periods

Professionals who are retiring or have another legitimate reason to cancel or not renew their E & O insurance might still want a limited amount of coverage in case an earlier error or omission comes back to haunt them. In these cases, it might be appropriate for the professional to purchase what is sometimes referred to as either "tail coverage" or an "extended reporting period."

Some errors and omissions products include a very small amount of tail coverage free of charge. For instance, if the insured voluntarily cancels or decides not to renew an E & O policy, the insurer might still respond to claims reported within 60 days after the policy's expiration or cancellation date.

Then, for an additional charge, the insurer might agree to respond to claims reported over a much lengthier period, such one or five years after the policy's expiration date. The insured will usually need to purchase this extra coverage within a limited time after the cancellation or nonrenewal. The cost will depend on the length of the extended reporting period and will often be based on a percentage of the insured's most recent annual premium.

Reporting a Claim

Within the context of errors and omissions insurance, a "claim" is generally defined as a written demand for money in response to an insured's alleged incompetence. Unless an extended reporting period applies, errors and omissions insurance will only cover claims that are reported to the insurer during the policy period.

Policy language will specify the deadline for reporting claims to the insurer. For example, a policy might say a claim must be reported within 30 days after the insured becomes aware of it. Ideally, claims should be reported as soon as possible so the insurance company's legal team can evaluate the situation and begin collecting any relevant evidence. The sooner the defense team can speak with witnesses (especially the insured), the clearer those witnesses' recollections are likely to be.

If an insured is planning on cancelling or not renewing an errors and omissions policy and is aware of a situation that has the potential to produce a later claim, it's generally unwise to ignore the situation until a written demand for money actually materializes. Instead, the insured should inform the insurance company as soon as possible and provide all known specifics (including what happened and to whom) to the carrier. Depending on the policy, this preemptive notice to the insurer might be treated as a claim and can make the insured eligible for insurance protection even if a written demand for money isn't made until after the policy period.

E & O Settlements

After the E & O carrier becomes aware of a claim, it will attempt to determine the strength of the insured's case and whether it makes sense to settle the matter.

Be aware that the carrier's job is to help limit liability-related costs for itself and its policyholders. So even if the insured has a good chance of prevailing in a court of law, the E & O carrier might determine that a quick settlement is the least expensive and best option.

Hammer Clauses

An E & O policy's "hammer clause" is meant to address situations in which the insured disagrees with an insurer's recommendation to settle a claim. In general, the insured won't be forced to settle a claim against his or her wishes but will be held responsible for any eventual settlement or judgment beyond the carrier's originally proposed settlement amount.

For example, suppose an insurance company believes the insured should settle a dispute for $75,000. If the insured refuses to settle, loses his or her case in court and is ultimately ordered to pay $100,000 to the plaintiff, the insurance company would contribute no more than $75,000. The insured would need to pay for the rest out of pocket.

Chapter Key Points

- Professional liability insurance is a broad category of liability insurance that includes malpractice insurance, errors and omissions insurance and more.

- Errors and omissions insurance is a type of liability insurance that covers various professionals when their services don't meet clients' or customers' expectations.

- "Malpractice insurance" is another name for errors and omissions insurance specific to doctors, lawyers and a few other professions with a long tradition of needing professional liability insurance.

- In general, errors and omissions insurance is only applicable in cases in which the insured is performing professional services or professional acts.

- Most forms of errors and omissions insurance include a duty to defend the insured. Unless a scenario is obviously unrelated to professional services or the performance of professional acts, the duty to defend obligates the insurer to provide competent legal counsel.

- Within the context of errors and omissions insurance, a "claim" is generally defined as a written demand for money in response to an insured's alleged incompetence. Policy language will specify the deadline for reporting claims to the insurer. For example, a policy might say a claim must be reported within 30 days after the insured becomes aware of it.

CHAPTER 18: CYBER INSURANCE

Concerns about computer viruses, malware, hackers and other forms of cybercrime have become a major concern for businesses. Recognition of these sorts of risks has inevitably led to changes in the insurance industry. Carriers specializing in commercial lines have attempted to protect themselves by adding and clarifying cyber-related exclusions in their basic property and casualty products. Yet they've also acknowledged the demand for an insurance-related solution to cyber risks and have introduced new options for security-conscious organizations. These options are part of an emerging market for what's sometimes known as **cyber insurance**.

It's important for producers to understand how cyber risks might be addressed by insurance products. Note, however, that generalizations about cyber insurance are difficult to make and might become inaccurate in the years to come. This chapter was written at a point when the market for this type of coverage was still finding its footing and hadn't produced much uniformity.

Contemplating First-Party and Third-Party Losses

A business concerned about cyber risks should consider its susceptibility to "first-party losses" and "third-party losses."

First-party losses are the financial losses or costs a business might encounter after a cyberattack or data breach regardless of whether any of its customers, clients or other third parties might have been harmed. Examples of first-party losses include the following:

- The business's temporary loss of income resulting from the unexpected shutdown of its computer systems.

- The business's temporary or permanent loss of valuable proprietary information (such as trade secrets) due to cyber theft.

- The cost to replace stolen or misplaced computer hardware.

- The cost to repair and re-secure the business's breached computer systems.

- The amount demanded by a hacker in exchange for either "unfreezing" a business's computer systems or agreeing to not disclose sensitive data.

Third-party losses are the financial losses or costs a business might encounter if it's held liable for a potentially harmful cyberattack or data breach. Examples of third-party losses include the following:

- Amounts paid to customers, clients or other third parties in lawsuits stemming from a cyberattack or data breach.

- Amounts paid by the business to defend itself in lawsuits stemming from a cyberattack or data breach.

- Amounts paid as part of "crisis management" in order to minimize potential lawsuits stemming from a cyberattack or data breach (such as the cost of notifying impacted customers and providing credit-monitoring services to them).

- Amounts paid to the government in the form of regulatory fines.

Be aware that even an excellent cyber insurance product is unlikely to address all of these potential losses. Some losses (such as the first-party loss of data) are difficult to translate into dollar amounts and are therefore practically uninsurable. Others (such as amounts paid to criminals and amounts paid in the form of regulatory fines) are potentially incompatible with insurance because compensation for them could be perceived as an indirect endorsement of illegal activity.

Regardless of the specific loss being contemplated, producers who advise businesses about cyber insurance should carefully review all policy language before recommending a particular product.

Notice to Potential Victims

If a security incident has made it possible for someone's personal information to be accessed inappropriately, the impacted business should take steps to notify everyone whose information may have been compromised. In some cases, this might be a legal requirement. In others, it's simply a smart form of crisis management that keeps clients and customers informed of the situation. As much as customers don't like having to cope with breaches of their data, their opinion of a business is likely to deteriorate even more if they believe the business is trying to hide a very serious problem.

The cost of notifying potential victims of a cyber breach can be expensive, particularly if there are thousands of people to contact. In many cases, those costs will be covered by cyber insurance.

Identity Theft Protection

In order to reduce the amount and impact of class-action suits after a data breach, cyber insurers will often provide a limited form of identity-theft protection to a business's customers who might have been affected by a cyber-security incident. This protection is typically in the form of credit-monitoring services, which are meant to catch instances in which exposed data is used to take out loans or create other forms of debt in a victim's name. Depending on the policy, the carrier might get to choose the vendor who'll provide the credit-monitoring services.

Defense Costs

A cyber insurance policy should include coverage of defense costs in case the policyholder is sued for wrongdoing. Ideally, coverage of defense costs shouldn't reduce the policy's overall dollar limit and should be based on a "duty to defend" rather than a "right to defend." A duty to defend is broader than a right to defend and allows the insured to receive paid legal counsel even if the carrier later determines that a claim for damages shouldn't be covered by the policy. A mere right to defend might force the insured to pay out of pocket for legal assistance in cases where liability is relatively ambiguous.

Chapter Key Points

- Unlike many of the major types of property and casualty insurance being sold, cyber insurance still has no standard form with common provisions and exclusions that are worded similarly from carrier to carrier.

- A business concerned about cyber risks should consider its susceptibility to first-party losses and third-party losses. First-party losses are the financial losses or costs a business might encounter after a cyberattack or data breach regardless of whether any of its customers, clients or other third parties might have been harmed. Third-party losses are the financial losses or costs a business might encounter if it is held liable for a potentially harmful cyberattack or data breach.

- The costs of notifying potential victims of a cyber breach can be expensive, particularly if there are thousands of people to contact. In many cases, those costs will be covered by cyber insurance.

- In order to reduce the amount and impact of class-action suits after a data breach, cyber insurers will often provide a limited form of identity-theft protection to a business's customers who might have been affected by a cyber-security incident. This protection is typically in the form of credit-monitoring services.

CHAPTER 19: MISCELLANEOUS CASUALTY INSURANCE PRODUCTS

Several categories of casualty insurance products make up a relatively small portion of the market but still deserve attention from people who are planning an insurance career. Summaries pertaining to many of those miscellaneous products appear in this chapter.

Crime Insurance

Although some kinds of commercial property insurance can insure a business against theft, that coverage might be limited to theft of property by outsiders rather than by employees. It also might include a limit on coverage of stolen money. Crime insurance policies can fill some of those gaps.

There are many different kinds of crime insurance, with separate forms used to insure against different kinds of illegal behavior, such as check forgery and theft from safes. Although we won't go into the details of the many crime insurance options available for concerned businesses, here are some basics to remember:

- Crime insurance sometimes applies to crimes detected within the policy's "discovery period." The discovery period is often up to one year after the end of the policy period. This means there might be coverage for a crime that is committed during the policy period but wasn't detected until a year after the policy ended.

- Crime insurance typically doesn't apply to indirect losses (such as business interruption after a robbery) and acts committed by an insured (such as a business partner).

- Crime insurance typically covers money at its face amount. Securities are covered based on their value at the time a crime is discovered. Other property impacted by a crime is generally covered at actual cash value.

Certain policy provisions might differentiate between theft, robbery and burglary:

- Theft is any kind of stealing.

- Robbery is theft by violence or threat of violence.

- Burglary is theft by forced entry.

Forgery and alteration coverage can insure a business in case of forgery of checks against its accounts. In general, forgery is signing someone's name without permission. Although the business might be covered for defense costs if it refuses to pay someone based on an allegedly forged document, permission must first be obtained from the insurer. The insurer may request a copy of the forged document or at least require a sworn affidavit from the business.

When a business is covered for crimes committed by an employee, an employee is generally defined as someone who provides services under the business's direction. For the sake of crime insurance, an employee continues to be an employee for 30 days after work for the employer has ended. This definition is intended to help protect a business if a disgruntled former worker decides to steal from the business soon after being terminated.

Regardless of whether a loss is insured, all dishonest acts committed by employees must be reported to the insurance company. Upon learning of such acts, the business will no longer have coverage against any future crimes committed by the reported person.

Personal Umbrella Policies

A **personal umbrella policy** is excess liability insurance that kicks in when a person's primary insurance policies for personal liability (auto or homeowners insurance) have reached their limits. It also fills in some of the circumstantial coverage gaps in many homeowners and auto insurance policies when the insured is accused of property damage or bodily injury. It usually insures the policyholder against $1 million in damages or more.

Umbrella policies provide relatively inexpensive insurance protection, but coverage is conditional in some respects. For the umbrella policy to pick up where the primary policy left off, the insured needs to remain covered by a company-mandated amount of primary liability insurance as part of an auto and/or homeowners policy. If the primary liability insurance is ever canceled or reduced below the mandated amounts, the insured might need to pay out of pocket for some or all of the loss.

In some cases, an umbrella policy will cover losses that are excluded by other forms of liability insurance. In those circumstances, the insured might be responsible for paying a fraction of losses, sometimes known as a **self-insured retention amount**. This amount is similar to a deductible but applies when a loss is only covered by the umbrella policy and not also by the person's primary auto or homeowners insurance. If a loss is covered by both the umbrella policy and the person's primary auto or homeowners insurance, a deductible will typically be paid under the primary insurance policy. Then, if the size of the loss exceeds the dollar limits of the primary policy, the umbrella will cover the rest without forcing the insured to pay the self-insured retention amount.

Whereas personal umbrella policies are intended to supplement the liability protection in personal auto and homeowners insurance, commercial umbrella policies offer liability insurance for businesses. As with personal umbrella products, a commercial umbrella policy can include excess insurance when the size of a liability loss is greater than a primary policy's dollar limits and can serve as primary insurance when a liability loss isn't covered by an underlying policy. Losses not commonly covered by umbrella policies include but aren't limited to intentional or criminal acts and punitive damages.

Directors and Officers Insurance

To an extent, **directors and officers (D & O) insurance** is malpractice insurance for high-ranking decisionmakers at public, private or non-profit companies. The insurance is meant to protect directors and officers when they perform their duties in good faith but are still personally sued by shareholders or other parties.

Over time, D & O insurance has evolved into a product that also repays companies when they indemnify their directors and officers directly for any loss of personal assets. It even sometimes covers the company as a whole against losses incurred in securities disputes.

Coverage for individuals is limited to the liability that stems specifically from their roles as directors and officers and usually doesn't extend to any rendering of professional services. If, for instance, doctors serve on a company's board of directors, they may be covered for the unpopular business decisions they make at board meetings. However, they won't have coverage under their D & O policy for any mistakes they make in treating or advising patients.

For the purpose of another example, consider a person who has multiple roles in a company, serving as a board member and as general counsel. A D & O policy might cover the person for legal advice given to the board but leave the individual uncovered for the services and advice provided beyond the boardroom.

Sides of D&O Insurance

There are generally three types of coverage available as part of a D & O policy. They're known as "sides," and each side will have its own dollar limit:

- "Side A" protects directors and officers' personal assets by paying for defense costs, settlements and court-awarded damages when a company can't or won't compensate or "indemnify" its directors and officers for those losses.

- "Side B" of a D & O insurance policy provides money to a business when it has already paid to protect or defend its directors and officers in a dispute.

- "Side C" of a D&O policy is intended to be used when both a business and its directors are jointly named in a lawsuit.

Garage Coverage Form

Businesses operating as parking garages, gas stations, car dealerships or auto mechanics are likely to need specialized coverage due to their high exposure to auto-related risks. This is often obtained via some version of the ISO's Garage Coverage Form.

Under the Garage Coverage Form, the business typically gets liability coverage if it hits a person or another vehicle but isn't covered for damage to other people's vehicles that are in its care (such as a customer who has taken a car into a mechanic for repair). This risk can be addressed by adding "garagekeepers coverage" to the Garage Coverage Form. The Garage Coverage Form also typically excludes liability for defective auto parts that were defective at the time of sale.

Bonds

Bonds are contractual guarantees that something will or won't happen. There are often three parties involved in a bond:

- The **principal** is the party who promises to do or not do something.

- The **obligee** is the person who is compensated when a promise is broken.

- The **surety** is the party who will compensate someone if the principal breaks the promise.

A **surety bond** is a bond guaranteeing something will be done. For example, some insurance professionals are required to obtain a surety bond in conjunction with a guarantee that they'll faithfully account for all the premiums they might collect from the public on an insurer's behalf. A surety bond is obtained and paid for by the principal (the person making the promise) NOT by the obligee. The principal might need to put down collateral for this bond.

A **fidelity bond** is a bond guaranteeing loyalty and faithfulness, often by an employee to an employer. It's obtained and paid for by the obligee (the person who will be compensated if a promise is broken) and might exist without the principal's knowledge.

Unlike insurance, which is based on a degree of uncertainty and outside factors, a bond often involves at least one party (the principal) who has control over whether a loss will occur.

Liability Insurance for Farmers

As mentioned in an earlier chapter, liability insurance for farmers can be purchased as part of a package along with many types of property coverage. Common liability/casualty coverages for farms may include:

- Coverage H: Bodily injury and property damage liability (when liable for harm to another person or someone else's property).

- Coverage I: Personal and advertising injury liability (when liable for violating someone's rights or doing harm as part of an advertisement).

- Coverage J: Medical payments (intended as no-fault medical insurance for a third party who is injured on the farm and intended to prevent a protracted legal dispute).

Chapter Key Points

- Crime insurance can fill in some of the coverage gaps in commercial property insurance, particularly when a business's money or property is stolen.

- Crime insurance sometimes applies to crimes detected within the policy's discovery period. The discovery period is often up to one year after the end of the policy period.

- Crime insurance typically covers money at its face amount. Securities are covered based on their value at the time a crime is discovered. Other property impacted by a crime is generally covered at actual cash value.

- Theft is any kind of stealing.

- Robbery is theft by violence or threat of violence.

- Burglary is theft by forced entry.

- Forgery is signing someone's name without permission.

- A personal umbrella policy is excess liability insurance that kicks in when a person's primary insurance policies for personal liability have reached their limits.

- To an extent, directors and officers (D & O) insurance is malpractice insurance for high-ranking decision makers at public, private or non-profit companies. The insurance is meant to protect directors and officers when they perform their duties in good faith but are still personally sued by shareholders or other parties.

- A surety bond is a bond guaranteeing that something will be done. It's purchased by the person who will be making the guarantee (the principal) and not by the person who will be compensated if a promise is broken.

- A fidelity bond is a bond guaranteeing loyalty and faithfulness, often by an employee to an employer. It is often purchased by the person who will be compensated if loyalty is broken (the obligee).

CHAPTER 20: INSURANCE REGULATION

The primary goal of laws, rules and other forms of insurance regulation is to protect the public. Due in large part to a federal law known as the **McCarran-Ferguson Act**, most aspects of insurance regulation are left up to the individual states rather than the federal government. Specifically, according to the law, "No act of Congress shall be construed to invalidate, impair, or supersede any law enacted by any state for the purpose of regulating the business of insurance (…) unless such act specifically relates to the business of insurance."

State insurance departments are generally intended to protect the public by monitoring market conduct and enforcing the state's various insurance requirements. More specifically, the insurance department is likely to concern itself with the following issues:

- Solvency of local insurance companies.
- Licensing of insurance producers and insurance companies.
- Consumer education regarding insurance topics.
- Fair sales and claims practices in the local insurance market.

The insurance department in most states is headed by an **insurance commissioner**. In some parts of the country, this person might instead have the title of "director" or "superintendent." The commissioner is responsible for managing the insurance department, setting its priorities and enforcing the state's insurance rules and laws. He or she might also have the power to hold hearings and either approve or reject insurance rates and products.

Company Licensing

Insurance companies that want to do business in a particular state generally must have the appropriate license. Among other things, the licensing process might involve auditing the company's finances and investigating the financial and personal histories of its top-level personnel.

Specific licensing requirements might depend on whether the company is a domestic insurer, foreign insurer or alien insurer. These terms relate to where an insurer is incorporated as a legal entity.

In regard to licensing, a licensed insurance company is considered a **domestic insurer** in the state where it is incorporated but is a **foreign insurer** in any other state where it also has a license. An **alien insurer** is an insurance company from another country. Since they are all licensed entities, domestic, foreign and alien insurers are collectively known as **admitted carriers**.

When insurance can't be easily obtained in a given state, a consumer might be able to purchase coverage from a **non-admitted carrier**. Although they might be licensed elsewhere, non-admitted carriers aren't licensed to sell insurance in the buyer's state. In order to provide some consumer protections against an unlicensed carrier, insurance from a non-admitted carrier can only be purchased with the help of specially licensed professionals and only under special circumstances. In general, the producer selling the insurance must be licensed as an **excess-and-surplus-lines** broker in the buyer's state and be able to show that adequate coverage from an admitted carrier wasn't reasonably available.

Insurer Solvency

When an insurer's assets are enough to honor its liabilities, the company is considered to be "solvent." Solvency is an immeasurably important issue because financially mismanaged carriers might not have enough assets to pay legitimate claims. An insolvent insurer harms consumers, of course, who might not receive fair compensation for insured losses, but it also has a negative impact on the other insurers in the market. When one carrier fails, other companies might be required to contribute to a state fund in order to pay for the insolvent insurer's liabilities or absorb some of the insolvent insurer's customers.

Fraudulent activities that impact an insurer's financial health can be prosecuted at the state or federal level. If false statements or the misappropriation of funds are deemed to impact interstate commerce, maximum prison sentences of 10 to 15 years can be imposed.

Private Rating Organizations

If a producer or consumer wants an independent evaluation of an insurance company's financial health (and ability to pay claims), several private ratings organizations can be consulted. Entities such as Standard and Poor's and A.M. Best provide their opinion of an insurer's financial health in the form of letter grades. Each organization will use its own grading scale.

Guaranty Funds

Guaranty funds are used to compensate claimants whose insurance is from an insolvent company. These funds might be financed through periodic fees paid by all insurers in the state, or they might require financial contributions from all carriers once an insolvency actually occurs.

Regardless of how they're structured, guaranty funds aren't ideal for consumers or insurers. They often limit a harmed consumer's compensation to a certain amount (such as $100,000) and involve long waiting periods (usually including a liquidation process) before any benefits become available. They also risk penalizing responsible insurers by making them pay for the mistakes of irresponsible carriers. For these reasons and more, regulators and insurance professionals should take solvency requirements very seriously.

The Gramm-Leach-Bliley Act and Insurer Privacy

The Gramm-Leach-Bliley Act (GLBA) is a federal law that deregulated the financial services industry and made it easier for different kinds of banks, securities firms and insurance companies to join forces or consolidate. By allowing those entities to become more tightly intertwined, the GLBA also made it more likely that people's personal information would be shared among businesses. To protect against the possibility that these businesses would infringe upon individual privacy rights, the GLBA includes provisions to protect consumers' personal financial information. Note that each state also has its own privacy requirements for producers and insurers.

There are three principal parts to the privacy requirements:

- The Financial Privacy Rule.
- The Safeguards Rule.
- The pretexting provisions.

The Financial Privacy Rule governs the collection and disclosure of customers' personal financial information by financial institutions. It also applies to companies that aren't financial institutions but still receive such information. It allows consumers to opt out of certain forms of information sharing.

The Safeguards Rule requires all financial institutions to design, implement and maintain safeguards to protect customer information.

The pretexting provisions of the GLBA protect consumers from individuals and companies that obtain personal financial information under false pretenses, a practice known as "pretexting." An example of pretexting would be a phone survey that claims to be gathering information to help insurance companies create new products but, in truth, will be using the acquired information to either sell insurance to the consumer or steal the person's identity.

As part of Gramm-Leach-Bliley, insurers and their agents might be required to provide certain privacy notices to consumers.

Producer Licensing

Insurance producers, including agents and brokers, must be licensed in order to sell insurance. Despite a push for greater uniformity and reciprocity in the licensing process, each state is responsible for enforcing its own licensing requirements.

According to the Federal Insurance Office, more than 2.3 million individuals are licensed to sell insurance. Those 2.3 million people hold over 6 million licenses. The difference in those numbers is the result of many individuals having licenses in multiple states. A license from a producer's home state is the person's **resident license**, and any licenses from other states are known as **non-resident licenses**.

In order to become licensed as a producer, a person usually must complete pre-license education, pass a state exam, pay various fees and undergo some kind of background check. A few states also require a licensee to already be affiliated with a particular insurance company. This relationship is sometimes called an "appointment." Even if an appointment isn't a mandatory part of the licensing process, each insurance company might have its own requirements and procedures before a licensee can sell the company's products.

Individuals who are interested in obtaining a producer license must choose one or more **lines of authority**. The line of authority is the kind of insurance (usually life, health, property or casualty) that a license allows someone to sell. The chosen line of authority can dictate the kinds of pre-license coursework that must be completed and the type of state exam that must be passed.

Upon the conclusion of a license term, a producer can usually renew his or her license by submitting documentation to the department of insurance, paying required fees and completing continuing education. Many states have followed the NAIC's continuing education standard, which requires a producer to complete at least 24 hours of continuing education (including three hours of ethics training) every two years. Individuals selling annuities or long-term care insurance are likely to have additional continuing education requirements. And of course, as in most things related to insurance regulation, each state is likely to have its own rules regarding hours, course content and course delivery.

Chapter Key Points

- The goal of insurance regulation is to protect the public.

- Due to the McCarran-Ferguson Act, most aspects of insurance regulation are left up to the individual states rather than the federal government.

- State insurance departments are generally intended to protect the public by monitoring market conduct and enforcing the state's various insurance requirements.

- The insurance department in most states is headed by an insurance commissioner. In some parts of the country, this person might instead have the title of director or superintendent. The commissioner is responsible for managing the insurance department, setting its priorities and enforcing the state's insurance rules and laws. He or she might also have the power to hold hearings and either approve or reject insurance rates and products.

- A licensed insurance company is considered a domestic insurer in the state where it is incorporated but is a foreign insurer in any other state where it also has a license. An alien insurer is an insurance company from another country. Since they're all licensed entities, domestic, foreign and alien insurers are collectively known as "admitted carriers."

- When insurance can't be easily obtained in a given state, a consumer might be able to purchase coverage from a non-admitted carrier. Non-admitted carriers are not licensed to sell insurance in the buyer's state. In general, the producer selling the insurance must be licensed as a surplus-lines broker in the buyer's state and be able to show that adequate coverage from an admitted carrier was not reasonably available.

- When an insurer's assets are enough to honor its liabilities, the company is considered to be solvent.

- Fraudulent activities that impact an insurer's financial health can be prosecuted at the state or federal level. If false statements or the misappropriation of funds are deemed to impact interstate commerce, maximum prison sentences of 10 to 15 years may be imposed.

- State guaranty funds are used to compensate claimants whose insurance is from an insolvent company. These funds might be financed through periodic fees paid by all insurers in the state, or they might require financial contributions from all carriers once an insolvency occurs.

- The Gramm-Leach-Bliley Act sets privacy requirements for financial institutions that collect consumer information. It allows consumers to opt out of certain forms of information sharing.

- Insurance producers, including agents and brokers, must be licensed in order to sell insurance.

- To become licensed as a producer, a person usually must complete pre-license education, pass a state exam, pay various fees and undergo some kind of background check.

- Individuals who are interested in obtaining a producer license must choose one or more lines of authority. The line of authority is the kind of insurance that a license allows someone to sell.

- Upon the conclusion of a license term, a producer can usually renew his or her license by submitting documentation to the department of insurance, paying required fees and completing continuing education.

CHAPTER 21: INSURANCE STATE LAW AND RULES

Missouri insurance producers have many laws and rules to follow when conducting business. Most requirements for Missouri producers can be found in Title 20 of the State Code of Regulations and chapters 374 to 385 of the Revised Statutes of Missouri.

This chapter summarizes some of the most important sections of the Missouri code and statutes. It first addresses information that is relevant to practically all Missouri producers regardless of the type of insurance being sold. Later sections are specific to certain lines of insurance (property-only, casualty-only etc.). Students who are attempting to pass a state licensing exam should carefully read all sections that are applicable to their situation.

Although the information provided here was compiled carefully for an audience of insurance licensing candidates, it should be treated as an important study tool rather than a comprehensive authority on compliance issues. Readers looking for practical guidance on a particular aspect of Missouri insurance regulation should review the laws and rules in greater detail with assistance from a qualified attorney.

General Information For All Producers

The next several sections should be reviewed carefully by all prospective Missouri producers regardless of whether they hope to specialize in life, health, property or casualty insurance.

The Missouri Department of Insurance

As part of the McCarran-Fergusson Act, the U.S. Congress decided that most aspects of insurance regulation should be handled by the individual states rather than the federal government. In Missouri, the responsibilities of protecting insurance consumers and enforcing the state's various insurance laws belong to the Missouri Department of Commerce and Insurance (DCI).

Missouri Insurance Director

The DCI is overseen by a director who is appointed by the governor. The director must be a Missouri resident and have a professional background in insurance. Other than as policyholders, the director and his or her deputies can't work for, be affiliated with or have any financial interest in an insurance business while working for the DCI.

In general, the director has the authority to take the following actions:

- Make reasonable rules and regulations to enforce the state's insurance laws.
- Conduct reasonable investigations to determine possible violations of state insurance requirements.
- Issue cease-and-desist orders to halt illegal insurance practices.
- Issue subpoenas in order to obtain insurance documents.
- Require individuals to testify under oath about insurance matters.
- Issue, deny, suspend or revoke insurance licenses for individuals and businesses.
- Contract with third parties to perform ministerial duties on the DCI's behalf (including but not limited to the collection of fees from licensed entities and the maintenance of a registry of all Missouri-licensed insurance producers).

At least 15 days before implementing any changes to insurance rules, the director must provide advance notice of a hearing. Members of the public can obtain copies of insurance rules from the director in exchange for a reasonable fee.

The director can employ examiners to investigate potential violations of state insurance laws and rules. The cost of an investigation can be charged to the party being investigated. Regulated entities, including insurance producers, generally have the right to a hearing when the director accuses them of illegal conduct.

Failure to abide by a subpoena from the director to appear, testify or produce documents can result in a $50,000 fine and the loss of an insurance license.

Failure to comply with a cease-and-desist order from the director can result in a maximum fine of $100,000 and up to 10 years imprisonment. License suspension or revocation are also possibilities.

Regardless of the reason for their use, documents submitted to the director can't contain any false or misleading information.

Financial Examinations of Insurers by the Director

The director must order a financial examination of each licensed insurance company at least once every five years. Financial examinations can be ordered on a more frequent basis at the director's discretion. Financial examinations will be based on standards from the National Association of Insurance Commissioners.

People or businesses that are the subject of a financial investigation by the director must receive a copy of any resulting report and will, in some cases, have 30 days to submit a rebuttal to the director. The director might then have another 30 days to take action based on the report and any rebuttals.

Recordkeeping and DCI Access (General)

Examiners working on behalf of the director must be provided free and convenient access to records. In general, requested records must be provided within 10 days of a request. Failure to cooperate in an examination can result in license suspension or revocation.

Policy records must be maintained for the duration of their current policy term plus an additional two calendar years.

All records related to insurance claims must be maintained for the year in which a claim is closed plus an additional three calendar years.

Records of consumer complaints must be maintained for at least three years. Complaint records must include the following information:

- The nature of each complaint.
- The category of insurance associated with each complaint.
- The outcome of each complaint.
- The amount of time it took to process each complaint.
- The total number of received complaints.

Recordkeeping and DCI Access (Personal Insurance)

Specifically regarding insurance for individuals and families (as opposed to businesses), a producer must keep records of all policies that he or she has sold. The records generally must be kept for the duration of a policy plus three additional years. These records must be provided to the director within five days of a request.

The records must include:

- Declarations pages.
- Endorsements.
- Applications.
- Binders.

- Written correspondence related to the transaction.
- Documents related to claims.
- Receipts for premium payments.

Upon written agreement, an insurance company can maintain these records on a producer's behalf.

Insurer Authorization Required

Insurers selling insurance in or intended for use in Missouri must be authorized to do so by obtaining a certificate of authority from the DCI. (Limited exceptions exist for insurers that operate in the excess and surplus, reinsurance or marine insurance markets.)

An insurer that fails to obtain a certificate of authority in Missouri might not be able to enforce an insurance contract in the state. Also, if an unauthorized insurer fails to pay a legitimate claim, any person who helped facilitate the transaction can be held liable for the loss.

Special "excess and surplus" licenses can be issued to producers who want to sell insurance from an unauthorized insurer. In general, this is only possible when insurance for a risk isn't obtainable from authorized insurers.

Producer License Requirement

In general, an individual who sells, solicits or negotiates insurance in exchange for compensation must have a producer license.

For licensing purposes, "selling" includes issuing certificates, binders or policies or indicating that requested coverage has or will be issued. Selling doesn't include the following activities:

- Receiving insurance-related requests that will ultimately be transmitted to a licensed producer.
- Obtaining or filling out information on an application that will be reviewed by a licensed producer.
- Obtaining information that will be used in the underwriting process.
- Receiving payment for an insurance product at a "place of business." (However, a "place of business" must be the principal office of at least one licensed insurance producer.)

For licensing purposes, "negotiating" includes the following activities:

- Providing price information about insurance.
- Recommending the purchase of specific coverage from a specific insurer.
- Recommending additions or deletions from an existing insurance policy.
- Explaining the impact of certain risk factors on the affordability or availability of insurance.
- Analyzing a person's insurance needs.
- Interpreting insurance policy language.

Negotiating doesn't include obtaining necessary information that will be used by a licensed insurance producer as part of an insurance evaluation.

For licensing purposes, "soliciting" includes the following activities:

- Providing information about insurance pricing from a list or database.
- Initiating phone conversations with insurance prospects (other than to set appointments with a licensed insurance producer).

- Evaluating someone's existing insurance coverage.
- Upon collecting payments for existing coverage, encouraging people to purchase additional coverage.

Soliciting generally doesn't include the following activities, as long as the terms of an insurance contract aren't discussed:

- Distributing brochures and general insurance information.
- Providing forms to the public upon request.
- Receiving or recording information from consumers for review by a licensed insurance producer.
- Scheduling an appointment to discuss insurance with a licensed insurance producer.

Licensing Qualifications

An applicant for a producer license in Missouri must satisfy the following criteria:

- Be at least 18 years old.
- Pay a $100 licensing fee.
- Submit an honest and complete license application to the DCI.
- Pass the applicable state exam(s) for the desired line(s) of authority. A line of authority is a category of insurance products that a producer is allowed to sell. The most common lines of authority in Missouri are:
    - Life.
    - Accident and health.
    - Property.
    - Casualty.
    - Personal lines (which allows a producer to sell property and casualty insurance intended for individuals and families but not for businesses).
    - Limited lines (which might allow a producer to sell insurance solely in conjunction with the offering of credit or solely intended to manage travel-related risks).

If the director takes no action within 25 days after all the licensing requirements have been met, the applicant is deemed approved and may begin work as a producer. However, this general rule doesn't apply if an application has indicated that the person has been convicted of a crime.

If the director refuses to issue or renew a license for any reason, a written explanation must be provided to the applicant.

Contents of a License

A producer license must contain the following information:

- Producer's name.
- License number.
- Date of issuance.
- Date of expiration.

- Address.
- Line(s) of authority.

Producers Licensed in Other States

In general, producers who are licensed in the same line of authority in another state can be issued a Missouri license without needing to pass a state exam. To avoid having to pass a Missouri exam, all of the following statements must be true:

- A producer's license from another state is in good standing and has not been canceled, suspended or revoked.

- The producer has paid the $100 fee for a Missouri license and submitted the required paperwork.

- The state that issued the producer's license has a similarly streamlined process for Missouri-licensed producers who also want to be licensed in that state.

A producer who resides in Missouri is generally considered a "resident producer" in Missouri. A producer who is licensed in Missouri but doesn't live there is generally considered a "nonresident producer" in Missouri.

If a producer is licensed in another state and becomes a Missouri resident, the producer must apply to become a resident producer within 90 days. Producers who move to Missouri but fail to apply within 90 days of residency will need to pass a state exam for each desired line of authority.

The fees charged by the DCI can't be increased solely because a producer resides in another state.

State Licensing Exams

The state has the power to contract with a third party as part of offering its insurance licensing exams. In general, a licensing exam must be passed for each desired line of authority. Exam fees are nonrefundable.

Limited Lines Producers

A limited lines producer is a specially licensed insurance producer who can only sell very particular kinds of insurance that make up a very narrow portion of the insurance market. In Missouri, a limited lines producer might only sell travel insurance or various forms of credit insurance. A limited lines producer doesn't need to pass a state licensing exam but must abide by nearly all other requirements for Missouri producers.

License Terms and Renewals

Producer licenses are issued for two years and can remain in force for subsequent two-year periods if the producer remains in good standing with the DCI, pays a $100 renewal fee and satisfies continuing education requirements.

Continuing Education

In general, Missouri insurance producers must complete 16 hours of continuing education during each two-year licensing period. At least three hours must relate to ethics and Missouri law. Limited lines insurance producers are exempt from continuing education requirements.

Continuing education courses must be completed prior to a producer's license renewal deadline. The director has the authority to issue extensions of up to one year.

A producer can apply for a waiver of the continuing education requirements under any of the following circumstances:

- The producer is disabled.
- The producer is living in another country.
- The producer is serving in the military.
- The producer is 70 or older.

No more than 16 hours of continuing education credit can be earned via completion of any single course. No credit can be earned by taking the same course twice during the same two-year licensing cycle. If a producer earns more than 16 hours of continuing education credit during a licensing cycle, excess hours can be carried over to the subsequent two-year licensing cycle.

A producer who teaches a course on behalf of a continuing education provider can receive the same amount of credit as a student.

No continuing education credit can be granted for courses pertaining to the following topics:

- Prospecting, sales and marketing techniques.
- Motivation or psychology.
- Recruiting.
- Office skills.
- Management training.
- Subjects unrelated to a student's producer license.

A non-resident producer is exempt from Missouri's continuing education requirements if both of the following statements are true:

- The non-resident producer has satisfied the continuing education requirements for his or her home state.
- The non-resident producer's home state grants a similar exemption to Missouri resident producers.

Education Providers

Continuing education courses must be approved by the DCI. Education providers must submit a $50 fee for each course. Course approvals are valid for one year at a time.

Upon a producer's successful completion of a continuing education course, education providers must submit completion records to the DCI within 30 days. Courses completed via self-study must include a closed-book final exam. Courses completed in a classroom or interactive webinar setting don't require a final exam.

License Reinstatement

A producer who fails to renew a license by the renewal deadline must immediately stop selling insurance but can reinstate the license by completing any remaining continuing education requirement and paying a reinstatement fee. The reinstatement fee will be equal to $100 plus an additional $25 for each month that has passed since the renewal deadline.

A license that isn't reinstated within 12 months will be terminated, and the individual can only operate as a producer again by repeating the entire licensing process (including successful completion of state exams).

Changes of Address or Legal Name

A producer must report any change of address or legal name to the DCI within 30 days. Failure to comply can result in a fine of $10 per month.

If a complaint from the DCI cannot be mailed to a producer due to an unreported change in address, the producer's license can be suspended until the issue is resolved.

Business Licensing and Insurer Liability

A business entity performing the same services as an individual producer (such as an insurance agency or an insurance brokerage firm) must have its own producer license. The business must pay all applicable licensing fees and designate one Missouri-licensed producer who will be ultimately responsible for its compliance with state insurance laws and rules. None of the business's owners, directors or officers can have committed any activities that would result in the denial, suspension or revocation of a producer license.

As part of an application for a producer license, a business must submit the identities of all producers who will be selling on its behalf and anyone else who will be compensated for helping to sell, negotiate or solicit insurance. The information must be updated with the DCI within 20 days of a change. The DCI can't charge a fee for these updates.

If any of a business's owners, directors or officers become aware of an illegal act by a producer, the business must take corrective action or report the violation to the DCI. A business that doesn't comply with this requirement can have its own license suspended or revoked.

Similar recordkeeping requirements and liabilities exist for insurers. Within 30 days of authorizing a producer to sell on its behalf, an insurer must enter the producer's name and license number in a register. Upon terminating its relationship with a producer, an insurer must update the register to reflect the date of termination.

Authorization to sell on behalf of an insurer is known as an "appointment." An appointment can apply to the relationship between either an insurer and an individual producer OR an insurer and a business entity (such as an insurance agency). For the purposes of maintaining a register of all appointed producers, an appointment exists as soon as a producer engages in any of the following activities:

- Providing applications to the public (other than a sample application).
- Collecting premiums.
- Accepting an application for underwriting.
- Having an oral or written employment agreement with an insurer.
- Receiving "binding authority" from an insurer. (Binding authority exists when a producer has the power to accept a risk on an insurer's behalf.)

A producer's appointment with an insurer will terminate automatically in any of the following cases:

- The producer is no longer licensed.
- The producer is no longer employed by a business entity that otherwise has an appointment with the insurer.
- The producer is employed by a business entity that no longer has an appointment with the insurer.

If an insurer terminates a relationship with an appointed producer for an illegal act, the DCI must be notified within 30 days. If illegal activity is discovered at a later date, the DCI must be notified immediately. The insurer will be shielded from liability for reporting someone's activities as part of these requirements if the reporting is done in good faith.

License Suspensions, Revocations and Refusals

The DCI can suspend, revoke, refuse to issue or refuse to renew a license in response to many prohibited activities, such as:

- Lying on a license application or other document submitted to the director.
- Violating Missouri insurance laws or rules.
- Violating another state's insurance laws or rules.
- Violating an order or subpoena from either the DCI or an insurance regulator in another state.
- Mishandling money that was obtained while transacting insurance business.
- Misrepresenting the terms of an insurance product or application.
- Committing a felony.
- Committing fraud.
- Demonstrating untrustworthiness, incompetence or financial irresponsibility in business.
- Having a license disciplined in another state.
- Signing another person's name on an insurance document without permission.
- Cheating on an insurance exam.
- Working as or with an unlicensed insurance producer.
- Failing to comply with an order to pay taxes or child support.

Denial, suspension or revocation of a license is also possible if someone commits an "unfair insurance trade practice." Examples of unfair insurance trade practices are listed next:

- Attempting to force an insurance sale via boycott, coercion or intimidation.
- Committing libel, slander or other forms of defamation. (Libel is defamation in writing. Slander is spoken defamation.)
- Not maintaining appropriate records of consumer complaints.
- False advertising.
- Knowingly making false statements about an insurer's business or financial condition.
- Misrepresenting the benefits or conditions of an insurance policy.
- Misrepresenting the shares or dividends payable to policyholders by a "mutual insurance company." (A mutual insurance company is owned by its policyholders. Those policyholders might receive dividends in the form of credits or discounts when the insurer accumulates a surplus.)
- Misrepresenting the name of an insurance product.
- Misrepresenting information in order to encourage someone to purchase, surrender or exchange an insurance product.
- Misrepresenting insurance as shares of stock.
- Misrepresenting information on an insurance application.

- "Rebating." (Rebating generally means providing something of value to a buyer other than what's specified in an insurance contract [such as a share of a producer's commission] as an incentive to buy insurance.)
- Engaging in unfair insurance discrimination.

If the director denies, suspends or revokes a license due to an illegal act, the disciplinary action must be made public.

Other Penalties

Many Missouri insurance laws and rules mention maximum penalties and prison sentences for noncompliance. However, those penalties and sentences can often be increased by the director or a court if a person committed an act knowingly and in conscious violation of the law. Conversely, penalties are supposed to be downgraded when a violation is caught as part of a self-audit and reported immediately to the director.

Disciplinary actions that are limited to fines of less than $200 and don't involve denial, suspension or revocation of a license will be expunged from a person's record after five years.

In accordance with the Missouri state constitution, most monetary penalties collected from producers and other insurance entities must be sent to the state treasurer and used to fund public schools.

Compensation and Fees

It's illegal for an unlicensed person to accept compensation for activities that require a producer license. Similarly, a producer or insurer can't compensate an unlicensed person for selling, soliciting or negotiating insurance.

A formerly licensed producer may receive renewal commissions or deferred compensation if the person was licensed at the time of the initial sale. However, note that an insurance carrier can impose its own additional rules regarding who can or can't receive compensation.

Compensation for a licensed producer can't be shared with a policyholder ("rebated") as an incentive to purchase insurance.

In general, compensation that must be paid by the consumer to a producer (other than commission on an insurance transaction) must be disclosed in advance. For example, if a producer will be charging fees for financial planning rather than earning a commission on an insurance sale, the fees must be disclosed in writing before services are provided. The nature and amount of each fee must be specified. If the financial planner will be recommending insurance, the disclosure must address whether the planner will be also be earning a commission on the insurance transaction. If a commission is possible, the person receiving fee-based advice must be told that the recommended insurance can be purchased from another producer.

Copies of compensation disclosures must be kept for three years.

Compensation Based on Insured Losses

In some cases, a producer's commissions or other compensation might be impacted by the amount of losses suffered by policyholders. In these cases, the authority to approve or deny claims must be left to the insurer. If a Missouri producer is ever given the power to approve or deny claims, the producer's decisions can't have any impact on his or her compensation.

Handling Money

Money obtained from insurance consumers must be held by producers in a fiduciary capacity (requiring a heightened level of care) and can't be misappropriated, converted, mixed or commingled with other funds. If a producer is allowed to deposit premiums for any length of time, it might be possible to keep all deposited premiums in a single account (separate from non-premium money). However, the intent and source of each deposited amount must be unambiguous.

Money held by a producer must be provided to its rightful owner as soon as possible but no later than 30 days.

If a producer accepts cash as part of a premium payment, the consumer must receive a receipt containing the following information:

- The name of the insured person.

- The name of the insurer (if applicable).

- The policy number (if applicable).

- The type of coverage (if applicable).

- The payment amount.

- The fact that it is a receipt.

- The signature of the producer or the producer's designated employee.

If no specific insurer has agreed to insure a risk associated with the cash payment, this must be made clear on the receipt. Copies of cash receipts must be maintained by the producer.

Collecting Late Fees

Although producers may collect late fees or reinstatement fees for premiums that are overdue, those fees must be disclosed in advance.

Handling Applications

Producers are required to provide and deliver applications for insurance on a schedule that allows coverage to be issued promptly. If insurance can't be issued within 30 days of a completed application, the producer must immediately provide written notice to the applicant. If additional documentation is needed to secure the coverage, the applicant must be informed in a timely manner.

Once coverage is issued, evidence of insurance must be provided to the applicant within 30 days. If insurance is denied, producers must inform the applicant as soon as possible and include the insurer's reason for the denial.

Providing Binders

A "binder" provides temporary coverage to an insurance applicant while a policy is in the process of being reviewed and issued. Unless special requests are made by the applicant, a property and casualty insurance policy that is intended to replace a binder must go into effect no later than the binder's expiration date.

If a binder is ultimately not replaced by an insurance policy, the cost of the binder can be no higher than the pro-rated cost of an insurance policy that would've provided similar coverage (based on the duration of the binder). This general rule doesn't apply when the cost of a binder is $20 or less.

Advertising

In general, insurance advertising that is conducted over the internet must comply with the same legal requirements as advertising conducted in other formats. However, website homepages must include the following items about the producer or insurer:

- Name.

- Phone number.

- Address.

- States in which the producer or insurer is licensed.

Titles and Designations

Producers must represent their qualifications accurately to the public. Terms such as "financial planner," "financial consultant," investment adviser," "financial counselor" or other titles that indicate expertise can't be used if a producer merely sells insurance. However, a producer who legitimately earned a designation through a professional course of study may indicate it on stationery and business cards.

Producers cannot advertise themselves as having special certifications or designations pertaining to senior citizens if any of the following statements are true:

- The producer hasn't actually obtained the certification or designation.

- The organization providing the certification or designation is primarily in the business of offering marketing and sales training.

- The organization providing the certification or designation does not have a reasonable way to determine the person's competency.

- The organization providing the certification or designation does not have continuing education requirements for its members.

- The organization providing the certification or designation does not have a method of monitoring and enforcing standards of ethical conduct.

Prohibition on Loans

In order to reduce conflicts of interest, producers are not allowed to accept loans from current, former or prospective policyholders. Possible exceptions exist if those policyholders are regularly in the business of making loans.

Discrimination

In general, insurance in Missouri can't be refused, canceled or non-renewed based on the following factors:

- Race.

- Gender.

- Color.

- Religion.

- National origin.

- Age of the insured.

- Location of the insured's residence.

- Ancestry.

- Occupation (as long as the insured's occupation is legal).

- Military service.

- The fact that a consumer has been denied insurance or had insurance canceled or non-renewed in the past.

In all lines of insurance, it's also illegal in Missouri to limit coverage amounts, refuse to offer insurance or refuse to renew insurance on the basis of:

- Gender.

- Marital status.

Disability Status

Property and casualty insurers in Missouri can't discriminate against consumers on the basis of disability.

Note that unlike some of the other antidiscrimination requirements in Missouri, this prohibition forbids discrimination in pricing and isn't merely limited to decisions about cancellations, nonrenewals or whether to offer insurance to someone at all.

Previous Nonrenewal or Denial of Insurance

Applicants for insurance in Missouri can't be denied solely because they've had insurance denied or non-renewed by another insurer.

Although applicants can't be required to disclose whether they've been denied insurance or non-renewed by another carrier, they can be required to disclose the name of their previous insurer so that the new insurer can obtain information about previous losses.

Redlining

Redlining occurs when insurance or other financial products are made intentionally unavailable in a particular geographic area due to residents' demographics (such as a higher-than-average population of ethnic or racial minorities).

In part to combat redlining, property and casualty insurers in Missouri can't limit coverage amounts, refuse to issue insurance, cancel insurance or non-renew insurance based solely on the location of the risk.

Unfair Claims Practices

In addition to facing potential lawsuits from consumers, insurance companies can be fined by the DCI for engaging in "unfair claims settlement practices." Fines are possible whenever an insurer knowingly engages in an unfair practice or unknowingly engages in such behavior on a routine basis. A "claim," in this context, is a demand for money from the insurance company.

Prohibited claims practices in Missouri include:

- Misrepresenting facts or policy provisions related to a claim.

- Not responding to communication from a claimant within a reasonable time.

- Failing to implement standards for the prompt investigation and payment of claims.

- Not offering fair and prompt settlement when the insurer's liability for a claim is reasonably clear.

- Frequently prompting claimants to sue in order to receive the full amount owed to them.

- Being named in a disproportionately high number of consumer complaints.

- Denying claims without conducting a reasonable investigation.

- Refusing to decide about a claim within a reasonable time after a claimant has provided proof of a loss.

- Requiring additional proof of a loss in order to delay payment.

- Failing to explain why a claim was denied.

- Failing to pay an amount that a reasonable person would expect based on advertising materials that were provided with an insurance application.

- Denying a claim due to alterations on an insurance application that were made without the insured person's knowledge.

- Not providing forms and instructions to claimants within 15 days of a request.

- Failing to ensure prompt and competent repairs of insured property (if repairs are being done by either the insurer or a vendor affiliated with the insurer).

If the victim of an accident might be entitled to insurance benefits under his or her own policy, the insurer can't force the person to first sue the at-fault person or make a claim with the at-fault person's insurer.

If an insurer is negotiating a settlement with a claimant, the insurer must keep the claimant informed of any deadlines that could impact either the person's ability to receive benefits or the ability to take legal action against an at-fault party.

When a consumer notifies the insurer of a claim, the insurer must acknowledge the notice. Acknowledgment can be done by paying a claim within 10 days, sending notice of acknowledgement within 10 days or orally acknowledging the notice and then documenting it in the insurer's files. Notice of a claim that is provided to an insurance agent (such as a producer who sells on behalf of the insurer) must be treated as notice to the insurer.

Upon receiving notice of a claim, an insurer must provide any necessary documents (such as proof of loss forms) to the claimant within 10 days. Requirements for providing proof of loss must be reasonable.

Within 15 days of receiving all completed documentation from a claimant, the insurer is expected to decide whether to pay the claim in full, in part or not at all. If an insurer needs more than the stated 15 days to decide, it must notify the claimant in writing and explain the situation. An additional written explanation must be provided to the claimant for every 45-day period of delay.

If the insurer decides to deny any portion of the claim, the specific grounds for the denial (such as the specific policy language used as a justification) must be disclosed to the claimant in writing. If a claim is denied because a property owner refused to allow for a reasonable inspection of the loss, the insurer must document the reasonable requests and the owner's refusal.

Regardless of the reason for the contact, insurers must reply to all communication from a claimant within 10 days unless a reply isn't reasonably expected.

The requirements mentioned here regarding claims apply to nearly all kinds of insurance in Missouri. Products exempt from the requirements might include (but aren't necessarily limited to) workers compensation insurance, boiler and machinery insurance, fidelity bonds and surety bonds.

The Missouri Property and Casualty Insurance Guaranty Association

All property and casualty insurers that are authorized to do business in Missouri must participate in the Missouri Property and Casualty Insurance Guaranty Association. If an insurer becomes insolvent and can't honor its claims-paying responsibilities, the association can compensate the impacted claimants.

The association is funded by fees charged to each Missouri insurer. The size of fees will generally depend on the amount of earned premiums that an insurer collected in the previous calendar year. Upon determining that an insurer has become insolvent, the director must notify the association within three days and then provide similar notice to producers who sell on the insurer's behalf.

Before making a claim with the association, the consumer must've exhausted all other sources of insurance that might pay for the loss, including any other policies that are otherwise intended to be excess, supplemental or secondary insurance.

Other than for workers compensation claims, the association is not obligated to pay any claims larger than $300,000.

Information For Property Producers

The next several sections should be reviewed carefully by all prospective Missouri producers who intend to sell property insurance. For purposes of study, they can be ignored by people who only intend to be licensed as casualty insurance producers.

General Property Insurance Requirements

Property insurance forms (including policy language) must be filed and approved by the DCI. In general, property insurance in Missouri must provide benefits and protections that are greater than or equal to the New York Standard Fire Policy of 1943.

A property insurance policy in Missouri must include an address where the insurer will receive notice of losses from the public. In general, consumers must be allowed to report property insurance losses at least 60 days from the time of loss.

A property insurance policy with a coinsurance clause must result in a reduced rate compared to a policy without a coinsurance clause. In property insurance, a coinsurance clause can make policyholders responsible for a portion of an otherwise insured loss if they fail to purchase coverage equal to an insurer-set dollar amount (such as 80% of a home's replacement cost).

If cancellation of property insurance results in a refund owed to the policyholder, the refund must be provided within 30 days.

Marine Insurance Definition

For regulatory reasons, marine insurance has its own definition that separates it from many of the rules for other kinds of property insurance.

In Missouri, marine insurance includes a specified group of policies for risks associated with imports and exports while in transit, domestic shipments, bridges, tunnels, docks, pipelines, power lines and radio towers.

Marine insurance products also include (but aren't limited to) personal property floaters (such as personal insurance for jewelry, stamps, furs, fine art and musical instruments), machinery and equipment floaters, commercial property floaters, builders risk insurance, installation insurance, bailee insurance and insurance for signs and accounts receivable.

Age of Residential Property

Carriers insuring residential property in Missouri aren't allowed to cancel, non-renew or limit dollar amounts for coverage based on the property's age.

Cancellations or Nonrenewals of Certain Homeowners Policies

Missouri enforces several requirements that limit an insurer's ability to cancel or non-renew certain homeowners insurance policies. In general, these requirements apply to insurance for owner-occupied property where no more than two families reside.

Homeowners insurance that has already been in effect for at least 60 days cannot be canceled by the insurer except for the following reasons:

- Nonpayment of premiums.

- Fraud or material misrepresentation by an insured.

- Violations of policy terms or conditions.

- Crimes committed by an insured (if a crime reasonably increases the risk to the insurer).

- A physical change to the property (if a change reasonably increases the risk to the insurer).

If an insurer intends on cancelling or not renewing a homeowners insurance policy, notice must be sent to the named insured's address 30 days prior to the cancellation or nonrenewal unless cancellation is for nonpayment. For cancellation in response to nonpayment, the notice must be provided at least 10 days prior to the effective date of the cancellation.

Proof of mailing can be used by the insurer to show compliance with these requirements. The required notices must include a clear reason for the cancellation or nonrenewal and information about the Missouri Basic Property Insurance Inspection and Placement Program.

Missouri Basic Property Insurance Inspection and Placement Program (FAIR Plan)

The Missouri Basic Property Insurance Inspection and Placement Program (sometimes known as Missouri's "FAIR Plan") can insure residential or commercial buildings when coverage can't be obtained in the regular market. Since the properties utilizing the program generally represent a higher risk of loss, the available insurance will generally be less comprehensive and more expensive than traditional property insurance.

Upon a request by a property owner, the program will conduct an inspection of residential or commercial property to determine its insurability. Within five days of receiving a full inspection report, the program can take any of the following actions:

- Agree to insure the property.

- Refuse to insure the property.

- Agree to insure the property if the owner makes specified repairs.

- Agree to insure the property at one price but inform the owner that a lower price is possible if specified repairs are made.

Although the program has the authority to issue coverage against additional perils, a policy must at least cover property against the following "basic" perils:

- Fire.

- Lightning.

- Windstorm.

- Civil commotion.

- Smoke.

- Hail.

- Aircraft or other vehicles.

- Volcanic eruption.

- Explosion.

- Riot or civil commotion.

- Vandalism and malicious mischief.

Limited coverage for theft and sinkhole collapse is also available, but the insurance against sinkhole collapse only applies to residential property where people actually reside. It can't be used in cases where sinkhole collapse causes damage to commercial property or non-residential structures (such as a detached garage where no one actually resides).

Maximum coverage limits for structures and contents insured by the program are $200,000 combined for residential property and $1 million combined for commercial property. Policies issued by the program will be in effect for one year.

If the program determines that property is uninsurable, it must disclose necessary improvements or repairs to the owner and then agree to reinspect the property if those improvements or repairs are ever made. If the program refuses to insure property or will only do so on the condition of certain repairs, the owner can appeal the decision to the director within 30 days. The program can't refuse to issue insurance based solely on property's location or an environmental factor beyond the owner's control.

Once a policy has been issued, the program can't cancel it without approval from the program's governing committee, except for the following reasons:

- Nonpayment of premiums.

- Arson.

- Fraud or misrepresentation by an insured.

- A changed condition that has increased the level of risk at the property.

In the event of a proposed cancellation or nonrenewal by the program, the property owner must receive notice at least 30 days prior to the cancellation or nonrenewal. The notice needs to include a clear reason for the decision and information about how to appeal. Appeals can generally be made to the director within 30 days.

Producers who facilitate insurance transactions through the program can receive commissions of 12% for new business and 10% for policies that are being renewed.

<u>Structure of the Missouri FAIR Plan</u>

All property insurers operating in Missouri must participate in the program as part of a joint reinsurance entity. Expenses and responsibilities pertaining to insuring property via the program will be shared by all members based on the amount of property insurance business they do in the state. Regardless of their market share, each participating insurer must contribute to a public education plan that highlights the existence of the program for high-risk properties.

The program is overseen by a governing committee of 13 members. The committee creates the program's budget and is generally authorized to disburse funds on behalf of participating insurers. If a participating insurer wants to cancel insurance issued by the program for reasons other than nonpayment, fraud, misrepresentation, arson or a change in the risk posed by a property, the insurer must receive approval from the committee.

Information For Casualty Producers

The next several sections should be reviewed carefully by all prospective Missouri producers who intend to sell casualty insurance. <u>For purposes of study, they can be ignored by people who only intend to be licensed as property insurance producers.</u>

Approval of Auto Coverage Forms

Auto insurers in Missouri must file their policy forms with the DCI prior to use.

Auto Liability Insurance Requirements

In accordance with Missouri's Motor Vehicle Financial Responsibility Law, vehicle owners can't operate, register or allow someone else to drive a vehicle without adequate liability insurance or some other state-approved method of compensating accident victims.

In most cases, the law will be satisfied by purchasing at least a state-mandated minimum amount of auto liability insurance. However, certain vehicle owners or drivers might be allowed to comply with Missouri requirements by obtaining a bond, depositing a large sum with the state and/or providing state-approved evidence of self-insurance.

Regardless of how the law is satisfied, vehicle owners are required to prove that they can compensate accident victims at least up to the following amounts:

- $25,000 for bodily injury sustained in an accident per person.
- $50,000 for all cases of bodily injury per accident.
- $25,000 for all property damage per accident.

Nonresidents can't operate or allow someone else to operate a vehicle in Missouri unless they're covered for minimum amounts of liability in accordance with auto insurance laws in their home state.

It may be illegal for a non-owner to operate a vehicle in Missouri while knowing that the owner hasn't complied with the state's financial responsibility law. In this case, the non-owner can only operate the vehicle if the non-owner has satisfied the state's financial responsibility law on his or her own.

For a first offense, failure to abide by the state's financial responsibility law is a Class D misdemeanor (a fine of up to $500). Subsequent violations can result in a $500 fine and up to 15 days in jail.

Upon being made aware of a violation of the state's financial responsibility law, the Missouri Department of Revenue can either suspend the person's license or require the person's insurer to impose "points" on the driver. (Too many points can ultimately lead to license suspension.)

License suspension will be automatic if a driver is liable for more than $500 of bodily injury or property damage and hasn't provided proof of financial responsibility to the Department of Revenue within 90 days.

Missouri's financial responsibility law generally doesn't apply to vehicles in storage or not in use.

SR-22 Requirements for Suspended Drivers

Following a license suspension, a driver must provide proof of financial responsibility to the state for at least the next three years. If a license has been suspended more than once, proof of financial responsibility will need to be provided to the state indefinitely.

In most cases, proof of insurance for a previously suspended driver will be provided by the person's insurance company on a form known as an "SR-22." When proof of insurance from an SR-22 is no longer valid or needed, the person's insurance company files another form, known as an "SR-26," with the Department of Revenue. If insurance associated with an SR-22 will be canceled by the insurer, the cancellation can go into effect no earlier than 10 days from the filing of an SR-26. (This general rule doesn't apply when an SR-22 is no longer mandatory for the driver or when coverage is being replaced.)

Fees for filing an SR-22 or SR-26 on a policyholder's behalf must be reasonable and must generally be one-time fees.

Uninsured Motorist Coverage Requirements

Uninsured motorist coverage compensates harmed parties when an accident is caused by someone without insurance. In Missouri, uninsured motorist coverage must also respond when a victim is hit by someone whose insurer has become insolvent.

Missouri drivers must have uninsured motorist coverage for bodily injury up to the following minimum amounts:

- $25,000 for bodily injury sustained in an accident per person.
- $50,000 for all total cases of bodily injury per accident.

Uninsured motorist coverage for property damage isn't required in Missouri.

Underinsured Motorist Coverage Requirements

Underinsured motorist coverage compensates accident victims under their own insurance when an at-fault driver has enough liability insurance to satisfy state requirements but still not enough to fully compensate harmed parties. This coverage isn't mandatory in Missouri.

Medical Payments Coverage

Medical payments coverage is a part of an auto insurance policy that pays for the policyholder's own medical expenses after an accident.

If an injured person in an auto accident is covered by an auto policy's medical payments coverage and by separate health or disability insurance, the medical payments coverage in the auto policy should generally act as primary insurance. If the medical payments coverage is intended to be excess or secondary insurance that only pays when other health or disability policies have been exhausted, the intent must be specified in the policy language, and the policyholder must be charged a reduced rate.

Comprehensive (Other-Than-Collison Coverage)

Comprehensive/other-than-collision coverage compensates a vehicle owner when a covered automobile is lost or damaged by something besides a collision. For example, it might cover a vehicle in cases of fire or theft.

If a driver is insured for comprehensive/other-than-collision coverage, the policy must include loss-of-use coverage that goes into effect after a theft. Benefits must be provided under this portion of the policy after a waiting period of no more than 48 hours after the theft. Benefits pertaining to the loss of use must be equal to at least $10 per day and $300 overall.

Covered Parties in Personal Auto Insurance

Personal auto insurance policies in Missouri must at least cover the following parties:

- The named insured.
- The named insured's spouse who lives in the same household.
- Someone who drives a vehicle with the permission of either the named insured or the named insured's spouse.

If an auto policy intends to exclude accidents involving specific drivers (as opposed to accidents involving specific vehicles regardless of who's driving), the excluded drivers must be specified by the insurer. The named insured must sign an acknowledgment pertaining to any excluded drivers.

Auto Insurance Coverage Territory

Auto insurance policies sold in Missouri must cover accidents anywhere in the United States, U.S. territories and Canada.

Additional Replacement Vehicles

If an auto insurance policy provides coverage for additional or replacement vehicles that are acquired during the policy period, the insurer must give the named insured at least 30 days to report ownership of a new vehicle.

Property Damage Coverage and Installed Items

In general, if a vehicle is covered for property damage, an auto policy can't exclude factory-installed equipment that is attached to the vehicle. However, electronic equipment that is stored in a vehicle but not installed by the manufacturer might be excluded.

Auto Insurance Discrimination

Exclusions in auto insurance policies can't relate directly or indirectly to a driver's:

- Age.
- Place of residence.
- Race.
- Gender.
- Religion.
- Color.
- National origin.
- Ancestry.
- Lawful occupation.

If an auto insurer wants to deny insurance to all people within a particular class or geographic area, it must inform the DCI in advance and provide a rationale for its decision.

Auto Insurance Identification Cards

Auto insurers need to provide an identification card for every vehicle they insure. The card can be a hard copy or in an electronic format but must be kept in the vehicle at all times and shown to law enforcement or anyone investigating an accident. The fact that a card is stored electronically on a driver's phone cannot be used as an excuse by law enforcement to access other information on the phone.

An auto insurance card must contain all of the following information:

- The named insured.
- The insurer's name and address.
- The insurance's effective date.
- The policy number.
- The vehicle's year, model and identification number.
- A statement that the card must be kept with the vehicle and provided on demand.

The insurer must provide a replacement card under the following circumstances:

- When a vehicle is replaced.
- When an additional vehicle is purchased by the insured.
- When the policy number has changed.
- When the named insured requests a replacement card.

In cases where an owner has been allowed to satisfy the state's financial responsibility law by means other than insurance, the Missouri Department of Revenue will issue a card. A binder, receipt or copy of an insurance policy can be used in place of a card as long as it contains the required information.

False Auto Insurance Cards

Creating or distributing false proof of auto insurance in Missouri is a Class E felony (with maximum penalties of $10,000 and four years in prison). Displaying false proof of auto insurance (regardless of who created or distributed it) is a Class B misdemeanor (with maximum penalties of $1,000 and six months in prison).

Insurance for Ridesharing Services

Missouri has special auto liability insurance requirements for drivers who are affiliated with ridesharing services (also known as "transportation network companies"). Unless this special insurance is obtained, a driver's personal auto insurance generally won't cover cases in which a vehicle is being used as part of a ridesharing service.

The amount of required liability insurance will depend on whether a driver is in the process of transporting passengers or is driving alone while still connected to ridesharing technology.

While transporting passengers, drivers providing ridesharing services must be covered for liability up to $1 million. If a driver is connected to ridesharing technology but has no passengers in his or her vehicle, this special insurance must have liability limits of at least the following amounts:

- $50,000 for bodily injury per person.
- $100,000 for bodily injury per accident.
- $25,000 for property damage per accident.

After an accident, drivers must disclose whether they were in the process of transporting passengers or were connected to ridesharing technology. Like other forms of auto insurance, proof of ridesharing liability coverage must be kept with the vehicle and provided upon request.

If one of its drivers doesn't maintain the required amount of ridesharing liability insurance, a ridesharing service must have its own insurance that satisfies the requirement.

Auto Insurance Renewals

Any documents related to renewal of auto insurance (including a bill to renew a policy) must include the following information:

- The policy number.
- The named insured.
- The policy period for the proposed renewal.
- A liberalization clause, unless similar language is already part of the policy. (A liberalization clause essentially states that if additional benefits are provided to new auto insurance policyholders at no cost [either by law or by the insurer's choice], existing policyholders will also receive those benefits.)

Auto Insurance Cancellations

Auto insurance that has been in force in Missouri for at least 60 days can't be canceled by the insurer except for the following reasons:

- Nonpayment.
- A suspended or revoked driver's license. (If a policy insures multiple people, it must remain in force for drivers whose license was not revoked or suspended and can exclude the suspended or revoked driver by name.)

Note the difference between cancellation and nonrenewal. In a cancellation, insurance is ended prior to the policy's stated expiration date. In a nonrenewal, insurance ends as scheduled on the policy's expiration date but can't be extended for another policy period.

Missouri Automobile Insurance Plan

A decision by an insurer to deny, cancel or non-renew someone's auto insurance must be made in writing and include information about the Missouri Automobile Insurance Plan. The plan is intended for high-risk drivers who can't obtain insurance in the regular market.

Auto-Specific Claims Rules

Along with aforementioned claims-related requirements that apply to nearly all Missouri insurers, auto insurers in the state need to comply with the following restrictions:

- An auto insurer can't force accident victims to make a claim on their own insurance rather than seek reimbursement from the at-fault driver's insurer.

- Auto insurers can't force a policyholder to travel an unreasonably long distance to obtain an estimate or repair.

- If an auto insurer sues another driver after an accident, the amount of any deductible paid by an accident victim must be included as part of the insurer's suit. If the insurer obtains a settlement that includes the deductible amount, the amount must be refunded to the victim. (The process by which an insurer takes the place of a policyholder and sues an at-fault party for an accident is generally known as "subrogation.")

- Estimates of auto repairs from the insurer must be reasonable and can include estimates from recommended repair shops. If the insurer will be handling repairs, the vehicle must be restored to its pre-accident condition in a timely manner.

- If a repair estimate is based on the installation of parts that aren't made by the vehicle's manufacturer, the specific parts must be disclosed and be of like kind and quality compared to the originals.

Commercial Casualty Insurance Requirements

Certain requirements in Missouri apply to most kinds of commercial casualty insurance (other than some types of professional malpractice insurance).

Commercial casualty insurance generally can't be canceled without 60 days' notice except for the following causes:

- Nonpayment of premiums.

- Fraud or material misrepresentation by an insured.

- Violations of policy terms and conditions.

- A change in the hazards related to a risk.

- Insurer insolvency.

Similarly, 60 days' notice is required before commercial casualty insurance can be non-renewed by the insurer. Proof of mailing can serve as compliance with this requirement.

Notices of cancellation or nonrenewal must include a clear reason for the insurer's decision. After either a cancellation or nonrenewal, a policyholder can request information about his or her losses over the past three years. The insurer must provide the loss-related information within 30 days of a request.

If an insurer wants to cancel or non-renew commercial casualty insurance for an entire segment of business or an entire class of people, the director must be notified at least 90 days in advance.

Workers Compensation Insurance Required

Missouri businesses generally need to obtain workers compensation insurance if they have five or more employees. Construction businesses need the insurance if they have even one employee.

For the purpose of counting employees, the number generally doesn't include sole proprietors or partners unless they want to be protected by workers compensation in case of injury. Members of an LLC, family members of sole proprietors, family members of business partners, and shareholders with more than a 40 percent ownership interest in a corporation are included in the number by default but might be excludable if certain actions are taken.

Certain large employers in Missouri might be allowed to self-insure for workers compensation and don't necessarily need insurance form an insurance company. Eligibility requirements and application procedures for self-insurance are set by the Missouri Department of Labor.

Workers Compensation Exemptions

Workers compensation benefits in Missouri might not apply to farm workers, domestic employees, real estate agents, certain independent contractors and volunteers at non-profit organizations. However, be aware that a business might be liable for workplace injuries sustained by a contractor if the contractor was performing tasks that were part of the business's regular activities.

Workers Compensation Enforcement for Construction Firms

Cities and counties in Missouri that issue licenses to construction firms can't do so unless a construction firm has provided a certificate of workers compensation insurance or an affidavit indicating that it is exempt from workers compensation requirements.

Workers Compensation Notices

Employers must post a notice of workers compensation protections in a workplace location where it is likely to be seen by all protected employees. If a particular employee is unlikely to see the notice, the information must be provided to that employee in writing. The notice must include the following information and disclaimers:

- That the employer must comply with Missouri workers compensation requirements.

- That workplace injuries should be reported immediately.

- That failure to report workplace injuries within 30 days might jeopardize the person's right to workers compensation.

- That workers compensation fraud is illegal.

- That additional information is available from the Missouri Workers Compensation Division.

- Contact information for the employer's workers compensation insurer (or, if the business is allowed to self-insure for workers compensation, the person designated by the employer to report workplace injuries).

- Contact information for the Missouri Workers Compensation Division.

Issuing Workers Compensation Insurance

Workers compensation insurance policies and endorsements must be issued within 60 days of receiving a completed application for insurance. If insurance is being renewed, the renewed coverage must be issued within 60 days of collecting a deposit premium from the policyholder.

If premiums for workers compensation will increase, the business must receive 60 days of advance notice. If the premiums for workers compensation might change due to an experience modification factor or other variables during the policy period, the potential for an increase must be disclosed as part of a special endorsement to the policy. (In general, an experience modification factor allows an insurer to adjust premiums based on a business's previous workers compensation losses over a particular time period, such as the previous three or five years.)

Premium audits in workers compensation must be completed no later than 120 days after a policy's expiration or cancellation. Premium audits allow an insurer to adjust the cost of insurance retroactively after doing a careful review of a business's records and calculating the true size of the insured risk.)

Workers Compensation Determinations Review Board

A five-person Workers Compensation Determinations Review Board can be utilized if an employer disagrees with the amount it is being charged for workers compensation insurance.

Limits on Workers Compensation Benefits

In general, workers compensation won't provide benefits when a person's work wasn't the cause of an injury, illness or death. Similarly, benefits generally won't apply when an injury or illness occurs coincidentally at work but could've reasonably happened at any time.

Employees are generally not covered by Missouri workers compensation laws when they're injured in an auto accident while driving to or from work.

Workers Compensation and Lost Wages

Employees who lose income due to a workplace injury or illness won't be compensated for the first three days of an absence unless the injury or illness ultimately forces them to miss at least 14 days of work. Days of work are based on when an employer is otherwise open for business.

Payments for lost wages are to be made generally on the same schedule as the person's regular wage or salary but no less frequently than every two weeks. Payments for lost income that are more than 30 days late must be increased by 10 percent.

Workers Compensation and Total Disability

In Missouri, a "total disability" exists when a person is unable to perform any work (rather than just his or her regular job duties).

If a total disability is likely to be permanent, compensation for lost wages is generally expected to continue until the person dies and will be based on 2/3 of the person's pre-disability income (up to a maximum of 105% of the average wage in Missouri and with a minimum of $40 per week).

If rehabilitation eventually allows someone with a permanent total disability to perform work again, payments for lost income on this basis will stop, but the person's case will remain open with the potential for later review.

Workers Compensation Death Benefits

Death from a workplace injury can result in workers compensation benefits if death occurs within 300 weeks of the injury.

If a workplace accident or illness results in death, the employer must pay for reasonable end-of-life expenses up to at least $5,000.

If the deceased employee had dependents, death benefits must be paid based on 2/3 of the person's pre-accident compensation (up to a maximum of 105% of the average wage in Missouri and with a minimum of $40 per week). Death benefits might end or be reduced if a surviving spouse remarries or a surviving child reaches adulthood.

For the purpose of identifying appropriate recipients for death benefits, employers must maintain a list of each employee's dependents. Upon receiving death benefits, beneficiaries must periodically provide updates to Missouri's Workers Compensation Division regarding their continued eligibility for compensation (such as information about their marital status or age).

Workers Compensation and Certain Workplace Illnesses

Special calculations are used to compensate workers for lost income when they're exposed to toxic elements that result in cancer or serious lung diseases. In general, these workers will receive 200 percent of the average Missouri wage for 100 weeks. If a worker dies during the 100-week period, payments will continue for the person's dependents. If the person dies but leaves no dependents, the remaining benefits will be provided to the person's estate in a lump sum.

Required Safety Management Services

Each insurer offering workers compensation insurance in Missouri must provide safety management services to its policyholders upon request. An insurer can contract with a third party to provide these services. The insurer must keep records regarding the services' effectiveness and alert the state when a policyholder utilizes them.

Upon learning that a business has bought workers compensation insurance for the first time or has switched its insurance to another carrier, the state must make the business aware of available safety services. A state database of safety consultants will be maintained for this purpose.

Fraudulent Workers Compensation Claims

Workers compensation payments that are received fraudulently must be repaid to either the employer or the employer's insurance company.

Associations and Professional Liability Insurance

Certain types of licensed professionals have the option of forming an association for the purpose of providing malpractice or professional liability insurance to itself and its members. This requires the filing of the following items with the DCI:

- Documents establishing the formation of the association.
- Bylaws.
- Member eligibility requirements.
- Purpose of the association.
- Various explanations of how the association will be funded.
- A $100 licensing fee (payable every year).

In general, the association will be treated like a mutual insurance company under Missouri tax law. Individual members can't receive profits or income from the association except in the form of insurance payments. Insurance-related dividends can be provided to members but only if the association will continue to operate with a budget surplus after providing the dividends.

Missouri Medical Malpractice Joint Underwriting Association

The Missouri Medical Malpractice Joint Underwriting Association exists to provide malpractice insurance to medical providers who can't obtain affordable coverage in the regular market. The association can issue policies with limits of $1 million per claimant and $3 million for all claims per policy period. All casualty insurers in Missouri must assist in the association's funding and administration.

Chapter Key Points

- In Missouri, the responsibilities of protecting insurance consumers and enforcing the state's various insurance laws belong to the Missouri Department of Commerce and Insurance (DCI).
- The DCI is overseen by a director who is appointed by the governor.

- Examiners working on behalf of the director must be provided free and convenient access to records.

- Insurers selling insurance in or intended for use in Missouri must be authorized to do so by obtaining a certificate of authority from the DCI.

- In general, an individual who sells, solicits or negotiates insurance in exchange for compensation must have a producer license.

- In general, producers who are licensed in the same line of authority in another state can be issued a Missouri license without needing to pass a state exam.

- If a producer is licensed in another state and becomes a Missouri resident, the producer must apply to become a resident producer within 90 days.

- A limited lines producer is a specially licensed insurance producer who can only sell very particular kinds of insurance that make up a very narrow portion of the insurance market. In Missouri, a limited lines producer might only sell travel insurance or various forms of credit insurance. A limited lines producer doesn't need to pass a state licensing exam but must abide by nearly all other requirements for Missouri producers.

- Producer licenses are issued for two years and can remain in force for subsequent two-year periods if the producer remains in good standing with the DCI, pays a $100 renewal fee and satisfies continuing education requirements.

- In general, Missouri insurance producers must complete 16 hours of continuing education during each two-year licensing period. At least three hours must relate to ethics and Missouri law.

- A producer who fails to renew a license by the renewal deadline must immediately stop selling insurance but can reinstate the license by completing any remaining continuing education requirement and paying a reinstatement fee. The reinstatement fee will be equal to $100 plus an additional $25 for each month that has passed since the renewal deadline. A license that isn't reinstated within 12 months will be terminated.

- A producer must report any change of address or legal name to the DCI within 30 days.

- A business entity performing the same services as an individual producer (such as an insurance agency or an insurance brokerage firm) must have its own producer license. The business must pay all applicable licensing fees and designate one Missouri-licensed producer who will be ultimately responsible for its compliance with state insurance laws and rules.

- If an insurer terminates a relationship with an appointed producer for an illegal act, the DCI must be notified within 30 days.

- It's illegal for an unlicensed person to accept compensation for activities that require a producer license. Similarly, a producer or insurer can't compensate an unlicensed person for selling, soliciting or negotiating insurance.

- Compensation for a licensed producer can't be shared with a policyholder ("rebated") as an incentive to purchase insurance.

- In general, compensation that must be paid by the consumer to a producer (other than commission on an insurance transaction) must be disclosed in advance.

- Copies of compensation disclosures must be kept for three years.

- Money obtained from insurance consumers must be held by producers in a fiduciary capacity (requiring a heightened level of care) and can't be misappropriated, converted, mixed or commingled with other funds.

- Money held by a producer must be provided to its rightful owner as soon as possible but no later than 30 days.

- In general, insurance in Missouri can't be refused, canceled or non-renewed based on the following factors:

  - Race.

  - Gender.

  - Color.

  - Religion.

  - National origin.

  - Age of the insured.

  - Location of the insured's residence.

  - Ancestry.

  - Occupation (as long as the insured's occupation is legal).

  - Military service.

  - The fact that a consumer has been denied insurance or had insurance canceled or non-renewed in the past.

- In all lines of insurance, it's also illegal in Missouri to limit coverage amounts, refuse to offer insurance or refuse to renew insurance on the basis of:

  - Gender.

  - Marital status.

- In addition to facing potential lawsuits from consumers, insurance companies can be fined by the DCI for engaging in "unfair claims settlement practices." Fines are possible whenever an insurer knowingly engages in an unfair practice or unknowingly engages in such behavior on a routine basis.

- All property and casualty insurers that are authorized to do business in Missouri must participate in the Missouri Property and Casualty Insurance Guaranty Association. If an insurer becomes insolvent and can't honor its claims-paying responsibilities, the association can compensate the impacted claimants. Other than for workers compensation claims, the association is not obligated to pay any claims larger than $300,000.

- If cancellation of property insurance results in a refund owed to the policyholder, the refund must be provided within 30 days.

- The Missouri Basic Property Insurance Inspection and Placement Program (sometimes known as Missouri's "FAIR Plan") can insure residential or commercial buildings when coverage can't be obtained in the regular market. Since the properties utilizing the program generally represent a higher risk of loss, the available insurance will generally be less comprehensive and more expensive than traditional property insurance.

- Regardless of how the law is satisfied, vehicle owners are required to prove that they can compensate accident victims at least up to the following amounts:

- o $25,000 for bodily injury sustained in an accident per person.

- o $50,000 for all cases of bodily injury per accident.

- o $25,000 for all property damage per accident.

- Missouri drivers must have uninsured motorist coverage for bodily injury up to the following minimum amounts:

- o $25,000 for bodily injury sustained in an accident per person.

- o $50,000 for all total cases of bodily injury per accident.

- While transporting passengers, drivers providing ridesharing services must be covered for liability up to $1 million. If a driver is connected to ridesharing technology but has no passengers in his or her vehicle, this special insurance must have liability limits of at least the following amounts:

- o $50,000 for bodily injury per person.

- o $100,000 for bodily injury per accident.

- o $25,000 for property damage per accident.

- A decision by an insurer to deny, cancel or non-renew someone's auto insurance must be made in writing and include information about the Missouri Automobile Insurance Plan. The plan is intended for high-risk drivers who can't obtain insurance in the regular market.

- Missouri businesses generally need to obtain workers compensation insurance if they have five or more employees. Construction businesses need the insurance if they have even one employee.

- The Missouri Medical Malpractice Joint Underwriting Association exists to provide malpractice insurance to medical providers who can't obtain affordable coverage in the regular market. The association can issue policies with limits of $1 million per claimant and $3 million for all claims per policy period. All casualty insurers in Missouri must assist in the association's funding and administration.

PROPERTY AND CASUALTY GENERAL PRACTICE EXAMS

The following practice exams are intended to judge your understanding of some of the most important topics on insurance licensing tests regardless of your state. (Practice tests that are specific to your state appear in a later section.)

Answer keys can be found later in this book. However, to accurately determine your comprehension of the material, you should answer each question before looking up the correct response. If you answer a question incorrectly, we encourage you to review the relevant chapter(s) of the book carefully again. Don't just search for correct answers!

Property Exam: #1

1. Portions of premiums that might still be refunded to consumers upon a cancellation are known as:

    A. Deposit premium
    B. Earned premium
    C. Unearned premium
    D. Modified premium

2. Which of the following is an example of risk transfer?

    A. Refusing to fly on planes
    B. Installing a smoke alarm
    C. Diversifying a retirement portfolio
    D. Buying an insurance product

3. Which is the best definition of open-peril coverage?

    A. All losses will be covered up to a certain amount.
    B. All perils will be covered unless they are specifically excluded in the policy.
    C. All perils will be covered as long as they are specifically mentioned in the policy.
    D. Coverage will remain largely ambiguous until a loss actually occurs.

4. With respect to insurance contracts, what is generally considered to be an offer given to the insurer for acceptance?

    A. An application
    B. Premiums
    C. An endorsement
    D. A certificate of prior insurance

5. Who is the person who owns and controls an insurance policy?

    A. Anyone insured by the policy
    B. The policy beneficiary
    C. The policyholder
    D. The insurance agent of record

6. A contract in which there is an understood possibility that one party might benefit more than the other can best be described as a(n):

    A. Contract of adhesion
    B. Aleatory contract
    C. Unilateral contract
    D. Bilateral contract

7. In most states, what is the minimum age for entering into a contact?

    A. 15
    B. 16
    C. 18
    D. 21

8. A court has been presented with ambiguous language in an insurance policy. In general, the court will rule in whose favor and why?

    A. The insurer, because consumers have an obligation to read their policies and ask questions.
    B. The consumer, because insurance companies have more money to defend themselves in court.
    C. The insurer, because it must abide by solvency requirements by not paying all claims.
    D. The consumer, because the insurer is the party with control over the policy's exact wording.

9. In insurance, what is the difference between a representation and a warranty?

    A. Warranties must continue to be literally true throughout the insurance contract's duration.
    B. Representations must continue to be literally true throughout the insurance contract's duration.
    C. Unlike representations, warranties only involve material facts.
    D. Representations give the insurer broader authority to rescind a policy.

10. Which is the best example of a policy rescission?

    A. An insurer agrees to continue coverage until the end of the policy period but refuses to extend it.
    B. The consumer gets to keep insurance money already provided by the insurer but will have no coverage moving forward.
    C. An insurer charges a higher rate in order to renew someone's insurance policy.
    D. Premiums are returned to the consumer, and coverage is treated as if it never existed.

11. Which type of contract is only enforceable by one of the parties in a court of law?

    A. Unilateral contract
    B. Bilateral contract
    C. Contract of adhesion
    D. Waiver and estoppel

12. What type of consideration is given by the consumer as part of an insurance contract?

    A. An application
    B. A signature
    C. A referral
    D. Premiums

13. In return for not having to be subjected to a property inspection, a homeowner is expected to disclose relevant risk factors to an insurance agent before coverage is issued. This is based on the concept of:

A. Concealment
B. Waiver and estoppel
C. Adverse selection
D. Utmost good faith

14. Which type of insurer is owned by its policyholders?

A. Domestic
B. Foreign
C. Stock
D. Mutual

15. Which type of insurer is utilized when coverage is otherwise unavailable in the traditional market?

A. Domestic insurer
B. Foreign insurer
C. Mutual insurer
D. Excess and surplus insurer

16. Who is the principal in an agency relationship?

A. The party representing someone else
B. The party being represented by someone else
C. The party receiving services from someone else
D. The party paying compensation to someone else

17. Who is likely to have binding authority in an insurance transaction?

A. An actuary setting insurance rates
B. A public adjuster representing a claimant
C. An insurance broker representing a client
D. A property and casualty agent representing a carrier

18. Insurance professionals who evaluate applicants and decide whether to accept risks are known as:

A. Actuaries
B. Brokers
C. Underwriters
D. Agents

19. Which of the following is the best definition of a non-admitted carrier?

A. An unlicensed producer
B. An insurer from another state
C. An unlicensed insurer
D. An insurer from another country

20. Traditionally, what has been the basic difference between an insurance agent and an insurance broker?

    A. Brokers are more likely to issue binders.
    B. Brokers are less likely to work in commercial lines insurance.
    C. Agents do not have contractual relationships with carriers.
    D. Agents tend to represent carriers, whereas brokers tend to represent consumers.

21. A consumer provides information to an insurance agent. Under the common law of agency:

    A. The information is considered unknown to the insurer.
    B. The information is considered known to the insurer.
    C. The insurer can't charge a higher premium based on the information.
    D. The information can only be disclosed to the carrier with written consent.

22. What is the relationship between the covered perils in commercial property insurance policy and the covered perils in a business interruption policy?

    A. The insurance covering the business's property tends to address more perils.
    B. The insurance for business interruption tends to address more perils.
    C. The covered perils tend to be similar across both types of insurance.
    D. Only a business interruption policy is likely to respond to flood-related losses.

23. An insurer is allowed to sue someone for damages as if it were the policyholder. This is done through:

    A. Subrogation
    B. Arbitration
    C. Mediation
    D. Assignment

24. In exchange for covering high-risk properties as part of a FAIR plan, private insurance companies receive help with catastrophic claims. This help is provided in the form of:

    A. Premium subsidies
    B. Tax credits
    C. Reinsurance
    D. Advertising

25. A business that is repairing a customer's property and loses it cannot make a claim and be compensated by the owner's insurance. This is explained in which clause of a property policy?

    A. Subrogation
    B. Liberalization
    C. Mortgagee
    D. No benefit to bailee

26. What is the purpose of a FAIR Plan?

    A. To provide affordable insurance to low-risk applicants
    B. To provide needed property insurance to high-risk applicants
    C. To promote redlining among property insurance companies
    D. To prevent adverse selection in the property insurance market

27. What is the purpose of a guaranty fund?

    A. To compensate claimants from insolvent insurers
    B. To ensure that claimants receive the full amount owed to them
    C. To provide reinsurance for private insurance companies
    D. To provide insurance to high-risk drivers

28. Which term is used to describe when insurance coverage begins and ends?

    A. Policy period
    B. Elimination period
    C. Coverage territory
    D. Free-look period

29. Which clause explains how insurance benefits will be calculated when a loss is covered by multiple policies?

    A. Subrogation clause
    B. Coinsurance clause
    C. Loss payable clause
    D. Other insurance clause

30. Cancellation that is initiated by the policyholder and involves a smaller refund of premiums is known as a:

    A. Flat cancellation
    B. Pro-rata cancellation
    C. Short-rate cancellation
    D. Rescission

31. As part of a claims dispute, the insurer and the insured are required to abide by the decision of a third party. This is an example of:

    A. Mediation
    B. Arbitration
    C. Utmost good faith
    D. Loss valuation

32. As a new standard practice, an insurer decides to omit an exclusion in order to attract new buyers. Existing policyholders might also benefit from this change depending on the wording of the:

    A. Liberalization clause
    B. Other insurance clause
    C. Conditions clause
    D. Declarations page

33. Which part of a property insurance policy is the insurer's basic contractual agreement to provide benefits to the policyholder?

    A. Principle of indemnity
    B. Declarations page
    C. Insuring agreement
    D. Loss payable clause

34. A home has been damaged by multiple perils. This is known as:

    A. Catastrophic risk
    B. Concurrent causation
    C. Adverse selection
    D. Split limits

35. Which is the best definition of "residence premises" with regard to homeowners insurance?

    A. The dwelling where relatives of the insured reside
    B. Detached structures where residence employees reside
    C. The dwelling, structure and grounds identified on the declarations page
    D. The place where a homeowner has personal liability coverage

36. Which type of loss would typically still be excluded from an open-peril homeowners insurance policy?

    A. Windstorm
    B. Fire
    C. Flood
    D. Theft

37. A dwelling policy typically excludes losses related to:

    A. Fire
    B. Lightning
    C. Explosion
    D. Personal liability and theft

38. An HO-3 policy uses which cause-of-loss form?

    A. Basic
    B. Broad
    C. Special
    D. Named-peril

39. Which policy is historically considered a building block that led to today's homeowners insurance products?

    A. New York Standard Fire Policy
    B. Commercial package policy
    C. Personal property floater
    D. BOP

40. A loss caused by which of the following perils is most likely to have a separate, percentage-based deductible in some states?

    A. Fire
    B. Windstorm
    C. Snow
    D. Personal liability

41. Which type of loss is most likely to trigger a special limit of liability for valuables?

    A. Fire
    B. Theft
    C. Flood
    D. Hail

42. Assuming guaranteed-replacement-cost coverage is not an option, what is the greatest amount of coverage that is likely to be available for a home?

    A. Functional replacement cost
    B. Extended replacement cost
    C. Replacement cost
    D. Market value

43. A homeowner suffers a $50,000 partial loss after a fire. After the loss, the insurance company determines that the home's replacement cost is $200,000. However, the homeowner only has $190,000 of coverage. Has the consumer met the coinsurance requirement?

    A. Yes
    B. No

44. Most kinds of commercial property insurance won't cover losses caused by which of the following perils?

    A. Fire
    B. Windstorm
    C. Pollution
    D. Vandalism

45. A homeowner is carrying heavy furniture from one room to another and drops it after slipping on a wet floor. In regard to property insurance, the floor damage in this case is a(n):

    A. Direct loss
    B. Indirect loss
    C. Consequential loss
    D. Total loss

46. Which of the following parties would have an insurable interest in a home?

    A. The former owner
    B. A prospect who becomes interested in the home during an open house
    C. A family member who expects to inherit the home following a death
    D. A creditor who provided a mortgage loan as part of the purchase

47. A burglar broke into a home and stole the owner's jewelry. If the homeowner insured the dwelling for $500,000 with an HO-3 policy, what is the most the insurer would pay as compensation, assuming no deductible?

    A. $0
    B. $1,500
    C. $2,500
    D. $250,000

48. Coverage F in homeowners insurance will pay for medical expenses that are incurred for within how long after an accident?

    A. One year
    B. Two years
    C. Three years
    D. Five years

49. Which type of loss would be covered by an HO-1 policy?

    A. Wind
    B. Sudden discharge of water
    C. Damage by a stray creature
    D. Weight of ice, snow or sleet

50. In general, vacancy clauses in property insurance will go into effect if a vacancy is longer than:

    A. 10 days
    B. 30 days
    C. 45 days
    D. 60 days

Property Exam #2

1. Which of the following is considered a package policy for small businesses?

    A. Business income insurance
    B. BOP
    C. Commercial package policy
    D. Commercial general liability insurance

2. A business is concerned about what might happen if one of its important vendors were to temporarily shut down. Which type of insurance addresses this issue?

    A. Loss-of-use coverage
    B. Contingent business interruption insurance
    C. Builders risk insurance
    D. Block insurance

3. By default, commercial property insurance tends to cover a business's property up to its:

    A. Replacement cost
    B. Extended replacement cost
    C. Agreed value
    D. Actual cash value

4. With a broker's help, a business has chosen to insure its property by using the intermediate cause-of-loss form. Which ISO form was likely used?

    A. Basic
    B. Broad
    C. Special
    D. All-risk

5. In general, how will insurance respond when a loss involves electronic data?

    A. The insurer will immediately replace the hardware that stored the data.
    B. The insurer will inquire about the business's data security plan.
    C. The data will be covered by standard cyber insurance products.
    D. Traditional insurance products will only cover a small portion of the loss or not cover it at all.

6. Which of the following is the best definition of a direct writer?

    A. An insurer that only sells insurance to businesses
    B. An insurer that is licensed in only one state
    C. An insurer whose agents work as employees of the carrier
    D. An insurer whose agents work as independent contractors

7. What do commercial property insurers receive from the federal government in exchange for offering terrorism-risk insurance?

    A. Free onsite inspections of properties by anti-terrorism experts
    B. Tax credits based on each carrier's market share
    C. Federal reinsurance in case of catastrophic terrorism losses
    D. The ability to set rates for personal lines insurance without any state-level intervention

8. What is the typical coinsurance requirement for homeowners insurance?

    A. 50% of actual cash value
    B. 65% of market value
    C. 75% of functional replacement cost
    D. 80% of replacement cost

9. What is the definition of actual cash value?

    A. Replacement cost
    B. Reconstruction cost
    C. Market value
    D. Replacement cost minus depreciation

10. In order to receive compensation from an insurance company, which document must be completed after a loss?

    A. Proof-of-loss form
    B. Application
    C. Waiver and estoppel
    D. Endorsement

11. Which term relates to the manner in which consumers and insurers are expected to act in an insurance transaction?

    A. Exclusive remedy
    B. Indemnification
    C. Morale hazard
    D. Utmost good faith

12. Which of the following is the best definition of "risk"?

    A. Economic loss suffered by a policyholder
    B. Uncertainty surrounding an event
    C. The unlikely chance of something good happening
    D. A purely environmental factor influencing the severity of a loss

13. Which of the following is an example of a morale hazard?

    A. A homeowner feeling safe enough to leave the home's front door unlocked
    B. A life insurance beneficiary plotting to murder a policyholder
    C. A property insurance customer being forced to pay a deductible
    D. A landlord installing a burglar alarm at a rental property

14. Which cause-of-loss form covers a dwelling on an all-risk/open-peril basis?

    A. Basic
    B. Broad
    C. Special
    D. Modified

15. Which of the following describes a declarations page?

    A. A collection of information used to evaluate risk
    B. A consent document to transfer policy rights
    C. A first-page summary of an insurance policy
    D. The insurer's promise to insure a consumer

16. Rather than directly lying on an application, a consumer fails to disclose material facts. This is known as:

    A. Misrepresentation
    B. Warranty
    C. Estoppel
    D. Concealment

17. A captive insurance agent can sell insurance:

    A. From one company
    B. From multiple companies
    C. Only in one state
    D. Only to friends and family

18. Which structure would typically NOT be covered under Coverage B of a homeowners insurance policy?

    A. A barn
    B. A detached shed
    C. A fence
    D. An attached garage

19. Property insurance that subtracts for depreciation is called:

    A. Market value coverage
    B. Agreed value coverage
    C. Replacement cost coverage
    D. Actual cash value coverage

20. Which policy form is typically used to insure a condo unit?

    A. HO-1
    B. HO-2
    C. HO-5
    D. HO-6

21. An unexpected expense or decrease in value is known as:

    A. Depreciation
    B. A hazard
    C. A peril
    D. A loss

22. Which of the following is an example of a peril?

   A. Fire
   B. Carelessness
   C. Inferior building materials
   D. Leaving a window open while away on vacation

23. Who at an insurance company decides whether to accept a risk?

   A. A broker
   B. An actuary
   C. An underwriter
   D. A claims adjuster

24. The coinsurance requirements for business interruption insurance are based on a business's:

   A. Payroll
   B. Income
   C. Property values
   D. Credit rating

25. A homeowner suffers $1,000 in insured losses and has a $250 deductible. How much of the insured losses will be covered?

   A. $500
   B. $750
   C. $1,000
   D. $1,250

26. Which of the following is true about a certificate of insurance?

   A. It is also known as a "binder."
   B. It overrides the contents of an insurance policy.
   C. It is proof of insurance provided to a third party.
   D. It is most commonly used in personal lines property and casualty insurance.

27. Upon being asked to increase someone's insurance, a producer changes the dollar limit listed on a certificate of insurance and hands the certificate to the policyholder. What is the status of this change?

   A. The change will not go into effect until the policy is changed.
   B. The change is in effect if the certificate is notarized.
   C. The change is in effect right away if the agent is a captive agent.
   D. The change is in effect right away if the producer's license is active.

28. Owners of homes in special flood hazard areas generally:

   A. Must purchase flood insurance in order to get a mortgage loan
   B. Cannot obtain insurance from the National Flood Insurance Program
   C. Must remodel in order to make their home compliant with local building codes
   D. Can only obtain insurance from a FAIR Plan

29. A consumer wants to insure a residential, non-owner-occupied building with two units occupied by renters. Which type of insurance would likely be the most appropriate choice for this prospect?

    A. Homeowners insurance
    B. Renters insurance
    C. A dwelling policy
    D. Commercial property insurance

30. The Terrorism Risk Insurance Act requires that terrorism-risk insurance be made available for which type of insurance?

    A. Personal lines insurance
    B. Homeowners insurance
    C. Commercial property insurance
    D. Personal property floater insurance

31. Which type of loss is typically excluded from an all-risk homeowners insurance policy?

    A. Fire
    B. Theft
    C. Explosion
    D. Earth movement

32. Which of the following is included within the personal liability portion of homeowners insurance?

    A. Defense costs
    B. Pollution liability coverage
    C. Risk mitigation services
    D. Professional malpractice insurance

33. Which type of insurance insures each item in a collection on an individual, stand-alone basis?

    A. Blanket coverage
    B. Scheduled property coverage
    C. Pair and set coverage
    D. Mysterious disappearance coverage

34. An owner's dog has bitten a stranger and caused bodily injury. Which type of insurance is most likely to cover the owner?

    A. Coverage A of homeowners insurance
    B. Coverage E of homeowners insurance
    C. Coverage F of a dwelling policy
    D. A scheduled property endorsement

35. Which part of a dwelling or homeowners insurance policy is designed to cover personal property and belongings?

    A. Coverage A
    B. Coverage B
    C. Coverage C
    D. Coverage D

36. Which is the best definition of a domestic insurer?

    A. An insurer from another state
    B. An insurer from another country
    C. An insurer in its home state
    D. An unlicensed insurer selling in the excess and surplus market

37. Which of the following is another name for an insurance policy's dollar limit?

    A. Conditions
    B. Declarations
    C. Definitions
    D. Limit of liability

38. HO-2 and HO-3 policies are generally designed to cover the dwelling up to its:

    A. Replacement cost
    B. Market value
    C. Agreed value
    D. Actual cash value

39. DP-2 and HO-2 policies use which cause-of-loss form?

    A. Basic
    B. Broad
    C. Special
    D. Open-peril

40. In homeowners insurance, which coverage pertains to a dwelling?

    A. Coverage A
    B. Coverage B
    C. Coverage C
    D. Coverage D

41. Which type of loss might only be covered by dwelling insurance by adding the proper endorsement?

    A. Fire
    B. Loss of use
    C. Theft
    D. Damage to detached structures

42. Regarding business interruption insurance, what is meant by term "continuing operating expense"?

    A. An expense that is designed to reduce the size or duration of a loss
    B. An expense that is caused by an unexpected interruption
    C. An expense that would exist regardless of an interruption
    D. An expense paid by the insurer with no impact on the limit of liability

43. After a fire loss, a business and its insurer believe it will take approximately 120 days to reopen. Regarding business interruption insurance, the 120-day period is considered the:

    A. Policy period
    B. Period of restoration
    C. Extended reporting period
    D. Retroactive date

44. A sudden or prolonged event that results in a loss is a(n):

    A. Accident
    B. Occurrence
    C. Hazard
    D. Liability

45. A homeowner has $100,000 of contents coverage and suffers damage to property that is stored at another dwelling. The most that the insurer will likely pay to replace the damaged property would be:

    A. $0
    B. $10,000
    C. $50,000
    D. $100,000

46. Local authorities are prohibiting a homeowner from entering her property due to a natural disaster in the area. How long will she be covered for extra expenses associated with the loss of use?

    A. Three days
    B. One week
    C. Two weeks
    D. Indefinitely

47. What is Coverage F in homeowners insurance intended to cover?

    A. Medical costs incurred by the homeowner
    B. Property damage incurred by visitors
    C. Medical costs incurred by third parties due to the homeowner's negligence
    D. Medical costs incurred by third parties regardless of fault

48. Which peril would be covered by an HO-3 policy but not an HO-2 policy?

    A. Wind
    B. Freezing of pipes
    C. Weight of snow, ice or sleet
    D. Damage to the dwelling from a stray creature

49. A covered peril has resulted in a tree falling and blocking a homeowner's driveway. Assuming an HO-2 policy with $200,000 of dwelling coverage and no deductible, how much will the insurer to replace the tree?

 A. $500
 B. $1,000
 C. $200,000
 D. $205,000

50. The transfer of rights in an insurance policy from one party to another is called:

 A. Assignment
 B. Application
 C. Adhesion
 D. Endorsement

Property Exam #3

1. The typical coinsurance clause requires that homeowners insure their dwellings for at least which percentage of replacement cost?

    A. 50%
    B. 75%
    C. 80%
    D. 100%

2. Insurance is an example of:

    A. Risk retention
    B. Risk transfer
    C. Risk avoidance
    D. Risk shouldering

3. What consideration is given by the consumer to the insurance company as part of an insurance contract?

    A. Premium
    B. The application
    C. Utmost good faith
    D. Good field underwriting

4. Which of the following is an example of a moral hazard?

    A. Carelessness
    B. Forgetting to fix a leaky roof
    C. Failing to pay an insurance premium
    D. The temptation to commit insurance fraud

5. Which of the following is NOT an example of a peril?

    A. Fire
    B. Earthquake
    C. Flood
    D. Frayed wiring

6. Which type of insurance is used to insure a business in the event of an unexpected shutdown?

    A. Business interruption insurance
    B. Inland marine insurance
    C. Commercial package policies
    D. Business owners liability insurance

7. Which type of insurance is intended for people with a vested interest in a ship's safe journey?

    A. Block insurance
    B. Ocean marine insurance
    C. Personal indemnity insurance
    D. Personal property floater insurance

8. A family has rented a new apartment in an owner-occupied building. What type of insurance would most likely be used to insure their belongings?

    A. An HO-3 policy
    B. An HO-4 policy
    C. A personal property floater
    D. The landlord's homeowners insurance

9. Which of the following is an example of a speculative risk?

    A. The risk of fire
    B. The risk of disability
    C. The risk of gambling
    D. The risk of premature death

10. Cancellation that is initiated by the insured and involves a potentially smaller return of premiums is known as a:

    A. Full cancellation
    B. Short-rate cancellation
    C. Pro-rata cancellation
    D. Flat-rate cancellation

11. Which of the following is the least likely to be "an insured" under a homeowners insurance policy?

    A. The person named on the declarations page
    B. The spouse of the person named on the declarations page
    C. A young child living with another insured
    D. An adult child of the named insured while living offsite

12. Which of the following is the result of the McCarran-Ferguson Act?

    A. Insurance agents must obtain surety bonds.
    B. Insurance regulation is typically done by the individual states.
    C. Insurance regulation is typically done by the federal government.
    D. Insurance companies must implement privacy protection programs.

13. Which type of property will typically have a special limit of liability for coverage when a loss is caused by theft?

    A. Furniture
    B. Fixtures
    C. Jewelry
    D. Televisions

14. Insurance that is designed to cover all items in a collection is generally known as:

    A. Floater coverage
    B. Bailee coverage
    C. Blanket coverage
    D. Specific insurance

15. Insurance companies attempt to reduce morale hazard by making consumers responsible for a portion of losses. This is demonstrated by:

    A. Requiring policyholders to pay a deductible
    B. Waiving coinsurance requirements after a total loss
    C. Allowing consumers to add endorsement to standard policies
    D. Returning a portion of premiums after a cancellation

16. Which of the following is NOT a common exclusion in property insurance policies?

    A. Wind
    B. Flood
    C. War
    D. Earth movement

17. Which of the following is NOT a common responsibility of insurance producers?

    A. Selling insurance for insurance companies
    B. Analyzing the insurance needs of consumers
    C. Proper handling of funds intended for insurers
    D. Helping the public interpret insurance laws

18. An insurance consumer should be restored to the position he or she was in directly prior to a loss, no better and no worse. This philosophy is known as:

    A. Utmost good faith
    B. The law of large numbers
    C. The principle of indemnity
    D. The pooling of risks

19. What is a peril?

    A. The cause of a loss
    B. An environmental factor that increases the likelihood of a loss
    C. An environmental factor that increases the severity of a loss
    D. An unexpected decrease in economic value

20. Following a shutdown, business interruption insurance is intended to provide benefits until the coverage limit has been reached or until which date?

    A. The end of the policy period
    B. The policy's renewal date
    C. The end of the period of restoration
    D. The end of a federal disaster declaration

21. Which of the following is an example of a pure risk?

    A. The risk of flood
    B. The risk of gambling
    C. The risk of starting a new business
    D. The risk of introducing a new product

22. Insurance involves an element of chance. This makes an insurance policy which type of contract?

    A. Contract of adhesion
    B. Unilateral contract
    C. Aleatory contract
    D. Personal contract

23. The former owner of a home cannot collect insurance benefits when it burns down. This is based on which concept?

    A. Insurable interest
    B. Assignment
    C. Subrogation
    D. Attractive nuisance

24. Which type of insurance is typically purchased by businesses specializing in repairing other people's property?

    A. Bailee's insurance
    B. Block insurance
    C. Builders risk insurance
    D. Malpractice insurance

25. Which of the following businesses is most likely covered by homeowners insurance for liability?

    A. A lemonade stand run by a homeowner's child
    B. A valet service in a residential area
    C. A one-person business not engaged in professional advice
    D. A doctor performing medical procedures at a home office

26. A business buys insurance in case one of its suppliers needs to shut down due to property damage. The supplier's location is known as the:

    A. Dependent property
    B. Dominant property
    C. Contingent property
    D. Scheduled property

27. Which type of insurance is used to cover commercial property that will be shipped?

    A. Marine insurance
    B. Differences in conditions insurance
    C. Businessowners policy
    D. Personal articles floater

28. Builders risk insurance is intended for:

    A. A building under construction and the materials that will become part of it
    B. Construction firms who can't obtain workers compensation insurance
    C. A builder's tools and other equipment that will be used on building sites
    D. Homeowners associations that need to insure a community's common elements

29. What is the main difference between a commercial package policy and a BOP?

A. A commercial package policy is only intended for established businesses.
B. A commercial package policy only insures against various forms of liability insurance.
C. A BOP is only intended for certain types of small businesses.
D. A BOP combines property and casualty insurance into one policy.

30. In addition to having the appropriate license, producers generally must complete a special training course before selling:

A. Excess and surplus insurance
B. Inland marine insurance
C. Flood insurance
D. Builders risk insurance

31. In homeowners insurance, structures are generally covered if they are:

A. Used primarily for business
B. Rented to a third party for business purposes
C. Vacant and don't contain a family's personal property
D. Located on the residence premises shown on the declarations page

32. In a homeowners insurance policy, which type of personal property is most likely to have a special limit of liability?

A. Phones
B. Kitchen appliances
C. Valuable documents
D. Items kept in storage

33. In homeowners insurance, special limits of liability for jewelry are most likely to apply to instances of:

A. Water damage
B. Fire loss
C. Theft
D. Mysterious disappearance

34. Insurance that only insures one piece of property is known as

A. Blanket insurance
B. Personal insurance
C. Specific insurance
D. Umbrella insurance

35. Which of the following is generally NOT granted to a mortgage lender as part of a "loss payable clause"?

A. The right to force the insured to buy insurance from another carrier
B. The right to pay premiums if the insured fails to do so
C. The right to provide proof of loss if the insured fails to do so.
D. The right to receive a portion of an insurance settlement following damage to the property

36. Terrorism risk insurance must be offered to:

    A. Individuals wanting dwelling insurance
    B. Individuals wanting personal auto insurance
    C. Businesses wanting commercial property insurance
    D. Businesses wanting errors and omissions insurance

37. Commercial property insurance usually allows the insurer to deny or reduce benefits if a building has been vacant for:

    A. 3 days
    B. 7 days
    C. 20 days
    D. 60 days

38. For property insurance based on ISO forms, which type of coverage insures against the largest number of perils?

    A. Basic
    B. Broad
    C. Special
    D. Modified

39. Which of the following is the best definition of "loss" in insurance?

    A. An increase in economic value
    B. The chance of something good, neutral or bad happening
    C. An expense or decrease in value at an unpredictable time
    D. The normal rate of depreciation of property

40. When is a homeowner most likely to be impacted by a policy's coinsurance clause?

    A. When a home is insured for 100% of its replacement cost
    B. When a home suffers partial damage
    C. When a loss only involves personal property
    D. When a brand-new home is completely destroyed

41. Coverage F in homeowners insurance provides a limited amount of medical payments coverage:

    A. Regardless of fault
    B. After an auto accident
    C. For at-home businesses
    D. Only if negligence was likely

42. Which method of risk management is most associated with insurance?

    A. Risk reduction
    B. Risk transfer
    C. Risk avoidance
    D. Risk tolerance

43. An insurer agrees to rebuild a home without deducting for depreciation. However, many parts of the home will be made of cheaper material that serves the same essential function as the original. The home was likely insured for its:

A. Guaranteed replacement cost
B. Functional replacement cost
C. Actual cash value
D. Fair market value

44. Homeowners insurance generally covers personal property if it is damaged:

A. Worldwide
B. Only on the residence premises
C. Only in the insured's state of residency
D. Only at the address listed on the declarations page

45. In general, the applicant's promise to keep property protected by a security system would be considered a:

A. Waiver
B. Warranty
C. Representation
D. Contract of adhesion

46. A homeowner has insured a dwelling at $200,000. The homeowner also likely has contents coverage equal to:

A. $20,000
B. $100,000
C. $150,000
D. $200,000

47. A homeowner has a Coverage E limit of $100,000. After the owner's dog bites a neighbor, the owner spends $50,000 to defend himself and is ultimately ordered to pay the neighbor $75,000. How much of the total cost will the insurer cover?

A. $50,000
B. $75,000
C. $100,000
D. $125,000

48. In general, the various ISO coverage forms for homeowners insurance are most similar in the way that they cover:

A. Property damage
B. Contents
C. Dwellings
D. Personal liability

49. Dwelling coverage in an HO-4 policy is intended to cover:

    A. The landlord in case of damage by a renter
    B. The tenant in case of liability for a fire
    C. Visitors who are injured on rented property
    D. Improvements to the dwelling made by the tenant

50. A homeowner has her credit card stolen by her son. Assuming the son lives with her, how much will the insurer pay for losses due to unauthorized use of the card?

    A. $0
    B. $250
    C. $500
    D. $1,500

Casualty Exam #1

1. Which of the following is considered the cause of a loss?

    A. Peril
    B. Hazard
    C. Risk
    D. Inherent vice

2. In general, the previous owner of property can no longer collect insurance after a loss. This is largely because the previous owner:

    A. Isn't allowed to pay premiums
    B. Lacks an insurable interest in the property
    C. No longer lives in the coverage territory
    D. May have committed fraud

3. The dollar limits found in an insurance policy are in conflict with those on a certificate of insurance. Which dollar limit applies?

    A. The limit in the policy
    B. The limit on the certificate
    C. Whichever limit is higher
    D. Whichever limit is lower

4. An applicant attempts to hide facts from an insurer in order to receive a lower premium. This is known as:

    A. Twisting
    B. Concealment
    C. Adverse selection
    D. Utmost good faith

5. "Personal and advertising injury" is a component of

    A. Commercial general liability insurance
    B. Directors and officers insurance
    C. Workers compensation insurance
    D. Cyber liability insurance

6. An insurance company insists on evaluating a consumer's previous insurance history from a third-party database. In general, what is the insurer required to do?

    A. Obtain consent from the consumer.
    B. Share the information with the consumer's insurance broker.
    C. Verify the accuracy of the information with the DOI.
    D. Disregard loss histories that are more than three years old.

7. Which type of liability insurance typically requires that both a claim and the event leading up to it occur while the policy is in force?

    A. Occurrence policy
    B. Claims-made policy
    C. All-risk policy
    D. Excess and surplus policy

8. After an auto accident, an insurer provides benefits to a customer and then attempts to recoup the money by suing the at-fault driver. This is an example of:

A. Subrogation
B. Estoppel
C. Risk transfer
D. Contractual liability

9. A "discovery period" in a crime insurance policy refers to:

A. The period during which a crime must be committed
B. The period during which a crime must be detected
C. The period during which a business will have no coverage
D. The period during which underwriters will evaluate a business's level of risk

10. Which type of insurance is most likely to respond when a person is held liable for providing bad professional advice?

A. Personal liability insurance
B. Surety coverage
C. Professional liability insurance
D. Commercial general liability insurance

11. Which of the following is true of workers compensation claims involving lost income?

A. Employees will receive amounts equal to their regular salary during recovery.
B. Employees will typically receive wage compensation regardless of how much time they miss work.
C. Most workers compensation claims involve lost income rather than medical payments.
D. Employees will typically only receive a fraction of their regular income as workers compensation.

12. Which of the following is an example of a speculative risk?

A. A new business venture
B. An earthquake
C. A fire
D. A wet floor

13. Accusations involving which of the following are unlikely to be covered by employment practices liability?

A. Discrimination
B. Retaliation
C. Sexual harassment
D. Workplace injuries

14. A driver has been denied insurance by multiple insurance companies. Where will the driver likely be able to obtain required coverage?

A. The residual auto insurance market
B. An insurer in another state
C. A Lloyds of London syndicate
D. Nowhere

15. Another name for casualty insurance is:

    A. Liability insurance
    B. Malpractice insurance
    C. Commercial insurance
    D. Personal lines insurance

16. Which type of insurance is most likely to respond when a business is accused of discrimination in employment?

    A. Commercial general liability insurance
    B. Workers compensation insurance
    C. Employers liability insurance
    D. Employment practices liability insurance

17. Which type of insurance will most likely respond to losses when a business commonly accepts its customers' property for repairs or alterations?

    A. Bailee insurance
    B. Commercial general liability insurance
    C. Personal articles floater insurance
    D. Professional liability insurance

18. When is an auto insurance deductible most likely to be enforced?

    A. When a claim is made against the liability portion of the driver's policy
    B. When a claim is made against the comprehensive (non-collision) portion of the driver's policy
    C. When the parties involved in a collision are all covered by the same auto policy
    D. When an at-fault driver is accused of bodily injury to multiple people.

19. What is the general purpose of a hammer clause in an errors and omissions insurance policy?

    A. To explain how the policy will cover instances of intentional acts
    B. To void coverage in cases involving professional acts
    C. To provide coverage for independent contractors who are named in complaints
    D. To explain what will occur if the insurer and the insured disagree about whether to settle a dispute

20. A business that is concerned about coverage of claims that might arise soon after not continuing its liability insurance might have protection due to:

    A. An elimination period
    B. A retroactive date
    C. A short-rated cancellation
    D. An extended reporting period

21. Which describes a casualty insurer's duty to defend the insured?

    A. The insurer is not expected to pay for the cost of a defense.
    B. The insurer's duty to defend is broader than its duty to pay for settlements.
    C. The insurer's duty to defend is narrower than its duty to pay for settlements.
    D. Defense costs will always reduce the amount of money available to pay for settlements.

22. With respect to a surety bond, who is the principal?

    A. The person who promises to do or not do something
    B. The person who will be compensated if a promise is broken
    C. The person who will provide compensation when a promise is broken
    D. The person who issues the bond

23. Which type of insurance is most commonly included with workers compensation insurance as part of the same policy?

    A. Group health insurance
    B. Group short-term disability insurance
    C. Employers liability insurance
    D. Employment practices liability insurance

24. Which term is used to describe a scenario in which coverage is effectively canceled due to nonpayment of premiums?

    A. Warranty
    B. Misrepresentation
    C. Assignment
    D. Lapse

25. Which type of insurance is most likely to pay a claim after coverage has been canceled, as long as the event that led to the claim occurred while coverage was in force?

    A. Occurrence policy
    B. Claims-made policy
    C. All-risk policy
    D. Excess and surplus policy

26. Which type of policy only insures against perils that are specifically mentioned in it?

    A. All-risk
    B. Open-peril
    C. Named-peril
    D. Multi-peril

27. A piece of information that influences an insurer's decision to accept a risk is considered a:

    A. Misrepresentation
    B. Waiver and estoppel
    C. Material fact
    D. Proximate cause of loss

28. Which is the best definition of risk?

    A. The unknown consequences of an event
    B. A type of damage or loss
    C. A physical or environmental hazard
    D. An event that is certain to occur

29. Which is the best description of medical coverage within the context of workers compensation?

   A. Employees must miss at least three days of work for medical costs to be covered.
   B. Employees will likely have a deductible to pay after a workplace injury.
   C. Employees will likely have a coinsurance fee to pay for all related medical services.
   D. Employees' medical costs will generally be paid immediately after an accident and without any deductible or coinsurance requirements.

30. Rather than insure just one vehicle in an area, an insurer will insure multiple vehicles in the same area. This is an example of:

   A. Adverse selection
   B. Risk retention
   C. Insurable interest
   D. The pooling of risks

31. Which type of insurance is most likely to cover losses related to a business's automobiles?

   A. Personal Auto Policy
   B. Business Auto Policy
   C. Commercial general liability insurance
   D. Bailee insurance

32. Which type of claim is least likely to be covered by an insurance producer's errors and omissions insurance?

   A. A claim involving bad financial advice
   B. A claim involving failure to secure requested coverage
   C. A claim involving a slip-and-fall accident at the producer's office
   D. A claim involving failure to disclose risk-related information to a carrier

33. Which group of workers is typically not protected by workers compensation laws?

   A. Full-time employees
   B. Independent contractors
   C. Workers in supervisory positions
   D. New employees who are injured during a 90-day probationary period

34. Which type of insurance is most likely to cover the cost of identity-theft protection services after a data breach?

   A. Cyber liability insurance
   B. Errors and omissions insurance
   C. Commercial general liability insurance
   D. Employment practices liability insurance

35. How is commercial general liability insurance likely to respond to the loss of intangible property?

   A. Little to no coverage will be available.
   B. The insurer will pay for damages but not for defense costs.
   C. Coverage will apply if the business was at fault.
   D. Coverage will apply if the business purchased all-risk coverage.

36. Which type of cancellation will result in a smaller return of premium for the consumer?

    A. Short-rate
    B. Pro-rata
    C. Flat
    D. Rescission

37. A liability insurance policy states that the events leading up to a claim must have occurred no earlier than a specific date. This date is known as the:

    A. Policy period
    B. Restoration period
    C. Elimination period
    D. Retroactive date

38. Which type of insurance covers a business when a worker is injured but is not entitled to workers compensation benefits?

    A. Workers compensation insurance
    B. Commercial general liability insurance
    C. Employers liability insurance
    D. Employment practices liability insurance

39. Which type of auto insurance would respond if a driver is the victim of a hit-and-run accident?

    A. Comprehensive insurance
    B. Uninsured motorist coverage
    C. Underinsured motorist coverage
    D. Gap insurance

40. Which type of insurance would respond if a driver is hit by someone who has enough insurance to satisfy the law but not enough to pay all damages after an accident?

    A. Comprehensive insurance
    B. Uninsured motorist coverage
    C. Underinsured motorist coverage
    D. Gap insurance

41. What is likely the highest amount that a typical driver can obtain from the insurance company after a vehicle has been destroyed by fire?

    A. Replacement cost
    B. Actual cash value
    C. Guaranteed replacement cost
    D. Extended replacement cost

42. Which type of insurance is liability insurance purchased by ship owners in the ocean marine market?

    A. Protection and indemnity insurance
    B. Cargo insurance
    C. Hull insurance
    D. Inland marine coverage

43. Which of the following is an example of express authority?

    A. Power that is reasonably assumed to exist by the agent
    B. Power that is reasonably assumed to exist by the public
    C. Power that is specifically granted in a written contract
    D. Power that requires no consultation with the principal

44. Which of the following best explains an insurance agent's duty to consumers in an insurance transaction?

    A. The consumer is the agent's principal in the transaction and must be obeyed at all times.
    B. The products recommended by the insurance agent must be suitable for the consumer's situation.
    C. As a representative of the carrier, the agent owes no duties to the consumer.
    D. The agent is an independent contractor and doesn't represent or owe duties to anyone.

45. What is the basic formula for calculating loss ratios?

    A. Marketing expenses divided by premiums
    B. Marketing expenses plus claims-related losses
    C. Agent commissions divided by claims-related losses
    D. Claims-related losses divided by earned premiums

46. A person who will never recover from an injury but is still capable of doing some work has which level of disability?

    A. Permanent total
    B. Permanent partial
    C. Temporary total
    D. Temporary partial

47. In premium calculations, which of the following is used to account for a business's own history of workers compensation claims and workplace accidents?

    A. Manual rate
    B. Industry classification code
    C. Experience modification factor
    D. Earned premium

48. Which of the following is likely to be covered as part of the supplementary payments section of an auto policy?

    A. Loss of a vehicle that is ordered demolished by the government
    B. Fines imposed by authorities for excessive pollution
    C. The cost of a bail bond associated with an accident
    D. The cost of renting a vehicle in Mexico or South America

49. According to the Personal Auto Policy, the cost of which type of auto is likely to be covered for up to $30 per day up to a maximum of $900?

    A. Owned auto
    B. Non-owned auto
    C. Temporary substitute auto
    D. A trailer being pulled by a covered auto

50. Which product is commonly purchased by an employer as a safeguard against disloyalty from employees?

    A. Fidelity bond
    B. Surety bond
    C. Employers liability insurance
    D. Employment practices liability insurance

Casualty Exam #2

1. Which of the following increases the likelihood or severity of a loss?

    A. Hazard
    B. Indemnity
    C. Speculative risk
    D. Insurable interest

2. Regarding commercial general liability insurance, when is a business most likely to have coverage for alleged copyright infringement?

    A. When the infringement is in non-promotional materials
    B. When the infringement is part of an advertisement
    C. When the infringement was committed on purpose
    D. When the infringement occurs after an extended reporting period

3. Which type of liability insurance allows for coverage of claims that are made after a policy has expired, as long as the event leading up to the claim occurred during the policy period?

    A. Claims-made policy
    B. Occurrence policy
    C. Errors and omissions insurance
    D. Intentional acts coverage

4. A business has renewed its claims-made liability insurance. What is most likely to happen to the policy's retroactive date?

    A. It will be reset based on the first date of the new policy period.
    B. It will remain the same as under the old policy.
    C. It will reflect the date of the business's most recent claim.
    D. It will be reset based on the last day of the new policy period.

5. Which policy feature allows for a limited amount of coverage if a claim arises soon after the cancellation of a claims-made policy?

    A. Hammer clause
    B. Duty to defend
    C. Extended reporting period
    D. Retroactive dates

6. Which of the following is an example of a third-party cyber liability loss?

    A. A business's loss of income due to a cyber-related shutdown of its operations
    B. A business's loss of proprietary information due to cyber-related theft
    C. The cost to repair or replace infected computer hardware
    D. Amounts paid to customers or clients when a business is sued for a cyber-related loss

7. Money paid for pain and suffering relates to which type of damages?

    A. Punitive damages
    B. Special damages
    C. General damages
    D. Liquidated damages

8. An insurance producer has been sued by a client. The producer's errors and omissions insurer wants to settle the matter for $200,000 but the producer refuses. The producer is ultimately ordered to pay $350,000 to the client. Based on the typical hammer clause and regardless of any deductible, how much will the producer's errors and omissions insurer pay?

    A. $0
    B. $150,000
    C. $200,000
    D. $350,000

9. Which of the following is least likely to be covered by employment practices liability insurance?

    A. Retaliation claims
    B. Discrimination claims
    C. Harassment claims
    D. Wage-and-hour disputes

10. In insurance, the possibility of a loss is sometimes known as a(n):

    A. Exposure
    B. Accident
    C. Speculative risk
    D. Proximate cause

11. The failure to act with reasonable care is known as:

    A. Fraud
    B. Negligence
    C. Liability
    D. Damages

12. Which type of insurance is most likely to respond when a customer suffers bodily injury at a place of business due to the business's negligence?

    A. Professional liability insurance
    B. Commercial general liability insurance
    C. Workers compensation insurance
    D. Employers liability insurance

13. Which type of accident is generally not covered by auto collision insurance?

    A. Two cars collide with each other.
    B. A driver hits a parked car.
    C. A driver hits a car door while it is being opened in traffic.
    D. A driver hits an animal that is running across a road.

14. Although it is still drivable, the cost to repair a vehicle is higher than its actual cash value. How will an insurer respond to a claim for property damage from the policyholder?

    A. Deny the claim.
    B. Pay for the repairs.
    C. Consider the vehicle "totaled" and pay the actual cash value.
    D. Require that repairs be done at the insurer's preferred dealership.

15. Which of the following is a characteristic of an insurance contract?

    A. Oral
    B. Bilateral
    C. Conditional
    D. Commercial

16. An insurer refuses to insure a consumer's supply of illegal fireworks. What is the likely reason for the refusal?

    A. Issuing coverage would likely be unprofitable.
    B. Issuing coverage would risk insolvency.
    C. An insurance contract must have a legal purpose.
    D. The property is an example of speculative risk.

17. Which of the following would most likely result in workers compensation?

    A. A worker is injured while driving home.
    B. A worker becomes ill with the flu and suspects that it came from a colleague.
    C. An employee experiences breathing problems after working with toxic chemicals.
    D. An employee needs to quit a new job due to a longtime heart condition.

18. Underinsured motorist coverage for the harmed driver would likely apply in which of the following scenarios:

    A. The policyholder is hit by someone without any auto insurance.
    B. The policyholder is hit as part of a hit-and-run accident.
    C. The policyholder is hit by someone with less insurance than is mandated by law.
    D. The policyholder is hit by someone who has complied with the state's auto insurance requirements but still lacks enough coverage to pay for the whole loss.

19. Which of the following is NOT a type of professional liability insurance?

    A. Errors and omissions insurance
    B. Malpractice insurance
    C. Jewelers block insurance
    D. Directors and officers insurance

20. Most types of liability insurance sold in today's market are:

    A. Claims-made policies
    B. Occurrence policies
    C. Umbrella policies
    D. Manuscript policies

21. Which of the following scenarios is least likely to be covered by a vehicle owner's auto insurance?

    A. The owner hits another vehicle.
    B. The owner's spouse hits a pedestrian.
    C. A thief hits a truck while stealing the owner's car.
    D. The owner's sibling, who lives in the same house, borrows the owner's car and hits a mailbox.

22. Which of the following is generally true regarding auto insurance deductibles?

    A. Higher deductibles tend to increase the premium.
    B. Deductibles tend to apply to the liability portion of the policy.
    C. Deductibles tend to apply to property damage to the insured's own vehicle.
    D. Deductibles are waived for a driver's first three accidents.

23. Uninsured motorist coverage for the harmed driver would likely apply in which of the following scenarios:

    A. The policyholder is hit by someone without any auto insurance.
    B. The policyholder suffers damage to his or her own car due to a hailstorm.
    C. The policyholder is hit by someone who is covered under the same policy.
    D. The policyholder is hit by someone who has complied with the state's auto insurance requirements but still lacks enough coverage to pay for the whole loss.

24. Which of the following tends to be used to insure the auto-related risks of gas stations, car dealerships and mechanics?

    A. Drive-other-car endorsements
    B. The Garage Coverage Form
    C. Commercial general liability insurance
    D. The Business Auto Policy

25. Which type of insurance is most likely to respond when theft is committed by an employee?

    A. Crime insurance
    B. Employment practices liability insurance
    C. Commercial general liability insurance
    D. Errors and omissions insurance

26. An insurer decides to draft an insurance contract specifically for an important customer rather than using one of its standard policies. The policy is known as a(n):

    A. Open-peril policy
    B. All-risk policy
    C. Manuscript policy
    D. Mutual insurance policy

27. Who is expected to engage in good field underwriting?

    A. Claims representatives
    B. Insurance agents
    C. Financial planners
    D. Fraternal benefit societies

28. Which of the following is possible evidence of negligence?

    A. No damages were suffered.
    B. An adult trespasser was harmed on private property.
    C. The allegedly negligent person reasonably fulfilled his/her duty of care.
    D. The allegedly negligent person's acts were the proximate cause of a loss.

29. An employer refuses to compensate an injured worker because the worker should've known that the job was dangerous. This defense is known as:

   A. Comparative negligence
   B. Contributory negligence
   C. Assumption of risk
   D. Statute of limitations

30. A homeowner whose backyard commonly contains a pool, a trampoline and a dog might be exposed to liability on the basis of:

   A. Operations liability
   B. Assumption of risk
   C. Attractive nuisance
   D. Contingent liability

31. A state has made changes to the way it calculates workers compensation requirements. What will happen to a business's workers compensation insurance?

   A. It will provide benefits as required by the updated requirements.
   B. It will provide benefits as required by the updated requirements if the business pays for and requests a special endorsement.
   C. The business will need to fill any coverage gaps by purchasing excess insurance.
   D. The new requirements won't apply to a business if workers compensation insurance is already in force.

32. After hitting a parked car, the at-fault driver would have coverage for his/her own property damage under which type of auto insurance?

   A. Liability insurance
   B. Collision coverage
   C. Underinsured motorist coverage
   D. Comprehensive (other-than-collision) coverage

33. In general, how much will an insurer pay when a policyholder's own car is damaged?

   A. The vehicle's replacement cost
   B. The vehicle's fair market value
   C. The vehicle's actual cash value
   D. The cost to repair or replace the vehicle or its actual cash value, whichever amount is lowest

34. Which type of liability doesn't require the existence of negligence?

   A. Absolute liability
   B. Vicarious liability
   C. Premises and operations liability
   D. Professional liability

35. Which of the following is generally not a covered vehicle with respect to personal auto insurance unless the proper endorsements are added to the policy?

    A. A van with a relatively low weight
    B. A vehicle with less than four wheels
    C. The vehicle listed on the declarations page
    D. A vehicle used temporarily by the policyholder while his or her regular vehicle is unavailable

36. Who pays for a surety bond?

    A. Principal
    B. Obligee
    C. Surety
    D. Agent

37. In insurance, what is the purpose of an independent rating organization?

    A. Evaluate an insurer's financial status and ability to pay claims
    B. Provide arbitration and mediation services for claimants
    C. Represent consumers in claims-related disputes
    D. Set rates that insurers will use to calculate premiums

38. Which type of liability involves being held responsible for somebody else's actions?

    A. Assumption of risk
    B. Comparative negligence
    C. Vicarious liability
    D. Commercial general liability

39. Which of the following best describes the relationship between punitive damages and insurance?

    A. Punitive damages are commonly covered by commercial liability insurance.
    B. Punitive damages typically have their own coverage limit.
    C. Punitive damages often can't be covered by insurance as a matter of law.
    D. Coverage of punitive damages tends to ensure that the related actions won't happen again.

40. Auto insurance for individuals tends to be based on which policy from the ISO?

    A. The Personal Injury Protection Policy
    B. The Personal Auto Policy
    C. The Commercial Package Policy
    D. The Comprehensive (Non-Collision) Policy

41. Which of the following best describes workers compensations laws in the United States?

    A. Workers are eligible for compensation related to workplace injuries regardless of fault.
    B. Workers are only eligible for compensation when they are injured due to employer negligence.
    C. Employers don't need to pay compensation when an injury is due to another worker's accidental acts.
    D. Workers are only eligible for compensation when they are injured while performing high-risk activities.

42. Which of the following is the best definition of a robbery?

    A. Any kind of stealing
    B. Theft by forced entry
    C. Theft by violence or threat of violence
    D. Stealing committed by an identifiable person

43. A family rents space at a restaurant for a private party and agrees to accept liability for any injuries that occur during the festivities, including cases in which the restaurant would ordinarily be liable. This is an example of:

    A. Vicarious liability
    B. Contractual liability
    C. Contingent liability
    D. Completed operations liability

44. An insurer agrees to continue coverage until the end of the policy period but won't insure a consumer beyond that point. This is known as:

    A. Renewal
    B. Nonrenewal
    C. Rescission
    D. Flat cancellation

45. What is the difference between a binder and a conditional receipt?

    A. A binder requires a signature from a licensed insurance broker.
    B. A conditional receipt is more common in property and casualty insurance.
    C. A binder binds the insurer to the risk and provides temporary coverage.
    D. A conditional receipt binds the insurer to the risk and provides temporary coverage.

46. Which of the following is an explanation of the principle of indemnity?

    A. The insurer should be made "whole" again after a loss.
    B. The consumer should be discouraged from attempting fraud.
    C. Understanding a risk requires adequate actuarial data.
    D. The insurer expects items on an application form to be true and accurate.

47. An addition to an insurance company's standard policy is known as a(n):

    A. Endorsement
    B. Representation
    C. Warranty
    D. Declaration

48. A driver already insures a vehicle against collision damage and buys an additional vehicle. In general, how long will the additional vehicle be covered for collision damage without needing to be reported to the insurer?

    A. 7 days
    B. 14 days
    C. 30 days
    D. Until the end of the policy period

49. The usual extended reporting period allows a business to report potential liability within how many days after the policy period?

    A. 3 days
    B. 30 days
    C. 60 days
    D. 5 years

50. A security camera reveals an employee entering the correct combination into a safe and stealing a business's cash. What has occurred?

    A. Theft
    B. Burglary
    C. Robbery
    D. Mysterious disappearance

Casualty Exam #3

1. Gambling is an example of:

   A. Pure risk
   B. Speculative risk
   C. Adverse selection
   D. The law of large numbers

2. Amounts awarded to harmed party for pain and suffering are generally categorized as:

   A. Special damages
   B. General damages
   C. Punitive damages
   D. Treble damages

3. What is the definition of a split limit in auto insurance?

   A. A policy with different limits for uninsured and underinsured motorist coverage
   B. A policy with different limits for bodily injury liability and property damage liability
   C. A policy that covers two vehicles owned by the same person
   D. A policy that combines personal auto and business auto coverage

4. The purpose of medical payments coverage in auto insurance is to:

   A. Compensate pedestrians who are struck by the insured driver
   B. Compensate the insured driver and his/her passengers for bodily injury
   C. Compensate the other driver when the insured lacks enough liability insurance
   D. Compensate workers who are injured while making deliveries for an employer

5. Which type of auto insurance would pay to repair a vehicle after it hits a mailbox?

   A. Collision
   B. Comprehensive (other than collision)
   C. Personal injury protection (PIP)
   D. Property damage liability

6. Which type of insurance pays the difference between what a borrower owes on an auto loan and the amount received after a total loss?

   A. Gap insurance
   B. Drive other car coverage
   C. Differences in conditions insurance
   D. Underinsured motorist coverage

7. Personal auto insurance generally doesn't cover situations in which a vehicle is transporting goods or passengers for money EXCEPT when:

   A. The vehicle is hailed by the customer of a ridesharing service.
   B. The vehicle is being used as part of a carpool.
   C. The driver only transports goods or passengers as part of part-time employment.
   D. The driver uses the same vehicle for personal and business activities.

8. An employee is hurt in an auto accident while performing his or her job duties. In general, benefits for the employee will come primarily from:

    A. The employer's auto insurer
    B. The employee's auto insurer
    C. The employee's health insurer
    D. Workers compensation

9. Which of the following is least likely to be covered by commercial general liability insurance?

    A. Premises and operations liability
    B. Personal and advertising injury
    C. Liability for injuries sustained by visitors at the business premises
    D. Liability for the loss of computer data belonging to a customer

10. For a claim to be covered by a claims-made policy:

    A. The claim must be reported after the policy period.
    B. The claim must be made before the policy period.
    C. The incident that led to a claim must occur before the retroactive date.
    D. The claim must be reported during the policy period, and the incident that led to it must occur after the retroactive date.

11. What is the purpose of an extended reporting period?

    A. To give consumers a chance to increase their coverage limits
    B. To allow the insurer extra time to examine an insured's books and records
    C. To let the insurer charge a more accurate amount of premium based on the business's actual risk
    D. To give the insured a limited opportunity to report claims even though coverage will otherwise end

12. What is the purpose of a policy's hammer clause?

    A. Determine what will happen if an insured refuses to settle a liability dispute
    B. Clarify that the insurer has an unlimited duty to defend the insured in court
    C. Provide compensation to the insured for assisting with court proceedings
    D. Allow the insurer to sue a third party on the insured's behalf

13. Which of the following is least likely to be covered by commercial general liability insurance?

    A. Liquor liability for a bar or restaurant
    B. Liability for libel or slander
    C. Liability for a slip-and-fall accident involving a customer
    D. Liability for using someone else's copyrighted information in an advertisement

14. What is meant by the term "exclusive remedy" regarding workers compensation and accidents?

    A. Workers must take their employers to court in order to receive workers compensation.
    B. Workers who are entitled to workers compensation generally can't sue their employers.
    C. Workers who receive workers compensation can't continue to earn work-related income.
    D. Workers compensation benefits cannot be paid by a private insurance company.

15. Which of the following is not required for an injury to be covered by workers compensation?

    A. The injury must have been accidental.
    B. The injury must have occurred in conjunction with the person's job duties.
    C. The injured person must be an employee.
    D. The injured person must be an independent contractor.

16. Which type of insurance is most likely to insure a business against data breaches and computer viruses?

    A. Equipment breakdown insurance
    B. Cyber liability insurance
    C. Commercial general liability insurance
    D. Professional liability insurance

17. What is the relationship between professional liability and commercial general liability insurance?

    A. Professional liability is commonly covered as part of premises and operations liability in the CGL form.
    B. Professional liability is typically not covered by commercial general liability insurance.
    C. Licensed professionals have little need for commercial general liability insurance.
    D. Licensed professionals must choose between commercial general liability insurance or professional liability insurance.

18. With respect to commercial general liability insurance, libel and slander are forms of:

    A. Personal injury
    B. Bodily injury
    C. Premises liability
    D. Exclusions

19. A distracted worker seriously injures himself on the job and is unable to work for several weeks. How will workers compensation insurance respond?

    A. The worker will likely be covered for medical bills and some lost earnings.
    B. The worker will be covered for medical bills but not lost earnings.
    C. The worker will be covered for a small fraction of medical bills because he contributed to the accident.
    D. The worker will have no coverage because he contributed to the accident.

20. Workers compensation pertaining to lost wages in most parts of the United States is typically capped at approximately which fraction of a worker's income?

    A. 1/3
    B. ½
    C. 2/3
    D. ¾

21. A worker dies in a workplace accident. How will workers compensation insurance respond?

    A. Death benefits will be available to survivors.
    B. Death benefits will only be paid if the worker had group life insurance from the employer.
    C. Death benefits will be reduced if the worker's negligence contributed to the death.
    D. Death benefits will be paid only if the worker was an independent contractor.

22. What can a business do if it can't obtain workers compensation insurance?

    A. Apply for coverage from the federal government
    B. Apply for coverage from a FAIR Plan
    C. Apply for coverage from the residual market
    D. Pay into a fund established by the DOI and obtain a yearly waiver.

23. In general, how long must an injured worker miss work in order to be eligible for lost wages as part of workers compensation systems?

    A. One day
    B. Three days
    C. One week
    D. 14 days

24. An injured employee is entitled to two years of workers compensation. What will happen if the employer cancels its workers compensation insurance after the first year and goes out of business?

    A. The employee will receive no more compensation.
    B. The employee will receive a reduced amount of compensation.
    C. The employee will continue to receive compensation from the insurer.
    D. The employee will receive compensation from the employer.

25. Workers compensation systems are based on which approach to liability?

    A. Negligence
    B. Comparative negligence
    C. Contributory negligence
    D. No-fault

26. With respect to a bond, who is the obligee?

    A. The person who issues the bond
    B. The person who promises to do or not do something
    C. The person who will be compensated if a promise is broken
    D. The person who will provide compensation when a promise is broken

27. Which type of coverage is generally not intended to be included as part of a Personal Auto Policy?

    A. Liability insurance
    B. Uninsured motorist coverage
    C. Underinsured motorist coverage
    D. Business auto coverage

28. Who generally doesn't have liability protection under a vehicle owner's liability insurance?

    A. A spouse
    B. A son or daughter who lives with the owner
    C. A friend who borrows the driver's car with permission
    D. A friend who borrows the driver's car without permission

29. Which of the following describes a proximate cause of loss?

    A. A loss that is preceded by another loss
    B. A loss caused by multiple perils
    C. Something that logically sets a loss in motion
    D. A hazard that makes the size of loss unpredictable

30. A consumer purchases insurance to manage a risk but will still be required to pay deductibles and other fees after a loss. This is an example of:

    A. Risk avoidance
    B. Risk sharing
    C. The principle of indemnity
    D. The law of large numbers

31. Rather than insure just one person, an insurer decides to insure several people who have similar amounts of risk and charges them a similar amount for coverage. This is an example of:

    A. Adverse selection
    B. Cost sharing
    C. Risk transfer
    D. Pooling of risks

32. Which of the following is usually a characteristic of insurance for personal property?

    A. All-risk
    B. Open-peril
    C. Named-peril
    D. Replacement cost

33. What is paid to the insurer in exchange for insurance?

    A. Rate
    B. Premium
    C. Deductible
    D. Coinsurance fees

34. Who is the consumer with the most control over the insurance contract?

    A. Beneficiary
    B. Principal
    C. Additional insured
    D. Named insured

35. An insurer decides to end its contractual relationship with a consumer before the end of the policy period. This is known as:

    A. Nonrenewal
    B. Cancellation
    C. Misrepresentation
    D. Waiver and estoppel

36. Where might insurance be available for consumers who are otherwise uninsurable?

    A. Reinsurance companies
    B. Stock companies
    C. The residual market
    D. Direct writers

37. What is a hazard?

    A. The cause of a loss
    B. The size of a loss
    C. The event being insured against
    D. Something that increases the likelihood or severity of a loss

38. What is the difference between a pure risk and a speculative risk?

    A. Only pure risks can include the possibility of something good happening.
    B. Only speculative risks can include the possibility of something good happening.
    C. Only pure risks can include the possibility of something neutral happening.
    D. Only speculative risks can include the possibility of something neutral happening.

39. An insurer worries that the only people who will buy flood insurance are those who are likely to suffer a loss. This concern is an example of:

    A. Risk reduction
    B. Adverse selection
    C. The pooling of risks
    D. Contingency planning

40. For something to be insurable, the risk usually must be spread across a larger population. This is known as:

    A. The principle of indemnity
    B. The pooling of risks
    C. Risk retention
    D. Morale hazard

41. Which type of hazard involves carelessness by a policyholder?

    A. Moral hazard
    B. Morale hazard
    C. Physical hazard
    D. Speculative risk

42. When must insurable interest exist in property insurance?

    A. At the time of loss
    B. Prior to the policy period
    C. After the policy period
    D. Prior to the payment of an insurance premium

43. Which concept is intended to prevent claimants from being in a better position after an insurance settlement than before a loss?

    A. Law of large numbers
    B. Principle of indemnity
    C. Adverse selection
    D. Risk management

44. A policy states that losses must occur within the United States or Canada. This is known as the policy's:

    A. Coverage territory
    B. Limit of liability
    C. Assignment clause
    D. Insuring agreement

45. Which portion of the policy stipulates various rules that must be followed when a loss occurs?

    A. Definitions
    B. Conditions
    C. Causes of loss
    D. Declarations page

46. Which right is generally given to the insurer as part of a commercial insurance policy?

    A. The right to prevent the business from introducing dangerous products
    B. The right to suspend the business's operations during a natural catastrophe
    C. The right to inspect the business's books and records
    D. The right to cancel the insurance for any reason with written notice

47. An agent is fairly certain that a particular insurer won't agree to cover a particular applicant and therefore doesn't recommend the insurer to that person. This is an example of:

    A. Binding
    B. Concealment
    C. Discrimination
    D. Field underwriting

48. How do casualty insurance products generally deal with defense costs?

    A. The insurer has the right to defend the insured.
    B. The insurer has the duty to defend the insured.
    C. The insured has the option to defend the insured.
    D. The insured generally doesn't cover defense costs unless an additional premium is paid.

49. What is the coverage territory for most personal auto policies?

    A. The United States, its territories and Canada
    B. North America
    C. The driver's home state
    D. Anywhere in the world

50. What is the purpose of the discovery period in a casualty insurance policy?

    A. Allow a business to report accidents that occurred after the policy period
    B. Allow a business to report crimes that aren't noticed until after the policy period
    C. Allow an insurer to investigate a business's books and records after the policy period
    D. Allow an insurer to audit the amount charged for workers compensation coverage

PROPERTY AND CASUALTY GENERAL PRACTICE EXAM ANSWER KEYS

Question	Property Exam #1	Property Exam #2	Property Exam #3	Casualty Exam #1	Casualty Exam #2	Casualty Exam #3
1.	C	B	C	A	A	B
2.	D	B	B	B	B	B
3.	B	D	A	A	B	B
4.	A	B	D	B	B	B
5.	C	D	D	A	C	A
6.	B	C	A	A	D	A
7.	C	C	B	B	C	B
8.	D	D	B	A	C	D
9.	A	D	C	B	D	D
10.	D	A	B	C	A	D
11.	A	D	D	D	B	D
12.	D	B	B	A	B	A
13.	D	A	C	D	D	A
14.	D	C	C	A	C	B
15.	D	C	A	A	C	D
16.	B	D	A	D	C	B
17.	D	A	D	A	C	B
18.	C	D	C	B	D	A
19.	C	D	A	D	C	A
20.	D	D	C	D	A	C
21.	B	D	A	B	C	A
22.	C	A	C	A	C	C
23.	A	C	A	C	A	B
24.	C	B	A	D	B	C
25.	D	B	A	A	A	D

Property and Casualty General Practice Exam Answer Keys

Question	Property Exam #1	Property Exam #2	Property Exam #3	Casualty Exam #1	Casualty Exam #2	Casualty Exam #3
26.	B	C	A	C	C	C
27.	A	A	A	C	B	D
28.	A	A	A	A	D	D
29.	D	C	C	D	C	C
30.	C	C	C	D	C	B
31.	B	D	D	B	A	D
32.	A	A	C	C	B	C
33.	C	B	C	B	D	B
34.	B	B	C	A	A	D
35.	C	C	A	A	B	B
36.	C	C	C	A	A	C
37.	D	D	D	D	A	D
38.	C	A	C	C	C	B
39.	A	B	C	B	C	B
40.	B	A	B	C	B	B
41.	B	C	A	B	A	B
42.	B	C	B	A	C	A
43.	A	B	B	C	B	B
44.	C	B	A	B	B	A
45.	A	B	B	D	C	B
46.	D	C	B	B	A	C
47.	B	D	D	C	A	D
48.	C	D	D	C	B	B
49.	A	A	D	C	C	A
50.	D	A	A	A	A	B

MISSOURI INSURANCE LAW PRACTICE EXAMS

A significant portion of your licensing exam(s) will relate to state-specific insurance material. The following practice exams are tailored specifically for your state. Answer keys can be found later in this book.

Missouri Insurance Law Exam #1

1. Who is primarily responsible for enforcing insurance laws and rules in Missouri?

   A. The federal government
   B. The Missouri Secretary of State
   C. The Missouri Department of Revenue
   D. The Missouri Department of Commerce and Insurance

2. A cease-and-desist order has been issued by the DCI director to an insurance producer. Which of the following best reflects the producer's rights in the situation?

   A. The producer can continue to sell insurance as long as disclosure of a pending regulatory investigation is disclosed to the public.
   B. The producer can ignore the order until his or her license has been officially suspended or revoked.
   C. The producer can enlist the services of legal counsel at the DCI's expense.
   D. The producer has the right to a hearing about the alleged wrongdoing.

3. How frequently must an insurer undergo a financial examination by the DCI?

   A. At least every year
   B. At least every five years
   C. At least every 10 years
   D. Whenever an insurer is named in a disproportionate amount of consumer complaints

4. A producer has sold insurance from an insurer that isn't authorized by the DCI. What will happen if the insurer fails to pay a legitimate claim?

   A. The claim will be paid by the state's guaranty fund.
   B. The insurer will owe double the amount of loss.
   C. The producer can be held liable for the loss.
   D. Nothing, since the consumer is expected to only do business with authorized carriers.

5. What is the minimum age for a producer license in Missouri?

   A. 16
   B. 18
   C. 21
   D. 25

6. A non-resident producer has recently moved to Missouri. If the person wants to remain licensed, what must he or she do?

   A. Successfully apply for a resident producer license within 90 days.
   B. Complete a pre-license course in all major lines of authority.
   C. Pay double the regular licensing fee.
   D. Pass a Missouri-specific insurance exam.

7. How much will it cost to reinstate a license after its renewal deadline?

    A. $100
    B. $200
    C. $100 plus an extra $25 for each month of lateness
    D. $100 for resident producers and $200 for non-resident producers

8. What is the penalty for failing to notify the DCI of a producer's change of address?

    A. $10 per month
    B. $20 per month
    C. $100
    D. $1,000

9. What must happen when a producer is no longer appointed to sell on an insurer's behalf?

    A. The producer must provide written notice to policyholders and provide a referral.
    B. The insurer must indicate the date of termination in a registry.
    C. The producer must be allowed to transfer his or her clients' insurance elsewhere.
    D. The insurer must provide any remaining compensation owed to the producer within 30 days.

10. A producer has been fined less than $200 for a violation and has avoided having his or her license suspended or revoked. Which of the following is true about the violation?

    A. It must be reported to the public by the DCI.
    B. It will be expunged from the person's record after five years.
    C. It will be ignored by the DCI if it relates to activities in another state.
    D. It will end the producer's appointment with authorized insurers in Missouri.

11. A producer's compensation will depend on how many of his or her customers suffer an insured loss during the calendar year. Which of the following is true about this arrangement?

    A. This type of compensation is illegal in Missouri.
    B. This type of compensation is legal in Missouri if it is disclosed to consumers.
    C. This type of compensation is an example of an unfair claims settlement practice.
    D. This type of compensation is legal in Missouri if the producer isn't the one who decides whether to approve or deny claims.

12. A binder will be replaced by a property insurance policy. Unless the policyholder makes a special request, when must the policy go into effect?

    A. No later than the binder's expiration date
    B. No later than the binder's effective date
    C. No later than the date when premiums were provided to a producer
    D. No later than 30 days after a property inspection

13. A producer needs a loan to purchase a home. Which of the following is true about the situation?

    A. The producer can never accept a loan from a customer.
    B. The producer can accept a loan from a customer who is regularly in the business of making loans.
    C. The producer can accept a loan from a prospect but not a policyholder.
    D. The producer can accept a loan from a prospect in exchange for a lower commission.

14. Which of the following reflects Missouri's stance on redlining?

    A. Insurers can refuse to offer any insurance to consumers who live in a particular neighborhood.
    B. Insurers can't refuse to offer insurance based solely on the location of property.
    C. Insurers must charge the same amount regardless of the loss histories of various ZIP codes.
    D. Insurers must record the racial identity of each insurance applicant.

15. In general, what is the maximum amount that can be obtained from the Missouri Property and Casualty Insurance Guaranty Association?

    A. $100,000
    B. $300,000
    C. $500,000
    D. $1 million

16. Which insurance product would generally not be considered marine insurance in Missouri?

    A. Personal property floater
    B. Insurance for shipments
    C. Builders risk insurance
    D. Dwelling insurance

17. Which level of perils must be covered by insurance from the Missouri FAIR Plan?

    A. Basic
    B. Broad
    C. Special
    D. Open-peril

18. What can a consumer do upon receiving a cancellation notice from the Missouri FAIR Plan?

    A. Appeal to the DCI director within 30 days.
    B. Demand a refund of all earned premiums within 30 days.
    C. Obtain a free property inspection from an unbiased third party.
    D. Apply for coverage from the Missouri Basic Property Insurance and Inspection Placement Program.

19. How much auto liability insurance must a Missouri driver have for property damage?

    A. $20,000
    B. $25,000
    C. $50,000
    D. $100,000

20. Which form must be filed when an SR-22 is no longer required or valid?

    A. SR-24
    B. SR-26
    C. SR-28
    D. SR-30

21. An auto insurance policy in Missouri must have a coverage territory of:

    A. Missouri and surrounding states
    B. The United States
    C. The United States and surrounding territories
    D. The United States, U.S. territories and Canada

22. How much special liability insurance must a driver maintain while driving for a ridesharing service?

    A. $20,000 for bodily injury and $20,000 for property damage
    B. $25,000 for bodily injury and $50,000 for property damage
    C. $25,000 for bodily injury per person, $50,000 for bodily injury per accident and $25,000 for property damage
    D. $50,000 for bodily injury per person, $100,000 for bodily injury per accident and $25,000 for property damage

23. Which type of business must have workers compensation insurance if it has one employee?

    A. A real estate office
    B. A non-profit organization
    C. A construction firm
    D. A staffing agency

24, Which of the following scenarios will most likely result in workers compensation benefits?

    A. An employee is injured in an auto accident while driving to work.
    B. An employee goes to work despite already being ill and passes out during a break period.
    C. A volunteer suffers an injury while intoxicated.
    D. An employee develops a lung disease after being exposed to toxic chemicals in the workplace.

25. What is the purpose of the Missouri Medical Malpractice Joint Underwriting Association?

    A. Provide compensation to patients who are harmed by medical malpractice.
    B. Step in when an medical provider's insurance company becomes insolvent.
    C. Offer medical malpractice insurance to professionals who can't obtain it in the traditional market.
    D. Reward medical providers who have not had any malpractice insurance claims over the past five years.

Missouri Insurance Law Exam #2

1. Which of the following statements is true regarding the DCI director's background?

    A. The director must be licensed as a Missouri insurance producer.
    B. The director must have an ownership interest in an insurance business.
    C. The director must have a professional background in insurance.
    D. The director must be elected by the residents of Missouri.

2. How long are insurers required to maintain records of sold insurance policies?

    A. During the current policy term
    B. During the current policy term plus an additional two calendar years
    C. Until the policyholder actively cancels the policy or causes it to lapse
    D. Until the conclusion of a financial audit for the year in which the policy was purchased

3. Which of the following activities generally can't be done without a producer license?

    A. Distributing general insurance information
    B. Setting appointments for a licensed producer
    C. Collecting premium payments at a producer's place of business
    D. Collecting premium payments from someone and then encouraging the person to buy more insurance

4. What is the fee for a producer license in Missouri?

    A. $100
    B. $150
    C. $180
    D. $200

5. Which of the following producers generally wouldn't need to pass a Missouri insurance exam?

    A. A nonresident life insurance producer who moves to Missouri and now wants to sell property insurance, too
    B. A limited lines producer
    C. A producer who has been appointed to sell on behalf of another licensed producer
    D. A certified financial planner who will be selling insurance as part of his or her business

6. Which of the following courses is most likely to result in continuing education credit for a Missouri producer?

    A. A course on prospecting and time management
    B. A course that a producer already completed during the same licensing cycle
    C. A course on Missouri insurance law and ethics
    D. A course that has been approved by an insurance regulator from a neighboring state

7. When must education providers report continuing education credits to the DCI?

    A. Immediately upon completion
    B. Within 5 days of completion
    C. Within 10 days of completion
    D. Within 30 days of completion

8. A business wants to be licensed as a producer but is partially owned by someone who has committed a felony. What will likely happen to the business's license application?

   A. It will be approved as long as the person has less than a majority ownership interest.
   B. It will be approved as long as a currently licensed producer is designated as the business's compliance officer.
   C. It will be approved as long as the felony wasn't committed in Missouri.
   D. It will be denied.

9. The DCI can't mail a complaint to a producer because the producer failed to report a change of address. How might the producer be penalized?

   A. The producer's license might be suspended until the change of address is resolved.
   B. The producer will be fined $100 per month until the change of address is resolved.
   C. The producer won't be penalized if he or she also has a valid phone number on file with the DCI.
   D. The producer will automatically have his or her license suspended for 90 days.

10. An illegal act has been caught by an insurer as part of a self-audit and was reported immediately to the DCI. What will happen to the insurer?

   A. The insurer will be penalized as if the self-audit had never happened.
   B. The penalty, if any, will be downgraded because of how the violation was caught.
   C. The insurer will lose its authorization to sell in Missouri.
   D. The insurer will be subjected to a detailed financial audit every six months until further notice.

11. A producer has collected an initial premium payment from an applicant but hasn't been able to procure requested coverage within 30 days. What must the producer do?

   A. Pursue coverage in the excess and surplus market.
   B. Provide an immediate return of premiums to the applicant.
   C. Immediately provide notice to the applicant.
   D. Immediately deposit the premium payment in a general operating account.

12. Which of the following must appear on the homepage of a producer's website?

   A. License expiration date
   B. License number
   C. Email address
   D. States in which the producer is licensed

13. Which of the following practices is prohibited in Missouri?

   A. Charging life insurance applicants different amounts based on gender
   B. Charging property insurance customers different amounts based on policy limits
   C. Charging property and casualty insurance customers different amounts based on disability
   D. Refusing to insure someone whose occupation is illegal

14. The victim in an auto accident wants to make a claim for property damage against his or her own policy. The insurer denies the claim by saying the policyholder must first take legal action against the at-fault driver. Which of the following is true?

    A. The insurer is exercising its right of subrogation.
    B. The insurer is engaging in an unfair claims settlement practice.
    C. The at-fault driver's insurer must compensate the victim within 15 days.
    D. The at-fault driver's insurer can't compensate the victim without the driver's written consent.

15. In general, property insurance in Missouri must provide benefits that are at least equal to those found in which policy form?

    A. HO-2
    B. HO-3
    C. HO-4
    D. New York Standard Fire Policy of 1943

16. Which of the following perils does NOT need to be covered by the Missouri FAIR Plan?

    A. Fire
    B. Lightning
    C. Explosion
    D. Flood

17. A policy for residential property from the Missouri FAIR Plan can have a maximum dollar limit of:

    A. $200,000
    B. $500,000
    C. $750,000
    D. $1 million

18. How much auto liability insurance must a Missouri driver have for bodily injury per person?

    A. $20,000
    B. $25,000
    C. $50,000
    D. $100,000

19. What is the fine for a first violation of Missouri's Motor Vehicle Financial Responsibility Law?

    A. $500
    B. $1,000
    C. $5,000
    D. $10,000

20. How much uninsured motorist coverage must be purchased in Missouri?

    A. $25,000 for bodily injury per person and $50,000 for bodily injury per accident
    B. $20,000 for bodily injury per person and $40,000 for bodily injury per accident
    C. $25,000 for bodily injury and $50,000 for property damage
    D. $50,000 for bodily injury and $50,000 for property damage

21. Which of the following is true about an auto insurance identification card?

    A. It must be kept in a vehicle in a hard-copy format.
    B. It must be issued by the Missouri Department of Revenue.
    C. It must be provided upon request of law enforcement.
    D. A request for a replacement card can increase a driver's premiums.

22. What is the purpose of the Missouri Automobile Insurance Plan?

    A. Provide lower premiums for perceivably safe drivers.
    B. Enforce Missouri requirements to obtain auto liability insurance.
    C. Provide auto liability insurance to high-risk drivers.
    D. Encourage Missouri drivers to purchase comprehensive auto insurance.

23. An accident victim has made a claim against his or her own auto insurance and has paid a deductible. What must occur if the insurer opts to exercise its right of subrogation?

    A. The insurer must seek reimbursement for the deductible on the victim's behalf.
    B. The insurer cannot seek reimbursement for the deductible on the victim's behalf.
    C. The accident victim is not required to reasonably assist the insurer in legal proceedings.
    D. Subrogation is not allowed in Missouri.

24. When must premium audits for workers compensation be completed?

    A. No later than 90 days before the end of a policy period
    B. No later than 30 days before a policy's effective cancellation date
    C. No later than 120 days after a policy's cancellation or expiration date
    D. No more than one year after a policy period

25. What is the definition of a total disability in Missouri?

    A. An inability to perform a person's regular job duties
    B. An inability to perform any work
    C. A loss of income due to a disability
    D. An inability to perform a portion of a person's regular job duties

Missouri Insurance Law Exam #3

1. Which of the following is generally NOT a typical power exercised by the DCI director?

    A. The power to issue licenses to individual producers and insurance businesses
    B. The power to create rules in order to enforce Missouri insurance laws
    C. The power to set standard commission rates for producers who sell auto insurance
    D. The power to issue subpoenas and cease-and-desist orders

2. How long must records of insurance claims be maintained?

    A. Until the end of the year in which a claim is made
    B. Until a claim has been paid by the insurer
    C. Until the applicable insurance policy is no longer in effect
    D. For the year in which a claim is closed plus an additional three calendar years

3. An unlicensed person will be designated to accept insurance payments from the public at a place of business and then forward them to a licensed producer. What must be true of the place of business?

    A. It must post signage regarding insurance antidiscrimination rules.
    B. It must be the principal office of at least one licensed producer.
    C. It must be identified clearly as an insurance agency to the public.
    D. It must store copies of all payment receipts for at least one year.

4. Which type(s) of insurance can be sold by a limited lines producer?

    A. Personal property insurance
    B. Excess and surplus insurance
    C. Credit and travel insurance
    D. High-risk auto liability insurance

5. How many hours of continuing education are required to renew a producer license?

    A. 12
    B. 16
    C. 24
    D. 30

6. Which of the following would be the least likely to qualify for a waiver of continuing education requirements?

    A. A producer who is more than 70 years old
    B. A producer who is serving overseas in the military
    C. A producer who is disabled
    D. A producer has been licensed for more than 15 years

7. An insurer has terminated its relationship with a producer due to illegal activity. What must the insurer do?

    A. Implement training procedures to address the activity.
    B. Perform an internal audit to detect similar activity by other producers.
    C. Inform the DCI within 30 days of the termination.
    D. Provide written notice to the producer's clients within 30 days.

8. A producer agrees to share a portion of his or her commission with a policyholder in exchange for a sale. What has occurred?

A. The producer has committed rebating.
B. The policyholder has sold insurance illegally without a license.
C. The producer and policyholder have executed a valid and mutually beneficial contract.
D. The insurer has engaged in an unfair claims settlement practice.

9. A financial planner charges a flat fee to evaluate someone's insurance. What must the planner do in order to charge a fee?

A. The planner must agree to a rebate of percentage-based commissions.
B. The planner must disclose the fee in advance.
C. The planner cannot also charge a commission for selling a recommended insurance product.
D. Nothing. Fees are standard practice in insurance.

10. A producer collects premiums that will ultimately be sent to the insurer. At the latest, when must the money be provided to the insurer?

A. 10 days
B. 15 days
C. 30 days
D. 45 days

11. A Missouri insurer is generally allowed to refuse insurance on the basis of an applicant's:

A. Gender
B. Loss history
C. Place of residence
D. Age

12. Which of the following is true regarding previous denials or cancellations of insurance?

A. Applicants can be asked whether they have been denied insurance in the past.
B. Applicants can be asked whether they have had insurance canceled in the past.
C. Applicants can be asked the name of their previous insurer in order to obtain loss histories.
D. Insurers cannot disclose the loss histories of consumers whose insurance has been canceled.

13. How is the Missouri Property and Casualty Insurance Guaranty Association funded?

A. Tax dollars obtained from Missouri residents
B. Licensing fees paid by producers
C. Fees charged to Missouri insurers
D. Financial penalties from disciplinary actions

14. How long do property insurance customers in Missouri have to report a loss?

A. 10 days
B. 30 days
C. 45 days
D. 60 days

15. How much notice must an insurer give to a consumer before cancelling a policy due to nonpayment?

A. None
B. 10 days
C. 30 days
D. 90 days

16. A policy for commercial property from the Missouri FAIR Plan can have a maximum dollar limit of:

A. $200,000
B. $500,000
C. $750,000
D. $1 million

17. How much auto liability insurance must a Missouri driver have for bodily injury to multiple people per accident?

A. $20,000
B. $25,000
C. $50,000
D. $100,000

18. In most cases, which form will need to be filed in order for someone with a suspended license to drive again?

A. SR-22
B. SR-24
C. SR-26
D. SR-28

19. A driver has other-than-collision coverage on a vehicle. How much loss-of-use coverage must the driver have after a theft?

A. None
B. $10 per day, up to at least $300 overall
C. $50 per day, up to at least $500 overall
D. $50 per day, up to at least $250 overall

20. A driver for a ridesharing service is connected to ridesharing technology but hasn't picked up a passenger. What is the status of the driver's auto insurance?

A. The driver's personal auto policy remains fully in force.
B. The driver must have special auto liability insurance while connected to ridesharing technology.
C. The driver remains covered by personal auto insurance for property damage liability but not bodily injury.
D. The driver remains covered by personal auto insurance for bodily injury but not property damage.

21. In general, a business with how many employees must have workers compensation insurance in Missouri?

    A. One
    B. Two
    C. Three
    D. Five

22. How must a business inform employees of their rights regarding workers compensation?

    A. Privately provide written notice to each employee.
    B. Post a notice in a portion of the workplace where all employees are likely to see it.
    C. Incorporate workers compensation information into formal employment contracts.
    D. Hold annual training sessions that include contact information for the Missouri Workers Compensation Division.

23. In general, what fraction of an employee's typical income will be provided as part of workers compensation?

    A. 1/3
    B. 2/3
    C. 100%
    D. 200%

24. Following a workplace death, Missouri employers must provide end-of-life expenses equal to at least:

    A. $1,000
    B. $5,000
    C. $50,000
    D. 105% percent of the state wage

25. Policies from the Missouri Medical Malpractice Joint Underwriting Association have coverage limits up to what amounts?

    A. $500,000
    B. $750,000
    C. $1 million
    D. $1 million per claimant and $3 million per policy period

MISSOURI INSURANCE LAW PRACTICE EXAM ANSWER KEYS

Question	Law Exam #1	Law Exam #2	Law Exam #3
1.	D	C	C
2.	D	B	D
3.	B	D	B
4.	C	A	C
5.	B	B	B
6.	A	C	D
7.	C	D	C
8.	A	D	A
9.	B	A	B
10.	B	B	C
11.	D	C	B
12.	A	D	C
13.	B	C	C
14.	B	B	D
15.	B	D	B
16.	D	D	D
17.	A	A	C
18.	A	B	A
19.	B	A	B
20.	B	A	B
21.	D	C	D
22.	D	C	B
23.	C	A	B
24.	D	C	B
25.	C	B	D

GLOSSARY

Absolute liability: A form of liability in which a person will be held legally responsible for losses even if he or she was technically not at fault.

Accident: An event that causes a loss at an unpredictable moment or in an unpredictable amount.

Accident and health insurance: A category of insurance that can assist with the payment of medical bills or replace a portion of someone's income after an illness, injury or disability.

Acts of civil authority: In property insurance, a type of indirect loss in which owners are temporarily prohibited from accessing or using their property by order of the government.

Actual cash value: The amount it would cost to replace property after subtracting for depreciation.

Actuaries: Professionals who determine the overall likelihood of losses for an insurance company and calculate an appropriate set of rates that insurers will use to charge their customers.

Additional living expenses: Costs that a homeowner or renter encounters as a direct result of not being able to use his or her home.

Admitted insurers: Insurance companies that are licensed to do business in a given state.

Adverse selection: In insurance, an undesirable scenario in which coverage is purchased disproportionately by people who are at the highest risk of suffering a loss.

Advertising injury: In commercial general liability insurance, committing an offense against someone in promotional materials.

Agency: The legal relationship created when one person represents another.

Agreed-value option: In commercial property insurance, an insurer's estimate of property's value at the time coverage is issued. Also, a dollar limit mutually agreed to by the business and the insurer that, if purchased by the business, will waive a policy's coinsurance requirements.

Aleatory contract: An agreement that incorporates elements of chance and thereby makes the exchange of compensation between the parties potentially unequal.

Alien insurer: A insurance company that is licensed in a particular state but located in another country.

Apparent authority: The public's reasonable belief—based on appearance, behavior or circumstances—that someone has the power to do something, regardless of whether such power was ever granted.

Application: The collection of documents used by an underwriter to evaluate a specific applicant for insurance.

Appraisal: A formal, expert opinion that pertains to an item's authenticity, condition and value.

Arbitration: A method of dispute resolution in which the parties generally agree to abide by the findings of an impartial third party without a chance to appeal.

Assignment: In insurance, the transfer of some or all of the rights contained within an insurance contract from the consumer to a third party.

Bailee insurance: Insurance for businesses that specialize in servicing other people's property, such as dry cleaners and repair shops.

"Basic" coverage: In regard to property insurance based on ISO forms, insurance that applies to only a small amount of perils.

Bilateral contract: An agreement in which both sides promise to do something, and both sides can use the courts to enforce the contract if a promise is not kept.

Glossary

Binder: A method by which an agent accepts a risk on a carrier's behalf and gives temporary coverage to a consumer while an insurance policy is still in the process of being issued.

Blanket insurance: Insurance that applies to multiple items within a collection.

Block policies: Specialized insurance products for businesses that specialize in selling highly valuable and very portable items, such as jewelry.

"Broad" coverage: In regard to property insurance based on ISO forms, coverage against an intermediate amount of perils.

Builders risk insurance: Insurance that covers a building while it is being rehabilitated or constructed and insures the building materials that have been purchased for the project.

Building and Personal Property Coverage Form: A document, created by the ISO, that contains the most common policy language for commercial property insurance.

Business income insurance: A form of business interruption insurance that pays business owners the amount of money they would have earned if a covered peril had not forced them to suspend normal operations.

Business interruption insurance: Insurance that reimburses businesses for lost income and the expenses they incur during a break in normal business operations.

Businessowners policy (BOP): An insurance policy that provides a combination of property and casualty coverage to businesses within relatively low-risk industries and below certain sizes.

Cancellation: The act of ending an agreement prior to its intended expiration date.

Captive agent: An insurance producer who tends to work as an independent contractor for a single insurance company.

Cargo insurance: In marine insurance, insurance for property being transported on a ship.

Casualty insurance: A category of insurance that provides financial protection to an insured who is potentially liable for someone else's losses.

Certificate of insurance: A document that provides proof of insurance by the insured to a third party.

Claims adjuster: An insurance professional who evaluates whether a loss should be covered at all and, if so, for how much.

Claims-made policy: A form of liability insurance in which coverage depends not only on when an accident occurs but also when a demand for money from a harmed party is made.

Coinsurance clause: In property insurance, a requirement that property be insured for at least a certain percentage of its value in order for the owner to be fully compensated for a partial loss.

Collision coverage: In auto insurance, insurance that pays for damage to the insured's own car due to a crash.

Combined ratio: In general, the insurer's losses and expenses divided by earned premiums.

Commercial general liability insurance: A broad form of liability insurance for businesses that addresses property damage, bodily injury, medical payments, personal injury and advertising injury.

Commercial lines insurance: Insurance intended to insure either a business or an individual within the context of his or her profession.

Commercial package policy: A special insurance policy for businesses that combines property insurance with various types of liability insurance as chosen by the insured.

Common policy conditions: In a commercial package policy, a set of responsibilities, duties and rights that govern the policy, regardless of which specific coverages are selected.

Common policy declarations form: In a commercial package policy, a set of basic information about the insured business and the selected coverages.

Comparative negligence: A form of liability in which responsibility for a loss is divided among all the negligent parties, often including the harmed party.

Compensatory damages: In casualty insurance, amounts paid by the responsible party in order to make the wronged party "whole" again.

Completed operations liability: A form of liability that arises when a business's poor performance causes harm even though the business's work has already been finished.

Comprehensive coverage: In auto insurance, insurance that compensates the insured when his or her own vehicle is damaged by theft, fire or several other perils other than a crash (also known as "other-than-collision insurance").

Concealment: Failing to disclose a material fact on purpose.

Concurrent causation: A scenario in which a loss is created by more than one peril.

Conditions: The portion of a property and casualty insurance policy that lays out many of the requirements for each party to the contract.

Consideration: Something of value offered in exchange for something else of value.

Contents coverage: Insurance for someone's belongings.

Contingent business interruption insurance: Insurance that provides lost income to a business when an offsite "dependent property" suffers physical damage and must shut down.

Continuing normal operating expenses: In business interruption insurance, costs that the insured would face regardless of damage to named property.

Contract of adhesion: A written agreement in which one party chooses the language of the contract and the other party merely has the option of either accepting the contract as written or rejecting it.

Contractual liability: Liability that's accepted as part of an oral or written agreement.

Contributory negligence: A legal theory stating that a third party isn't liable for damages if the injured party's own negligence contributed at all to a loss.

Controlled business: In Illinois, insurance sold by producers to themselves, their spouse, their business or their employer.

Coverage territory: The geographic area where a loss must occur in order for it be covered by an insurance product. In some cases, the coverage territory might not extend to another country or another state.

Cyber insurance: A broad category of property and casualty insurance that relates to losses from data breaches, computer viruses and other problems with technology.

Damages: Depending on the context, either harm suffered by someone or compensation provided by a liable party because of harm.

Declarations page: Often a first-page summary of an insurance policy.

Deductible: The amount of an otherwise insured loss that the consumer must pay out of pocket before a loss can be covered by the insurance policy.

Deposit premium: An amount paid to the insurer at the beginning of a policy period based on an estimate of the risk.

Detached structure: In homeowners insurance, a structure that is separate from a dwelling but still situated on the residence premises, such as a detached garage or barn.

Direct loss: In property insurance, a form of property damage.

Direct writer: An insurer that sells insurance solely through its employees rather than through independent contractors.

Differences in conditions insurance: Generally, insurance designed to cover perils that are commonly excluded by commercial property insurance, such as floods and earthquakes.

Directors and officers (D & O) insurance: Liability insurance for high-ranking decision makers at public, private or non-profit companies.

Domestic insurer: An insurer that is licensed and domiciled and incorporated in the same state.

Dwelling: In property insurance, the structure that a person lives in.

Dwelling policies: Limited insurance for a home that generally does not include coverage for theft or personal liability.

Earned premium: Money paid by consumers to insurance companies that can be kept in the event of a policy cancellation.

Earth movement: A broad term that can be used to describe earthquakes, mudslides, landslides and the formation of sinkholes.

Elimination period: A period, often expressed as a number of days, during which an insured will need to pay out of pocket for a loss before insurance benefits will apply.

Employers liability insurance: Insurance that pays for damages and defense costs when an employer is believed to be liable for an occupational injury that is not covered by workers compensation insurance.

Employment practices liability insurance: Insurance that is intended to protect businesses when they are accused of violating someone's employment rights.

Endorsement: An amendment to an insurance company's standard policy language.

Equipment breakdown insurance: Insurance used in response to unexpected damage to machinery caused by power surges, broken motors and defective parts rather than by fire, flood or other traditional perils.

Errors and omissions insurance: A type of liability insurance that covers various professionals when their services don't meet clients' or customers' expectations.

Estoppel: The inability of a party to exercise a right.

Excess-and-surplus lines: A special market for insurance that may be utilized when adequate coverage from an admitted carrier is not reasonably available.

Exclusions: Perils that aren't covered by an insurance product.

Exclusive remedy: In workers compensation systems, the inability of eligible workers to also sue their employers after an illness or injury.

Expense ratio: In general, an insurer's costs divided by earned premiums.

Exposure: The possibility of a loss.

Express authority: Powers granted explicitly by a principal to an agent, either orally or in writing.

Extended replacement-cost coverage: A type of homeowners insurance that will provide extra coverage (often capped at 120% or 125% of Coverage A) when the cost of replacing the dwelling is larger than the policy's Coverage A limit.

Extended reporting period: In casualty insurance, an amount of time during which a claim can be reported to an insurance company even though coverage has otherwise been canceled or not renewed.

Fair Credit Reporting Act: A federal law that requires insurance companies to inform consumers when negative action is taken against them based on reports from third parties.

FAIR plans: Arrangements whereby the property insurers in a given state provide property insurance in high-risk areas in exchange for federal help with catastrophic losses.

Fidelity bond: A bond guaranteeing loyalty and faithfulness, often by an employee to an employer.

Field underwriting: Evaluating the level of risk posed by an insurance applicant prior to completion of an application.

Floater: An insurance product designed to provide greater coverage for particular kinds of movable and valuable personal property.

Foreign insurer: An insurer that is licensed but not domiciled in a given state.

Functional replacement cost: The amount it would take to replace property with a new but potentially cheaper alternative that serves the same essential function.

Gap insurance: In auto insurance, insurance that covers the difference between the remaining loan balance on a totaled vehicle and its actual cash value.

General damages: In casualty insurance, compensation for losses that aren't easily quantifiable and might be awarded when someone is held liable for a death, a long-term disability, a reduced quality of life or a harmed reputation.

Gramm-Leach-Bliley Act: A federal law that sets requirements for the sharing of information among financial institutions, allows consumers to opt out of certain types of sharing and requires the delivery of various privacy notices to the public.

Guaranteed replacement-cost insurance: A formerly common type of homeowners insurance that made the insurer pay to replace the entire dwelling regardless of a policy's Coverage A limit.

Guaranty funds: Money used to compensate claimants whose insurance is from an insolvent company.

Hammer clause: In liability insurance, a clause that addresses what will happen if an insured refuses to settle a dispute against the insurance company's wishes.

Hazard: Something that increases a loss's likelihood or scope.

Homeowners insurance: A common form of insurance for owner-occupied dwellings that also includes personal liability insurance.

Hull insurance: Insurance for a commercial vessel, such as a ship.

Implied authority: Non-explicit power given to an agent in order to exercise his or her express authority.

Independent agents: Insurance producers who can represent multiple insurance companies.

Indirect loss: In property insurance, usually a loss of income or a consequential expense that results from not being able to use property.

Inflation protection: In homeowners insurance, a policy feature that will recalculate the dwelling's insured value on a regular basis and may increase the policy's Coverage A limit based on the increased cost of construction.

Inherent vice: Damage, spoilage or deterioration that is relatively natural in regard to the property and not caused by an unexpected force.

Inland marine insurance: Insurance for items shipped by land rather than by water. Also, insurance used to cover easily movable commercial property of great value.

Insurable interest: A desire for a person or thing to remain unharmed.

Insurance: A contractual arrangement whereby one party agrees to absorb a risk in exchange for compensation and in an attempt to pool several risks together.

Insurance agent: In general, an insurance producer who legally represents the interests of an insurer in an insurance transaction.

Insurance broker: In general, an insurance producer who legally represents the interests of consumers in insurance transactions.

Insurance commissioner: In most parts of the country, the person in charge of a state's insurance department.

Insurance producers: Licensed professionals who act as intermediaries between consumers and insurance companies.

Insured: In general, a person or other entity who is entitled to insurance benefits after a loss. Depending on the circumstances, also known as the "policy owner," "policyholder," or "named insured."

Insurer: The company issuing the policy, also known as the "carrier."

Insuring agreement: In an insurance policy, the insurance company's basic promise to the consumer.

Lapse: Cancellation of an insurance policy due to nonpayment of premiums.

Law of large numbers: The belief that the probability of an occurrence (such as a loss) becomes clearer as it is tested against an increasingly larger sample of data.

Liberalization clause: Part of an insurance policy that states that if the carrier decides to modify the policy in a way that gives additional insurance to new customers at no cost (either by choice or by law), its existing policyholders must also receive these free benefits.

Life insurance: A broad category of insurance that helps manage the financial consequences of premature death.

Limit of liability: The maximum amount of compensation that an insurance company must pay to an insured after a loss.

Lines of authority: Broad categories of insurance products (life, health, property, casualty, etc.) that a license allows someone to sell.

Loss: An expense or decrease in value.

Loss of use coverage: Property insurance that pays money to the insured when the residence premises or building is made uninhabitable by a covered peril.

Loss ratio: In general, the amount of claims-related losses divided by earned premiums.

Manuscript policy: An insurance contract that has been written with significant participation from the consumer or the consumer's representative.

Marine insurance: Insurance pertaining to trade and goods in transit.

Material fact: Information that, if known, would influence a decision regarding whether to enter into a contract in the first place.

McCarran-Ferguson Act: A federal law that places most aspects of insurance regulation under the jurisdiction of the individual states rather than the federal government.

Mediation: A form of non-binding dispute resolution in which attorneys, retired judges or other third-party participants attempt to get both sides of a dispute talking to each other in order to come to a resolution.

Medical payments coverage: In auto insurance, medical coverage for a driver or a driver's passengers.

Moral hazards: Conditions that increase the temptation to cause a loss on purpose.

Morale hazards: Circumstances that encourage people to feel indifferent about reducing or preventing losses.

Mutual company: An insurance company owned by the same individuals who have purchased insurance from it.

Named insured: With a few exceptions, usually the only person or entity who will be covered by insurance and the only party, besides the insurer, who can change the insurance.

Named-peril policy: An insurance contract that only insures the policyholder against those perils that are specifically mentioned as a covered peril.

National Flood Insurance Program (NFIP): A federal program intended to facilitate the selling of flood insurance.

Negligence: The failure to act with as much care as a reasonable person in a given situation.

New York Standard Fire Policy: A 1943 document that served as a basic template for modern homeowners insurance policies.

Non-admitted carrier: An insurer that is not licensed in a given state.

Nonrenewal: The insurance company's refusal to extend coverage beyond the previously agreed policy period.

Non-resident license: A license to sell insurance somewhere other than a producer's home state.

Notice of claim: Informing the insurer of a loss (or, in some cases, a potential loss) within a timeframe specified by the policy.

Obligee: With respect to a bond, the person who receives the promise and is compensated when it's broken.

Occurrence: An event that results in a loss.

Occurrence policy: In liability insurance, coverage that depends mainly on when an accident occurs rather than when a demand for money by a harmed person is made.

Ocean marine insurance: Property and casualty insurance for people who have a vested interest in a ship's safe journey.

Open-peril policy: An insurance contract that covers losses caused by any peril unless the insurance contract specifically excludes it.

Other insurance clause: Part of an insurance policy that explains how a loss will be handled if the same loss is insured under multiple policies and/or by multiple insurance companies.

Package policy: An insurance product designed to cover multiple kinds of risk and thereby containing multiple insuring agreements.

Peril: A cause of a loss.

Period of restoration: The amount of time during which a business will receive business interruption benefits, usually lasting until the point in time when the business has permanently relocated or should've been capable of rebuilding the premises.

Personal Auto Policy: An ISO-authored coverage form used to insure most private-passenger vehicles.

Personal injury: In commercial general liability insurance, a loss that occurs when someone's reputation or rights are taken away.

Personal injury protection (PIP): In no-fault auto insurance states, insurance that is intended to cover a driver's own medical costs after an accident.

Personal liability insurance: A portion of homeowners insurance that pays when third parties suffer accidental harm to themselves or their property because of something an insured did or failed to do.

Personal lines insurance: Insurance intended to insure one person or a family in non-business endeavors.

Personal umbrella policy: Excess liability insurance that applies when a person's primary insurance policies for personal liability have reached their limits.

Physical hazard: An environmental factor that increases the likelihood or severity of a potential loss.

Policy period: The time between an insurance policy's issue date and expiration date.

Pooling of risks: A method by which insurers attempt to spread either the same or similar risks across a larger group.

Premises and operations liability: In commercial general liability insurance, liability that arises from accidents at the insured's place of business or while the insured is conducting business.

Premium: Compensation given by the consumer to the insurer.

Premium fund trust account: In Illinois, a special account where money collected by producers from consumers must be deposited and held in a fiduciary capacity.

Principal: Regarding a bond, the person who promises to do or not do something. Also, in an agency relationship, the party being represented by someone else.

Principle of indemnity: A general rule dictating that policyholders be made financially "whole" again after a loss, but not any better than they were prior to a loss.

Professional liability insurance: A broad category of liability insurance that includes malpractice insurance, errors and omissions insurance, directors and officers (D & O) insurance and more.

Proof of loss: Documentation that must be provided by the insured to receive compensation from the insurance company.

Property insurance: A broad category of insurance that compensates businesses and individuals when they suffer losses pertaining to their physical assets, such as their building, home or belongings.

Pro rata liability: A manner of calculating each insurer's share of an insured loss when it could reasonably be covered by multiple existing policies. Typically based on each policy's fraction of the overall coverage limit for the loss.

Protection and indemnity insurance: Liability insurance in the ocean marine market.

Proximate cause of loss: When multiple perils might technically have contributed to a loss, the dominant peril that logically resulted in a loss.

Public adjusters: Insurance professionals who represent claimants during the claims process and do not work for or on behalf of an insurance company.

Punitive damages: Financial penalties intended to make an example of the liable party and discourage society from engaging in the activity that caused a loss.

Pure risk: A risk in which none of the potential outcomes are beneficial.

Rate: In premium calculations, generally the cost of insurance per amount purchased.

Rebating: Providing a thing of value, such as part of a producer's commission, in order to induce an insurance sale.

Reinsurance: Insurance sold to insurance companies in case of unexpected catastrophic losses or major miscalculations in an insurer's pricing models or underwriting guidelines.

Replacement-cost coverage: Property insurance that does not subtract for depreciation.

Representation: A statement of fact made by the consumer at the formation of a contract. It generally cannot result in insurance being voided unless it includes knowingly false information and pertains to a material fact.

Rescission: Treating a contract as if it never existed in the first place.

Residence premises: In homeowners insurance, the dwelling and all the land and other structures surrounding it.

Resident license: A license from a producer's home state.

Residual market: In auto insurance, arrangements by which high-risk drivers can obtain mandatory insurance despite being otherwise uninsurable.

Retroactive date: With respect to a claims-made liability insurance policy, the earliest date on which a covered accident can occur.

Risk: Uncertainty surrounding either the likelihood or impact of an event.

Risk avoidance: A risk management strategy in which a person entirely eliminates a risk by choosing not to engage in an activity.

Risk reduction: A risk management strategy in which steps are taken to reduce either the likely frequency or severity of a potential loss with the understanding that the risk can't be entirely eliminated.

Risk retention: A risk management strategy in which someone decides to accept a risk and live with the consequences.

Risk sharing: A form of risk transfer in which the original party still maintains a portion of the risk.

Risk transfer: A risk management strategy in which the consequences stemming from a risk are taken from one party and moved to another.

Salvage value: The worth of an item that can no longer be used for its intended purpose.

Scheduling: In insurance, itemizing a person's valuables and insuring each item for a specific amount.

Self-insured retention amount: In umbrella insurance, the amount of an otherwise insured loss that the policyholder will need to pay out of pocket.

Short-rate cancellation: Cancellation of insurance whereby the insurer will generally be allowed to keep an extra amount of the paid premium in order to compensate for administrative expenses caused by the unexpected cancellation.

"Special" coverage: In property insurance policies based on ISO forms, open-peril insurance that will respond to all perils other than those specifically excluded in the policy.

Special damages: In casualty insurance, damages that are easily quantifiable, such as those awarded to replace damaged property or to reimburse an injured person for medical bills that have already been paid.

Special flood hazard area: A place where there is at least a 1 percent chance of flooding each year, thereby usually requiring the purchase of flood insurance.

Special limits of liability: In property insurance, coverage limits on some highly valued items, such as jewelry, furs and documents.

Specific insurance: Insurance solely for a single piece of property rather than a collection or assortment of different items.

Speculative risks: Risks in which there is at least a chance of success or gain rather than just the chance of a negative or neutral outcome.

Split limit: In auto insurance, having different dollar limits for bodily injury liability and property damage liability.

Stock company: An insurance company that is owned by investors who haven't necessarily purchased insurance from that particular company.

Subrogation: The transfer of rights between parties who are already part of the contract (such as rights transferred from the policyholder to the insurer).

Suitability standard: A requirement that the insurance products, dollar limits, and recommendations given to consumers be appropriate for a given situation.

Supplementary payments and/or additional coverages: Parts of an insurance policy that allow the policyholder to receive benefits in addition to the main type of coverage that has been purchased.

Surety: With respect to a bond, the party who will compensate someone if a promise is broken.

Surety bond: A bond guaranteeing that something will be done.

Temporary substitute vehicle: A vehicle being driver because the driver's regular vehicle has been damaged or stolen.

Terrorism Risk Insurance Act of 2002 (TRIA): A federal law that mandates the availability of terrorism-risk coverage in various commercial lines of insurance.

Underinsured motorist coverage: Auto insurance that applies when an at-fault driver has the legal minimum amount of liability coverage but still lacks enough to fully compensate an accident victim.

Underwriter: An insurance professional who decides whether or not to accept a risk at a given price.

Underwriting: The process of evaluating each insurance customer's level of risk.

Unearned premium: Money paid to the insurer that is technically still refundable in the event of a policy cancellation.

Unilateral contract: An agreement in which only one of the parties makes a legally enforceable promise.

Uninsured motorist coverage: Auto insurance that applies when an at-fault driver hasn't purchased at least the legal minimum amount of liability insurance.

Utmost good faith: In insurance, acting with honesty and a willingness to disclose information about the risk being insured.

Vacancy clause: In property insurance, a provision that allows the insurer to deny or reduce coverage when property has been vacant for more than 30 to 60 days.

Valued policy: An insurance contract in which the insurer and the consumer agree to the specific dollar amount that will be received in the event of a loss.

Vandalism and malicious mischief: Causing intentional damage to another person's building or belongings.

Vicarious liability: Liability that exists when one party is held responsible for another party's actions.

Waiver: The intentional or unintentional relinquishment of a legal right.

Warranty: In insurance, a statement that must continue to be literally true in order for the insured party to keep the policy in force. Compared to a representation, a warranty is closer to being a promise to do or not do something during the policy period.

APPENDIX

Property Insurance Perils by Coverage Form

Peril	DP-1 (Basic Form)	DP-2 (Broad Form)	HO-1 (Basic Form)	HO-2 (Broad Form)	Commercial Property (Basic Form)	Commercial Property (Broad Form)
Fire or lightning	X	X	X	X	X	X
Internal explosion	X	X	X	X	X	X
Windstorm	With EC Endorsement	X	X	X	X	X
Civil commotion	With EC Endorsement	X	X	X	X	X
Smoke	With EC Endorsement	X	X	X	X	X
Hail	With EC Endorsement	X	X	X	X	X
Aircraft	With EC Endorsement	X	X	X	X	X
Vehicles	With EC Endorsement	X	X	X	X	X
Volcanic eruption	With EC Endorsement	X	X	X	X	X
Explosion (internal and external)	With EC Endorsement	X	X	X	X	X
Riot	With EC Endorsement	X	X	X	X	X
Vandalism and Malicious Mischief	With Vandalism Endorsement	X	X	X	X	X
Theft			X	X		
Falling Objects		X		X		X
Damage by Burglary		X				
Weight of ice, snow, sleet		X		X		X
Accidental discharge of water or steam		X		X		X
Sudden and accidental tearing, cracking, burning or bulging of heating and water systems		X		X		
Freezing		X		X		
Sudden and accidental artificial current		X		X		
Sinkhole collapse					X	X
Sprinkler leakage					X	X

Note: The HO-3 (Special form) insures the dwelling against all perils other than those specifically excluded and insures contents against the same perils as the HO-2. Similarly, the DP-3 (Special form) insures the dwelling against all perils other than those specifically excluded and insures contents against the same perils as the DP-2. Special coverage for commercial property insures property against all perils other than those specifically excluded.

Homeowners Forms by the Numbers

	Dwelling Coverage Limit	Other Structures Coverage Limit	Contents Coverage Limit	Loss of Use Coverage Limit	Notes
HO-1	Varies	10% of Dwelling Limit	50% of Dwelling Limit	10% of Dwelling Limit	Dwelling covered against basic perils at replacement cost; contents covered against basic perils at actual cash value.
HO-2	Varies	10% of Dwelling Limit	50% of Dwelling Limit	30% of Dwelling Limit	Dwelling covered against broad perils based on replacement cost; contents covered against broad perils based on actual cash value.
HO-3	Varies	10% of Dwelling Limit	50% of Dwelling Limit	30% of Dwelling Limit	Dwelling covered against non-excluded perils at replacement cost; contents have broad peril coverage based on actual cash value
HO-4	10% of Contents Limit	NA	Varies	30% of Contents Limit	Broad peril coverage based on actual cash value; intended for renters.
HO-5	Varies	10% of Dwelling Limit	50% of Dwelling Limit	30% of Dwelling Limit	Open-peril coverage on dwelling AND contents
HO-6	$1,000	$1,000	Varies	50% of Contents Limit	Broad peril coverage based on actual cash value; intended for condo owners
HO-8	Varies	10% of Dwelling Limit	50% of Dwelling Limit	10% of Dwelling Limit	Dwelling and contents covered at actual cash value against basic perils.

Note: The HO-7 (not shown) is intended to insure mobile homes.

Common Homeowners Insurance Figures and Limits

Type	Amount
Debris coverage	Additional 5% of Coverage A if Coverage A is exhausted.
Vacancy clause trigger	60 days
Trees	$500 per tree, $1,000 total
Personal property normally stored offsite	$1,000 or 10% of Coverage C (whichever is greater)
Jewelry theft	$1,500
Furs theft	$1,500
Silverware/goldware theft	$2,500
Money	$200
Valuable documents	$1,500
Firearms theft	$2,500
Watercraft and parts	$1,500
Trailers	$1,500
Electronic devices kept in vehicles	$1,500
Tombstones	$5,000
Coverage if property is inaccessible due to civil authority	2 weeks
No-fault damage to someone else's property	$1,000
Compensation for missing work to assist in legal proceeding	$250 per day
Common Coverage F no-fault medical payments	$1,000 for use within 3 years of accident
Common coinsurance requirement	80% of replacement cost
Business personal property at residence premises	$2,500
Unauthorized use of credit cards	$500

Common Commercial Property Insurance Figures

Type	Amount
Radius for covered business personal property	Within 100 feet of business premises
Common coinsurance requirement	80%
Fungus, rot and bacteria by a covered peril	$15,000
Temporary coverage for newly acquired building	Up to $250,000 for up to 30 days
Pollution cleanup by covered peril	$10,000
Loss of data by covered peril	$2,500
Vacancy clause trigger	60 days
Debris by covered peril	25%(deductible + non-debris portion of loss)

Common Business Interruption Insurance Figures

Type	Amount
Trigger for business income benefits	Interruption of at least 3 days
Trigger for extra expenses	Immediately at start of interruption
Coverage if premises is inaccessible due to civil authority.	4 weeks

Other Property Insurance Figures

Type	Amount
Minimum coverages for Commercial Package Policy	2
Special flood hazard area	1% chance of flood each year
Waiting period for flood insurance to go into effect	30 days
Common NFIP limits	$250,000 for dwelling, $100,000 for contents
Earthquake occurrence	All instances of movement within 72 hours

Appendix

Common Auto Insurance Figures

Type	Amount
Bail bonds	$250
Temporary coverage of new vehicle replacing another	Liability coverage for 14 days. For property coverage, vehicle will be covered for 4 days (if previous vehicle had no property coverage) or 14 days (if previous vehicle had property coverage).
Temporary coverage of new vehicle not replacing another	Liability coverage for 14 days. For property coverage, vehicle will be covered for 4 days (if previous vehicle had no property coverage) or 14 days (if previous vehicle had property coverage).
General requirements for personal auto	4 wheels, less than 10,000 pounds and not used for business
Temporary substitute auto if vehicle is stolen or damaged	$30 day up to $900 (if collision/comprehensive coverage is in place)

Other Casualty Insurance Figures

Type	Amount
Employers liability insurance policy limits (as part of workers comp policy)	$100,000 per injury, $500,000 overall limit for disease, $100,000 per employee for disease
Common discovery period for crime insurance	1 year after policy period
Umbrella policy limits	$1 million or more

www.ingramcontent.com/pod-product-compliance
Lightning Source LLC
Chambersburg PA
CBHW061351210326
41598CB00035B/5951